AMSTERDAMER PUBLIKATIONEN ZUR SPRACHE UND LITERATUR

herausgegeben von

COLA MINIS

11. BAND

RODOPI N.V.
Amsterdam 1974

THE RECAPITULATED FALL

A Comparative Study in
Mediaeval Literature

Brian O. Murdoch

RODOPI N.V.
Amsterdam 1974

ISBN-90-6203-021-1

Library of Congress Catalog Card Number: 73-91188

CONTENTS

Preface 1

Abbreviations, References and Translations 5

I The Typological Problem 7

II Scripture and Exegesis 23

III Vernacular Prose Writings 49

IV Early Vernacular Poetry 67

V Later Vernacular Poetry 95

VI The Dramatic Versions 119

VII Medieval Iconography 149

VIII Some Concluding Remarks 171

Bibliography 177

Index 201

PREFACE

This study seeks to examine the connexion drawn in medieval writing and art between the temptation and Fall of Man in Eden, and the temptation and victory of Christ in the desert. Of special interest is the manner in which the second event—as a typological recapitulation of the first—is seen as having cancelled out the effects of the first. It is, of course, unusual to have the moment of Redemption placed in the desert rather than on Calvary, but the idea is a widespread one. The best-known literary manifestation is, in fact, not a medieval work, but Milton's 'Paradise Regained,' this concept linking the 'brief epic' to 'Paradise Lost.' This monograph is not a study of Milton, however, although it might be of interest to students of 'Paradise Regained.' The view of the temptation in the desert as a recapitulation of the Fall is not usual, and the material background is therefore more closely circumscribed than it is for 'Paradise Lost.' I am not aware that the parallel has been the subject of close analysis as far as the medieval writings are concerned. Some works on other aspects of medieval thought have touched on the point, and some Milton-studies have treated the parallelism as such, but the medieval religious writings that are the primary basis of this study are usually considered footnote material.

A full survey of that medieval material has several points in its favour. It might contribute to comparative literature studies with special reference to the Middle Ages, and it might at the same time be of interest in the field of theological history, in that it can demonstrate the dissemination of an exegetical point that is of some importance in a Christian context. The study aims too, however, to throw light on the interrelationships and structures of the medieval works as such, and in some cases indicate the literary value of some little-studied texts.

No-one can, of course, pretend to be able to achieve completeness in this kind of study. I have tried to be as full as possible, but more material might doubtless have been included. I have, in fact, paid more attention than might be expected to monuments in the less well-known languages such as Irish (although availability of translations imposed here an artificial limitation). Similarly I have restricted to some extent the coverage of later medieval and renaissance texts, as much of this has been dealt with in Milton research. As an example, I have cited only 'Umanitá del figliuolo di Dio' of Teofilo Folengo, rather than use too his 'Palermitana.' One or two renaissance writings were simply not available to me.

By and large only printed texts have been used (although this does include a number of manuscript facsimiles). Such manuscripts as have been consulted have most frequently been cited with thanks to the generosity of friends and colleagues who have drawn my attention to the works in question.

In view of the range of material, I have drawn to a large extent on the generosity of my colleagues, and this has affected not only the study of texts in less common languages, but also such tasks as the obtaining of rare material. I am grateful in particular to the following: Mrs. E. Campbell (Chicago), Dr. G. P. Cubbin (Cambridge), Dr. R. W. Fisher (Christchurch, New Zealand), Dr. S. Harroff, (Fort Wayne, Indiana), Dr. Fernando Huerta-Viñas (Barcelona), Mr P. Hurst (Bangor), Mr. D. Maclaren and Miss S. Powell (Glasgow), Mr R. Walker (East Lansing, Michigan). I am especially grateful to my friend and collaborator in other studies in the same field, Mr Michael Benskin (Edinburgh), who has supplied me generously with material and ideas. Errors or readings of works that my informants might not agree with remain of course my own responsibility.

I am also grateful to various bodies and people for assistance of a more technical nature. The bulk of research for this study was completed with the help of a Faculty Fellowship from the Graduate College of the University of Illinois at Chicago Circle, which enabled me to have free the Summer Quarter, 1971. Publication of the book has been assisted too by a generous grant from the Carnegie Trust for the Universities of Scotland, and I have had other assistance from the German department of the University of Stirling. I owe also a considerable debt of gratitude to the staff of the interlibrary loan departments at Chicago Circle and, latterly, at Stirling. I am indebted finally to Professor Cola Minis, both for accepting the study for his series, and for his very ready assistance in all matters concerned with the publication of the work.

My wife, of course, has been of indispensable assistance from the start of the work. The book is dedicated to her.

Brian O. Murdoch
Stirling, February 1973

Abbreviations, References and Translations

Only the most frequently used works and series are given in abbreviated form and listed here. Full details of series in which individual studies have appeared are given in the bibliography. The Bible is cited, chapter and verse, according to the Latin Vulgate, and a translation is not always given. The edition used is that of Aloisius Gramatica, Bibliorum Sacrorum iuxta Vulgatam Clementinam nova editio, Vatican 1959. Other texts not in English are provided with a translation. This includes Old but not, except in difficult cases, Middle English. Unless otherwise stated, the translations are my own.

ATB   Altdeutsche Textbibliothek
BGPM   Beiträge zur Geschichte der Philosophie des Mittelalters
DTM   Deutsche Texte des Mittelalters
EETS   Early English Text Society. Ordinary (OS) and Extra
       (ES) Series
ITS   Irish Text Society
PG   J. P. Migne, Patrologiae cursus completus ... series
       Graeca, Paris 1857 -66.
PL   J. P. Migne. Patrologiae cursus completus ...[series
       Latina], Paris 1844 -64.

I   THE TYPOLOGICAL PROBLEM

A recent study of Milton's 'Paradise Lost' in the context of the various traditions linked with the Fall of Man concludes a survey of medieval Christian exegetical motifs with a brief reference to the connexion sometimes drawn between the Fall and the story, narrated in the synoptic Gospels, of the temptation of Christ in the desert. The chapter closes with a provocative comment:

> The Fall was . . . neutralized not on the Cross, but in the desert. It is in this typological tradition that 'Paradise Regained' had its origins . . .[1]

The tradition referred to—and the descriptive adjective "typological" will require separate treatment—lies, then, in the juxtaposing of two biblical events. The first book of the Old Testament relates how Adam and Eve, in Paradise, were tempted by the serpent—seen from pre-Christian times as the devil or his agent—and fell prey to that temptation, with disastrous results for mankind. Beside this is set the temptation of Christ in the desert, the Redeemer being tempted three times by Satan, and each time repulsing him, until at last he is driven away.

Evans' comment, that the second event neutralizes the first, draws the two events together in a way that goes far beyond merely incidental comparison. The notion is, of course, best demonstrated with Milton's epics, and their very titles make the point clear, although not all critics have agreed with the implications of the Atonement in his second great work.[2] While the internal evidence of 'Paradise Regained'—quite apart

1.   J. M. Evans, 'Paradise Lost' and the Genesis Tradition, Oxford 1968, p. 104. A comprehensive review of this work, by M. Benskin and B. Murdoch will appear in Neuphilologische Mitteilungen in 1973.

2.   See for example C. A. Patrides, Milton and the Christian Tradition, Oxford 1966, p. 145f. The point will be discussed further in chapter V.

from the title—that bears out this reading far outweighs that produced by the critics of the view, the very fact that there is, even with Milton, a variety of interpretative possibilities, is significant of itself. For the tradition as such—the precise manner in which the two narratives have been compared with one another—is a varied one. It is also a widespread one, culturally, geographically and temporally. The comparative tradition reaches from the earliest Christian writings to Milton as a continuous and living force. It is found, moreover, not only in Latin and Greek theological writings proper, but in vernacular sermons, in the vernacular poetic and dramatic tradition, and in art all through the Middle Ages and on into the Reformation and the Renaissance. The basic form of the motif becomes a commonplace of the medieval Christian tradition, and for this reason it is found all over Europe.

There have been some studies of this tradition, both in the context of Milton and outside this field. The most extensive attempt so far is the work of Elizabeth M. Pope on "Paradise Regained": the Tradition and the Poem', originally a doctoral dissertation from Johns Hopkins University, and published in Baltimore in 1947. This is, of course, essentially a Milton study, and the emphasis is on the later, immediately pre-Miltonic portion of the tradition. Reference to medieval vernacular literature is almost exclusively relegated to footnotes, or it is very brief. The same applies to Pope's comments on art— although it must be noted that the monograph does cover a wide cultural field. There is little or no reference to medieval literature, apart from Latin, written outside England. As far as the Latin background goes, the examination of the motif in theological writing does take account of the Fathers and of medieval exegesis, but here again, about twice as much space is devoted to Reformation and post-Reformation attitudes.[3] The work is concerned, finally, more with narrative details as they

3. See the chapter entitled 'The Triple Equation', pp. 51-69.

are found in Milton than with variations in pre-Miltonic attitudes to what Pope calls "the triple equation"— one, incidentally, of many felicitous turns of phrase in a study which is, within its own limits, exemplary: this description of the parallel has caught the attention of a number of subsequent critics.

The purely theological aspects—the exegetical history of this equation—have been dealt with in a more recent monograph, one which has received scant attention in studies of the point over the past decade, presumably because it is both outside literary studies, and in German. Klaus-Peter Köppen's book: 'Die Auslegung der Versuchungsgeschichte unter besonderer Berücksichtigung der Alten Kirche'[4] deals, however, with the entire exegetical history of this Gospel story, of which the "triple equation" is of course only one possibility. Other interpretations, indeed, are sometimes relevant in the present study. Köppen does, however, devote one full chapter (pp. 79-85) to the comparison of the two temptation scenes, and there are other relevant references elsewhere in his text. His analysis is a valuable one for the literary scholar in that it discusses the changes in the general outline of the exegesis made by the main figures of ecclesiastical history. In spite of the title of the study, the range is from Justin Martyr to Luther and Calvin: no vernacular literary texts are considered, however.

The most recent of the relevant studies is that of Donald R. Howard, 'The Three Temptations' (Princeton 1966), of which a chapter is devoted to this and other exegetical patterns related to the view of the Fall of Man in the Middle Ages. Howard links the equation of the two temptation-scenes with two other biblical and exegetical points: with the moralizing (Philonian-Ambrosian) interpretation of the Fall in terms of the way in which man in general is tempted and falls—with the *suggestio*, "the promptings" of the devil leading to attraction

4. Tübingen 1961. "The Interpretation of the Temptation Story with Special Reference to the Early Church."

(*delectatio*) and thence to consent (*consentio*); and with the three temptations of 1 John 2: 16—lust of the flesh (*concupiscentia carnis*), lust of the eyes (*concupiscentia oculorum*) and the pride of life (*superbia vitae*).[5] For all that Howard examines the use of the triple equation in a large number of Latin expositors of the patristic and medieval centuries,[6] several points may be raised regarding this work. First, the emphasis is once again on detail, rather than attitude: the analysis of superficial difference takes precedence over fundamental comparison. Secondly, his integration of the various different motifs, while they do overlap to some extent, as will be seen in the course of this study, does not make for a clear picture of any of them. Finally, although the work is not concerned with Milton, but with the Middle Ages (its subtitle is 'Medieval Man in Search of the World'), the bulk of the study is devoted to 'Troilus and Criseyde,' 'Sir Gawain' and 'Piers Plowman.' The last work is of course religious, but there is practically no reference to other religious poetry, particularly outside England. With the sole exception of a footnote reference to the fourteenth-century English 'Stanzaic Life of Christ' no vernacular literary treatment of the point is mentioned. This, indeed, is the case with other studies of medieval literature where the point is noted, such as D. W. Robertson's 'Preface to Chaucer.'[7] Only in Morton W. Bloomfield's study 'The Seven Deadly Sins' is the vernacular evidence of the triple equation mentioned, with reference to medieval English texts only and in a purely incidental context.[8]

Two other studies must be mentioned, however: Rosemary Woolf's full-length study of 'The English Mystery Plays'

5. The relevant portion is on pp. 43-75.
6. P. 48, n. 12. For Eucherius read Claude of Turin. See P. Glorieux, Pour revaloriser Migne, Lille 1952, p. 35.
7. Princeton 1963, p. 382f.
8. East Lansing 1952, p. 110 f. See p. 384 of the same work.

(London 1972) devotes some space to a discussion of the topic (pp. 219 -23) in the drama in England. A purely philological-methodological study of the exegesis in German (with reference too to Old and Middle English) appeared, by the present writer, in the yearbook of the Osaka-Kobe Japanischer Verein für Germanistik (Doitsu Bungaku Ronko 13, 1971, pp. 43 -63). Materials augmenting this paper may be found in chapter VI of the present study.

The lack of any full literary study of the vernacular versions of the motif as such is a curious omission. No-one would deny the validity—explored so fully in recent years—of looking at medieval secular poetry in terms of Christian exegetical traditions, just as it is equally apparent that some critics have been over-enthusiastic in the pursuit of this approach.[9] But to proceed from a fairly brief discussion of the Christian background to secular works which may or may not be connected with the point is at least to miss out an important step. The literary-religious poetry in the vernacular, and perhaps even more so the drama, sermons[10] and art[11] all provide potential bridges between theological writing proper and literary texts. Nor is the artistic value of the purely religious material negligible—for it is here where the academic prose of most of the theological material is given shape in the vernacular language. Exact source-study is of course rarely possible: we are usually as ill able to point to a religious work in the vernacular as the source of a motif in a secular poem as we are to point to one specific Latin commentary.

9. Some examples of the techniques are listed by J. Hillis Miller, Literature and Religion, in: Relations of Literary Study, ed. James Thorpe, New York 1967, p. 122f., n. 22. As an example of its exaggerated use, see H. B. Willson, Echoes of St. Paul in the 'Nibelungenlied' (MLN 84, 1969), pp. 699-715.

10. Well justified in G. R. Owst, Literature and Pulpit in Medieval England, Cambridge 1933.

11. See F. P. Pickering, Literatur und darstellende Kunst im Mittelalter, Berlin 1966.

But the examination of the vernacular religious writing can show some startling similarities with, or clear up obscure passages in its more widely studied literary contemporaries. One final justifi cation for this sort of study needs to be made. Many, if admittedly not all of these neglected religious works, have their own intrinsic literary value, and certainly in most cases an intrinsic interest. This applies even to the better sermons. Especially, however, it applies to some of the poetical and dramatic works. In our particular context, Milton is by no means the first artist to draw the parallel between the two temptation scenes. He is just the best-known in a continuous chain of creative religious writing that stretches from Ireland to Germany, from Iceland to Portugal, covering some eight hundred years.

The medieval approach to scriptural interpretation has been discussed in a number of key works such as those by Henri de Lubac, Friedrich Ohly, Beryl Smalley, Ceslas Spicq and others.[12] It need, therefore, only be reviewed briefly here. The best-known form of medieval scriptural interpretation allows for each individual verse of the Bible to be expounded accord- ing to any or every one of four senses, a literal or historical sense (*sensus litteralis*) and three spiritual senses. While the spiritual senses are wholly interpretative, this is, or may be, true to a certain extent of the *sensus litteralis,* which may not be taken as a literal reading in any modern sense.[13] As a concrete example of this point, the serpent of Genesis 3: 1 is invariably taken as the devil or his agent in early and medieval Christianity

12. Exégèse mediévale, Lyons 1959 -64; Vom geistigen Sinn des Wortes im Mittelalter (Zeitschrift für deutsches Altertum 89, 1958/9), pp. 1-23; The Study of the Bible in the Middle Ages, 2nd ed. Oxford 1952; Esquisse d'une histoire de l'exégèse latine au moyen age, Paris 1944. A glance at these shows how simplified the fourfold pattern is, and how often works do not conform.

13. See Anthony Nemetz, Literalness and the *sensus litteralis* (Specu- lum 34, 1959), pp. 76 -89.

13

and beyond, even though this is based on no Old Testament justification: this is not literal to a world which has absorbed the "higher criticism" of the nineteenth century into a part of its thought: but for the Middle Ages at least it is taken as historical fact, even though it is something *quod scriptura tacens intellegendum relinquit,*[14] "which Scriptures leaves out, to be assumed tacitly".

The spiritual senses fall into three forms. A verse may be interpreted as applicable to the general conduct of a Christian life—in the moral, that is, or the tropological sense (*sensus tropologicus*); it may be seen as containing some eschatological reference, as pointing to the last things (*sensus anagogicus*); or it may be seen in the allegorical[15] or typological sense (*sensus typologicus*)—perhaps the most important of all four senses, and that most relevant to the present study—the sense which points out the connexion between events in the New Testament and parallel events in the Old. This order for the four senses is arbitrary, and is deliberately circumspect in respect of a definition of the last, for reasons which will become apparent.

The connexion between the two temptation scenes, in Eden and in the desert, is, then, a typological one. A closer examination of precisely what this sense implies is, however, necessary. The various exegetical nuances apparent in parallels, all of which are considered as typological, have been considered by few of the scholars concerned with the two temptations, from the point of view of Milton or otherwise.[16] Once again,

14. Cited out of context from Augustine's 'De Genesi ad litteram' xi, 30, where it is used of Eve's persuasion of Adam to eat the fruit. See the edition in the Corpus scriptorum ecclesiasticorum latinorum 28/ii/2, Vienna 1894, p. 363,24f. It is also in PL 34. The point is repeated by Bede (PL 91, 54), Raban (PL 107, 488) and the Comestor (PL 198, 1072).

15. I have avoided the term "allegorical" here as this generally has a wider sense which might be confusing in the present context.

16. Exceptions are Barbara K. Lewalski, Milton's Brief Epic, Provi-

14

however, there are several standard studies of typology in general, both in a purely theological context, and also directly applied to literature: prominent among these are the works of Auerbach, Chydenius, Daniélou, Goppelt and Hanson.[17] A particularly clear consideration of the findings of many of these scholars is found, however, in the introductory chapter of a work by Heinz G. Jantsch entitled 'Studien zum Symbolischen in frühmittelhochdeutscher Literatur'.[18] As the title implies, this is a literary study of medieval German in the first instance, and it is regrettable that the body of Jantsch's book does not live up to his first chapter: the very serious faults in the rest of the work were pointed out by most of the reviewers,[19] and for this reason the work is likely to be less familiar. The grasp of the problem of typology is, however, valuable enough for it to serve as a useful starting-point here.

Jantsch offers a basic definition of typology in the following terms (translated here directly without the German text):

> "typological" is the approach that recognizes the Old Testament as prefiguring the New.

dence/London 1966, pp. 164-92, and a medieval study to which reference will be made again, Robert Longsworth, The Cornish 'Ordinalia', Cambridge/Mass. 1967, pp. 22-45.

17. Erich Auerbach, *Figura,* originally in his Neue Dantestudien, Istanbul 1944, pp. 11-71, but readily accessible in the translation by Ralph Manheim, Scenes from the Drama of European Literature, New York 1959, pp. 11-76; Johan Chydenius, The Theory of Medieval Symbolism, Helsinki 1960; Jean Daniélou, *Sacramentum futuri,* Paris 1950; Leonhart Goppelt, Typos, Gütersloh 1939, repr. Darmstadt 1969; R. P. C. Hanson, Allegory and Event, 1959.

18. Tübingen 1959. "Studies in the Symbolism of Early Middle High German Literature."

19. For example Roy Wisbey (The Year's Work in Modern Languages 22, 1960), p. 314.

To this must be added the point that

> at the starting-point of a typological exegesis stand the relevant facts
> concerned with the narration of the Redemption, facts taken up as
> *typoi* ... We are concerned in the last analysis with the under-
> standing of the Old Testament.[20]

The choice of the verb "recognize" (*erkennen*) is central here.
For this recognition can lead to an interpretation that is of
necessity adaptive. Given the New Testament as a starting-point,
if the Old Testament type offers a close, but not exact parallel
as it stands, it is sometimes interpreted in typological exegesis
to make for a closer parallel. The *locus classicus* is the interpretation of the selling of Joseph into slavery (Genesis
37: 28 f.) as a prefiguration of the betrayal of Christ. The sum
of money involved in Joseph's case has to be adapted before it
can prefigure that accepted by Judas. The typological sense of
Scripture, then, as far as it affects the Old Testament side, may
be doubly interpretative: once for the parallel itself, and again
to make that parallel fit. This phenomenon, which one might
term inverse typology, will be seen in the context of the
temptation parallel, although the picture is confused in this case
by the existence of certain pre-Christian traditions which may
have affected the way in which the adaptions are made.

The typological sense sees the Old Testament as prefigurative: this is the philosophical foundation—the role of the
old law was to prefigure the new. The notion of prefiguration
can, however, have various shades of meaning, and Jantsch has
listed a large variety of ways in which the terms *typos* and
figura are understood in New Testament and interpretative
Christian typology.[21] Not all of his findings are relevant here,
but some of them are central to our theme.

The basic form taken by the idea of typology is that the
Old Testament passage simply indicates what is to come in the

20. Studien, pp. 8 and 6.
21. Ibid. pp. 25 -9.

New Testament. Jantsch cites Romans 5: 14 as a (pertinent) example of this: [*Adam*] *est forma futuri* (= *typos tou mellontos*)—simply a picture-in-advance of something that will happen later.

Closely involved with the idea of typology, however, is the notion of fulfillment. A figure, a type, Jantsch points out, may be fulfilled or confirmed: *implere* or *confirmare*.[22] In a sense, all types are confirmed in their New Testament antitypes. The more relevant question is: what is meant by "fulfillment" in this context? The term implies that the New Testament event goes further, in some way, than its Old Testament parallel. Not only is the New Testament event indicated in the Old, but it improves on it in some way: Jantsch uses the term "augmented repetition" (*gesteigerte Wiederholung*).[23]

The notion of fulfillment needs, finally, to be taken one stage further. In certain cases, the Old Testament type is "recapitulated"—I use the term first employed in this context in the soteriological exegesis of the Greek Church Father Irenaeus of Lyons. Irenaeus means by recapitulation (*anakephalaiosis*) a case where a New Testament event not only has a parallel in the Old Testament, but where the two events have a causal link; further, that the New Testament event—usually in the Gospels— makes good (or in Evans' term, neutralizes) the (still prefigurative) earlier event.

We have, then, a progression in typological exegesis. Typology may imply simply prefiguration: event A told us that event B was going to happen. It may imply an augmented New Testament parallel to an Old Testament event: event A told us that event B was going to happen, but when event B did happen, things were added to it. Or the typology may be recapitulative: event A prefigured event B, but where event A was not a success, event B did the job properly. The recapitula-

22. Ibid. p. 33.
23. Ibid. p. 39.

tive typology envisions a reworking, then, of the Old Testament: the same numbers are used, the problem is set up in the same way, but in the second case the correct answer is achieved: the "equation" is made to balance.

It is, of course, often difficult to distinguish between these different forms. Indeed, there are sub-divisions even within these sub-divisions, and the ramifications of typology have long been the subject of debate. All of these forms, however, will be relevant to the study of the temptation equation. It might be added, incidentally, that, as Jantsch again points out, the concept of *typos* is sometimes used in the New Testament to mean something like "example". This concept, too, is relevant to our topic, but I have considered it proper to treat this point not as typology proper, but rather as tropology, as interpretation in a wider, moralizing sense.[24]

Let us then apply the various shades of meaning contained in the notion of typology to the two temptations. Our starting-point is, of course, the Gospel narrative: Christ overcomes the devil after three temptations in the desert. As an example of the first type of simple prefiguration in the context of Christ and Adam we may take the verse of Romans mentioned above. In very general terms, Adam is a simple prefiguration of Christ. Adam's divine creation and his direct link with God the Father prefigures that of Christ, also placed in the world by God. It must be noted, of course, that if we pursue the Adam-Christ parallel (which one philosopher at least-Kierkegaard—has seen as being more confusing than valuable)[25] we come into the other meanings of typology: Christ certainly augments or fulfils Adam—the latter is made by God, but of earth, where Christ is the literal son of God. And, as we shall

24. Ibid. p. 27. See no. 2 (*Vorbild*).
25. 'Begrebet angest', translated by Walter Lowrie as The Concept of Dread, Princeton 1944, p. 30. Kierkegaard recognizes that the concept is at least incomplete. See also Longsworth, 'Ordinalia,' p. 33.

see, Christ recapitulates Adam: whether it be in the desert, on the Cross, or in the Resurrection, Christ neutralizes Adam's sin.

For an example of fulfilled typology in this context, however, it will be clearer if we take two different Old Testament parallels. By taking two it can be made clear that the notion of fulfillment or improvement in this context may also be ambiguous. The two examples are both very familiar types of our Gospel story, widely known from such medieval compilations of typology as the 'Speculum humanae salvationis' and the 'Biblia pauperum'. The first example may be termed positive, the second negative. On the one hand, the temptation and victory of Christ is seen as having been prefigured in the victory of David over Goliath (1 Kings 17: 49). Christ's conquest of Satan is, of course, much the greater, although the parallel is a valid one, even if it requires some interpretation—David uses small stones, Christ small words, and so on. What is of interest, however, is that a parallel may readily be seen, however much interpretation goes into this.

On the negative side, we may cite the incident of Esau's selling of his birthright for food (Genesis 25: 29f.). This is linked with the first temptation of Christ, which the medieval exegete saw as a temptation—overcome by Christ—to gluttony. We are close here to recapitulation. Christ does rework the problem here—he takes the same point but conquers, where Esau is conquered. But this is only prefiguration in a negative sense, not in a completely fulfilled sense. There is no question of Christ neutralizing Esau's folly, and there is no causal connexion between the two incidents.

The causal connexion is seen, of course, in the juxtaposing of Adam's Fall with Christ's victory in the desert. Christ makes good what Adam did wrong. All three Old Testament passages—David and Goliath, Esau, and the Fall of Man, may be seen as prefiguring the temptation of Christ. Only the last implies—or need imply—a recapitulation. On the other hand, the Fall of Man may be seen purely as confirmative typology, simply pointing to the prefigurative aspects of the parallel; it may be seen as fulfilled typology—Christ improved on Adam, but did not neutralize Adam's sin until the Crucifixion; or it may be seen in the fully recapitulative sense.

In whatever sense the point is taken, of course, a certain amount of preliminary interpretation is necessary. The usual type of Christ is—after the passage in Romans—Adam himself. And yet the temptation in Eden is directed mostly at Eve. In our parallel, the pair in Eden are fused into one, although some vernacular writers (and indeed some theological ones) feel this as a problem, and have Eve as the type for Christ. In fact this does not, although it might be a danger, confuse the usual view of Eve as the type of the Virgin. Some vernacular writers even postulate that Adam himself overcame the devil prior to Eve's temptation: in this case Adam is a confirmative type of Christ, or one whose actions need to be augmented, rather than re-capitulated in the Irenaean sense.

This then is the purpose of this study: to examine the various forms the typological parallel may take, with special reference to vernacular literature in the Middle Ages. The chief concern is with the parallel in the recapitulative sense, although all the others—and also the quasi-tropological form—will be represented. But the centre of the tradition must be the balancing out of the equation, the neutralization that culminates in Milton's poems. For the point is of the greatest importance to medieval thought. The medieval mind—if such a generalization is admissible—saw history as a divine circle, God-organized and teleological:[26] the Fall prepares for the Redemption, and the latter is inherent in the former. We need to be saved, and to be saved we need to fall. The divine wholeness of history is felt at least by the religious writers of the Middle Ages, and it is here where, in the first instance, the

26. On the point see Sarah A. Weber, Theology and Poetry in the Middle English Lyrics, Ohio 1969, pp. 4 -6.

points will be expressed. That there should be a tradition that sees the Redemption as taking place in the desert rather than on Calvary is fascinating in itself. And for all the adaption that is needed to make the parallel fit, the connexion between the two temptation-scenes is typologically sounder than that which sets the tree of knowledge against the Holy Rood. Our parallel is more human, and as such it is more satisfying. Milton felt this, and he was by no means the first.

Two quotations may serve as the twin poles of this study, taken from two of the most important later literary monuments to be discussed. The first is from a sixteenth-century *auto* by the Portuguese court dramatist Gil Vicente, which has as its subject the "history of God"—the story, that is, of the divine plan, beginning with the Fall and closing with the temptation in the desert. In the expository opening passage we hear how the

> . . . ressurreição de Nosso Senhor
> tem as raízes naquele pomar,
> ao pé daquela árvore . . .
> onde Adão se fêz pecador . . .[27]

(The Resurrection of our Lord/ has its roots in the same orchard/ at the roots of the same tree . . ./ where Adam became a sinner)

The other pole is Milton, at the triumphant close of 'Paradise Regained', apostrophizing the victory of Christ:

> . . . now thou hast aveng'd
> Supplanted Adam, and by vanquishing
> Temptation, hast regain'd lost Paradise,
> And frustrated the conquest fraudulent:
> He never more henceforth will dare set foot
> In Paradise to tempt; his snares are broke:
> For, though that seat of earthly bliss be fail'd,

27. Gil Vicente. Breve Sumário da História de Deus, ed. João de Almeida Lucas, Lisbon 1943, p. 41, vv. 6 -9. The passage will be discussed in more detail in chapter VI.

A fairer Paradise is founded now
For Adam and his chosen sons, whom thou
A Saviour, art come down to re-install.[28]

28. Paradise Regained iv, 606 -15, cited from the Columbia University
Edition, ed. Frank A. Patterson, New York 1931-8, II/2/480f.

II   SCRIPTURE AND EXEGESIS

The three synoptic Gospels all offer accounts of the temptation of Christ in the desert by Satan. The briefest is that of Mark (1: 12f.) which simply mentions a period of forty days and adds—the only one of the Gospels to do so—that Christ *erat cum bestiis,* "was with the animals." The versions offered by Luke and by Matthew are substantially similar, and far more detailed. Up to Milton, the latter (which is also probably the earlier), is the version most commonly—indeed, almost invariably—utilized in vernacular paraphrase and exposition, as well as in art. I cite, for convenience, the Vulgate text of Matthew in full:

> Tunc Jesus ductus est in desertum a spiritu, ut tentaretur a diabolo: et cum ieiunasset quadraginta diebus et quadraginta noctibus, postea esuriit. Et accedens tentator dixit ei: si filius dei es, dic ut lapides isti panes fiant. Qui respondens dixit: scriptum est: non in solo pane vivit homo, sed in omni verbo quod procedit de ore dei. Tunc adsumpsit eum diabolus in sanctam civitatem et statuit eum super pinnaculum templi. Et dixit ei: si filius dei es, mitte te deorsum; scriptum est enim: quia angelis suis mandavit de te, et in manibus tollent te, ne forte offendas ad lapidem pedem tuum. Ait illi Jesus: rursum scriptum est: non tentabis dominum deum tuum. Iterum adsumpsit eum diabolus in montem excelsum valde et ostendit ei omnia regna mundi et gloriam eorum et dixit ei: haec omnia tibi dabo si cadens adoraveris me. Tunc dixit ei Jesu: vade Satanas: scriptum est enim: dominum deum tuum adoraberis et illi soli servies. Tunc relinquit eum diabolus, et ecce angeli accesserunt et ministrabant ei.

> (Matthew 4: 1-11)

The temptations hinge, then, upon three points: that Christ should turn the stones into bread; that he should throw himself from the temple; that he should gain the kingdoms of the world by worshipping the devil. The Lucan version (Luke 4: 1-13)

24

differs, apart from a few verbal points, primarily in the order of the temptations, for here the last two are reversed.[1]

It must be stressed at this point once again that the equation with the Fall is by no means the only exegesis of the Gospel narrative relevant to our works. Mention might be made, for example, of the very important notion of the devil's ignorance of Christ's identity, a point stressed by many of the early Fathers in the context of the doctrine of the dual nature of Christ. The soteriological implication is that the temptation of Christ is designed by the devil precisely to elucidate whether Christ is man or God.[2] This has a bearing on the question of the "devil's rights," and the devil loses his rights over man through the Redemption. The question of the devil's uncertainty, and the dual nature of Christ, can have an effect on certain aspects of the narrative, even when the Fall parallel is at the forefront. At the close of the temptation-scene the devil is sometimes portrayed as bewildered, although the sense of triumphant recapitulation is of course clearer in those versions where Christ is revealed as God to the devil.

It is difficult to estimate when the temptations in the desert came to be linked in any way with the Fall of Man as narrated in Genesis 3. The general typology of Adam and Christ is familiar and of course scriptural (Romans 5: 12 etc.). It has been suggested (though not universally accepted) that the Gospel narratives themselves rest in the first instance upon a deliberate typological parallel with the Fall. That there is a certain typological intent here seems to be undeniable; there is a

1. Pope, 'Paradise Regained,' discusses the narratives, pp. 1-12. It might be noted that the rebuttal of the devil familiar from the Authorized Version, "Get thee behind me, Satan," is not in the Vulgate, nor in the modern translations, and was adopted from the Bishops' Bible of 1568. See The New Testament Octapla, ed. Luther A. Weigle, Edinburgh/New York/Toronto 1962, p. 336f.
2. See Köppen, Auslegung, p. 85f. Also Woolf, Mystery Plays, p. 221.

conscious desire on the part of the creator of the desert story to
establish a connexion between this incident and the Mosaic era,
thus strengthening the claims of Jesus as the Messiah. Leonhard
Goppelt, in his standard study of New Testament typology,
cites the Old Testament examples of forty-day fasts (by Moses
in Exodus 34: 28 and Deuteronomy 9: 9 and 18, and by Elias
in 1 Kings 9: 5 and 8), as well as the link between the "stones
into bread" request and the manna miracle.[3] Evidence for a
direct link with the Fall, however, is less straightforward: the
difficulties are partly chronological and partly due to the fact
that the relevant material is mostly apocryphal rather than
canonical. There may be a link, for example, between the
forty-day penance in the desert and the forty-day period of
fasting undertaken as penance by Adam, standing in the river
Jordan, after the expulsion from Eden. This tradition is found,
however, in the fourth century Latin 'Life of Adam', the 'Vita
Adae et Evae', one version of a series of legends about the
post-Fall life of the first couple known throughout Europe for
most of the Middle Ages, and translated into nearly all of the
European vernaculars, from Irish to Old Church Slavonic, over a
period of many centuries. There are also numerous metrical
adaptions of these legends. It might be noted further that, apart
from the family of legends to which these works belong, there
arc other more or less closely related collections of Adam-
legends extant in such languages as Ethiopian, Arabic and
Syriac.[4]

3. Goppelt, Typos, p. 118f. See also p. 157f. For a variant view, see
Hans G. Leder, Die Auslegung der zentralen theologischen Aussagen der
Paradieserzählung, Diss. Greifswald 1961, pp. 814, 825, 831.

4. See Friedrich Stegmüller, Repertorium biblicum medii aevi, Madrid
1940 -61, I, 25 -35. Some vernacular versions are listed by L. S. A. Wells
in: Apocrypha and Pseudepigrapha of the Old Testament, ed. R. H.
Charles, London 1913, II, 133, and by Wilhelm Meyer, 'Vita Adae et Evae'
(Abhandlungen der Bayerischen Akademie der Wissenschaften, philos.-

The 'Vita' itself is a Christian text. The Greek apocryphon with which it is most intimately connected, the somewhat earlier 'Apocalypsis Mosis,' does not contain this particular motif.[5] In spite of this, it has been shown that the notion of the penance as such belongs to the Jewish core of the legends, and is therefore of some antiquity: this was demonstrated by internal linguistic evidence by Louis Ginzberg, in spite of an earlier assumption by Jewish scholars that the entire episode is Christian.[6] The episode in the 'Vita' has, however, a fairly strong Christian overlay in any case, and it is difficult to sort out what is originally Jewish here and what has been added.[7] Finally, the length of time that the penance is to take, while normally forty days, varies quite considerably in Jewish and indeed in the various Christian recensions. Any evidence that there is in these Adam-legends is, then, necessarily somewhat shaky.[8]

There is, however, one further piece of evidence for a pre-Christian link between the Fall and the temptations,

philol. Cl. 16/iii, 1878), pp. 185-200. The relevant Irish text is the 'Saltair na Rann,' which is rarely included in these and similar lists. It is a metrical work of the tenth century and has been edited by Whitley Stokes, A Collection of Early Middle Irish Poems, Oxford 1883. There is partial translation by Eleanor Hull in: The Poem-Book of the Gael, London 1912, pp. 1-52. A new edition and translation is in preparation at the hands of Professor David Greene of the Dublin Institute for Advanced Studies, to whom thanks are due for this information.

5. See Wells/Charles, Apocrypha II, 135 for the 'Vita' text in English. The Latin original ('Vita' vii, 2–viii, 3) is in Meyer, 'Vita,' p. 223.

6. The Legends of the Jews, Philadelphia 1913-38. V, 114f., n. 106. He refutes Israel Lévi, Eléments chrétiens dans le 'Pirké Rabbi Eliézer,' (Revue des études juives 18, 1889), pp. 86-9.

7 See Louis Ginzberg's own discussion of the 'Book of Adam' in: The Jewish Encyclopaedia, New York/London 1901-6, I, 179f.

8. Versions vary from a penance of 33 to one of 49 days—the latter being the case in the 'Pirkê de Rabbi Eliezer,' a Jewish text that is however

although this is again tenuous. In Jewish writings over a long period of time, three specific sins are ascribed to Adam which resemble very closely those with which the devil, according to later Christian exegesis, tried to tempt Christ. The earliest example is in the Babylonian Talmud, in the Mishnaic tractate 'Aboth', of the third century AD but stemming from an older tradition. It might be remembered incidentally that the entire form of the temptation in the desert is very like a rabbinic debate, citing text for text in dispute.[9] 'Aboth' contains the statement:

> Rabbi Eleazar Ha-Kappar said: Jealousy, cupidity and [the desire for] honour put a man out of the world.[10]

R. Travers Herford, in a different translation, renders the sins involved as "jealousy, desire and ambition."[11] This is echoed later in the Middle Ages, in the eighth century 'Pirkê de Rabbi Eliezer': Gerald Friedlander, translating this text, sees the man as Adam:

> Envy, cupidity and ambition remove man (Adam) from the world.[12]

Rather later still, the philosopher Moses Maimonides, writing in his 'Guide to the Perplexed' ('More Nebuchim') in the twelfth century, refers, this time in the specific context of the Fall, to

post-Christian. But see Evans, 'Paradise Lost,' p. 103. For further comment on the penance, see Brian Murdoch, The River that Stopped Flowing, to appear in Southern Folklore Quarterly, 1973.

9. See Ernst Lohmeyer, Die Versuchung Jesu, in: Urchristliche Mystik, Darmstadt 1956, p. 84.

10. The Babylonian Talmud, ed. I. Epstein, London 1935-52, vol. Seder nezikin 8, 1935, p. 55f. This is usually considered as Aboth iv, 21 (or 28).

11. In Charles, Apocrypha II, 706—here as iv, 28, and based on the Vilna edition of the 'Talmud Babli.'

12. Pirkê de Rabbi Eliezer. The Chapters of Rabbi Eliezer the Great, London 1916, p. 91 (= chapter 13 on the reckoning of Friedlander).

Adam's gluttony; this seems to represent the last stage in the Jewish view of Adam's sins—general cupidity turning into specific gluttony, which is the central pivot of the link between the temptation of Christ and of Adam in the Middle Ages at least.[13]

There is, then, a Jewish tradition imputing to Adam certain sins, and it may be that the three temptations of Christ make a deliberate parallel to this fact. But the parallel with the Jewish sins is by no means exact, and the other possibility remains that Christian exegesis interprets first the sins with which Christ is tempted, and then interprets Adams Fall to become a "prefiguration" of this. The typological approach, after all, starts with the Gospel, and consists frequently, as we have seen, of highly interpretative hindsight. The Jewish imputation of three similar sins to Adam may, then, be coincidental, and we may surmise, in this case, that here as with the forty-day fast, the New Testament has in fact shaped the exegesis of the Old Testament, or (partially) the apocryphal Adam-Legends, rather than vice versa.

The history of the development of the exegesis within Christian thought, specifically in the Greek and Latin patristic and post-patristic writers is a complex one. Nor is it desirable to duplicate here the findings of Köppen, Howard and Pope. None of these, however, groups the various interpretations of the temptations according to basic attitude. It seems appropriate here to review in outline the history of the exegesis, highlighting the most significant expositions, but mentioning too as many of the places where the exegesis is found as possible, to give an indication of the spread of the various ideas. Some individual motifs outside the mainstream of the exegetical history will also emerge, and these will be dealt with in detail when they are of relevance to the later study of vernacular writings. Most of the

13. The Guide of the Perplexed, transl. Shlomo Pines, Chicago 1963, pp. 23 -6.

material to be covered here will be taken from exegetical commentaries and theological tractates proper: but concordance-style works such as the 'Speculum humanae salvationis,' pious legend-collections of the order of the 'Legenda aurea', and some chronicles will also be relevant. Concentration will, moreover, be upon the direct parallelism of the two temptation scenes. While the other exegetical traditions mentioned, for example, by Howard—the three stages of sin, and the interpretations of 1 John 2: 16—will be of incidental importance, it would confuse the overall picture unnecessarily if they were to be treated in any detail here. The aim is primarily the investigation of a typology, and both of these lean at least towards the tropological, although they are used frequently in conjunction with our typological parallel in commentaries. Attention will be mainly on commentaries on Matthew (and sometimes on Genesis): those on Luke make the connexion less often, in view of the less suitable Lucan order of temptations. Certain figures may be taken whose work is either very influential, or clearly demonstrative of a certain approach. Thus attention will be paid especially to Irenaeus of Lyons, in whose soteriology of recapitulation the point reaches its zenith, or to Gregory the Great, one of the major figures of the Middle Ages—centuries which "followed the principles of St Augustine and the practice of St Gregory, or St Augustine, via the 'Moralia' of St Gregory."[14] Gregory's immediate predecessor in this point, John Cassian, is also important, and later in the Middle Ages Thomas Aquinas makes some interesting changes. But these are only the major figures. Almost as important are the many exegetes whose work follows, say, Gregory. It is necessary to document these as fully as possible, even if this overlaps to an extent with the findings of earlier researchers. The materials to be presented here augment those of Pope and Howard, but cannot, even so, claim to be nearly complete. There are bound to be gaps, particularly

14. Spicq, Esquisse, p. 11.

in the later Middle Ages: much material from this period remains unedited or in particularly rare editions. One is left, therefore, with the prospect that the 'Quadragesimale' of Johannes Gritsch, the 'Sermones dominicales' of Hugh of Prato, the 'Praedicationes' of Roberto Caracciola or the 'Sermonarium' of Michael de Carcano might well contain the point in some form.[15] To verify this, however, would involve much perhaps unprofitable travelling from library to library: but the material that can be obtained can demonstrate the extent to which a given motif was known. This is of course the main justification for offering at all evidence that at first sight seems to be superfluous—of adopting, perhaps, an approach more suitable to the doctoral dissertation. But it is rarely possible with a medieval work to determine the exact source of a given theological point. Gregory, let us say, may be the foundation of a widely-known exegesis. But a German work from the Fulda region some centuries after Gregory might equally well have taken the Gregorian idea from one of the commentaries of

15. There is no single bibliographical source that can provide a key to works of this kind. The necessarily fortuitous examples provided here are culled in the main from catalogues of antiquarian booksellers, as well as more orthodox sources. Special mention must be made of the excellent catalogues of William Salloch, of Ossining, New York. The works mentioned are all relatively rare. Gritsch was a friar minor whose Lenten sermons were published at Ulm in 1475, with later editions; Hugh was a Dominican who died in 1322, and whose works were published in Strasbourg in 1476; Carraciola, a Franciscan born in 1425, whose works appeared in Venice in c. 1475; Michael de Carcano, another Franciscan of the mid-fifteenth century, published his sermons in that city in 1476. We might add the sermons of John of Werden (d. 1437), whose sermons were published in Ulm in c. 1480; those of Jordan of Quedlinburg (fl. c. 1325), published in Strasbourg in 1483; the 'Quadragesimale' of his contemporary, François Mayron (Venice, 1491); the Quadragesimal sermons of Peter of Paludo (c. 1280-1342), published in Antwerp in 1572. See the Salloch catalogues nos. 186-7 (1971).

Raban Maurus. Even if Gregory is cited as the source in the vernacular, this is scarcely conclusive, as this may have been the case in the derivative work. Biblical exegesis from the time of Bede to, say, the early scholastics, remains enormously eclectic, dependent upon the Fathers, and making only the slightest adaptions to their commentaries.[16] In view of the usual difficulty of establishing conclusive internal evidence for a point, the documentation must try to be as broad as possible.

Of the three studies of the exegesis by Köppen, Howard and Pope, only the first deals to any extent with the earliest instances of the parallel. Köppen points to the very brief reference in the 'Dialogue with Trypho' of the apologist Justin Martyr, as well as to general parallels in the writings of Chrysostom and Theodoret of Cyrus.[17] The first clearly typological case that Köppen mentions, however, is in the Greek fourth-century apocryphon known in the Latin version in which the bulk of it has survived as the 'Passio Bartholomaei.' The stress here is on the notion of gluttony (although it is not named yet). Adam ate the fruit and fell; Christ did not turn the stones into bread, and so conquered: Christ allowed himself

se temptari a diabolo illo qui primum hominem uicerat suadendo ut de arbore uetita a deo manducare praesumeret. ipsum ergo permisit ad se acedere, ut sicut dixerat Adae, id est primo homini, per mulierem: Manduca, et manducauit, et sic de paradiso est proiectus et in isto mundo exiliatus, et sic genuit omne humanum genus ita et isti diceret: Dic lapidibus istis ut panes fiant, et manduca et non esuriis. Cui respondit: Non in pane tantum uiuit homo sed in omni uerbo dei. Hic ergo diabolus, qui per manducantem hominem uicerat uictoriam suam, per ieiuniantem et se contemnentem amisit. par enim erat ut qui filium uirginis uicerat a filio uirginis uinceretur.[18]

16. See Robert E. McNally, The Bible in the Early Middle Ages, Westminster/Md. 1959, pp. 11-17.

17. Auslegung, p. 79f.

18. Auslegung, p. 80. The text is from the Acta Apostolorum Apocrypha, ed. Richard Lipsius and Maximilian Bonnet, Leipzig 1891-1903,

(to be tempted by the devil, the very same who overcame the first man, persuading him to presume to eat from the tree forbidden by God. Therefore Christ permitted him to approach him, and just as he had said to the first man, Adam, via his wife, "eat,"—and he did eat, and was thrown from Paradise and exiled in this world, giving rise to the human race—thus he said to Christ: "tell these stones to become bread, and eat and do not hunger." And Christ replied: "man does not live by bread alone, but by all the words of God." Therefore the devil, who won a victory through a man who ate, was condemned by one who fasted. In the same way, then, the one who conquered the son of the virgin [earth] was conquered by the son of the Virgin.)

The 'Passio Bartholomaei" is typological, and in a Pauline sense: Köppen points out that Christ is referred to here as *deuteros anthropos* and as *deuteros Adam*—the second man, or the second Adam. Christ makes good by fasting what Adam lost through eating: the notion of recapitulation is there. But I have chosen to discuss this text here, out of chronological sequence, for a different reason. It is interesting in the stress on the actual eating, pointing to the greed of Adam. This stress on the fasting continues throughout the Middle Ages, and is often set off naturally against Adam's gluttony. There are, in fact, independent references to this particular sin from an early stage. The second-century Latin Father Tertullian has it, for example,[19] and it is natural that it would be mentioned in this context. An anonymous Irish compilation of the seventh or eight centuries, and ascribed to Jerome, echoes the 'Passio Bartholomaei' in concise form. Christ fasted for forty days *quia per haec peccatum Adae delere debuit,* "because this was necessary to eliminate the sin of Adam."[20]

But the notion of Adam's greed and Christ's fast, while

II/i, 136 (chapter 4 (10), 4 -15). See the introduction, p. xxiv on the text.

19. De ieiunio III, 2: see the edition in the Corpus Christianorum, series Latina, Turnhout 1954, II, 1259, 5ff.

20. Expositio quattuor Evangeliorum (PL 30, 541).

basically typological, may easily be adapted to a tropological approach, and for this reason it is appropriate to examine this idea first. The position of the Matthew pericope is at the beginning of Lent. Thus Maximus of Turin makes the point in a tropological sense in his 'Homilia de ieiunio quadragesimae I' (PL 57, 303), and other, later examples may be adduced.[21] The evidence of the twelfth-century 'Summa de arte praedicatoria' of Alan of Lille is perhaps the most telling in this context, however. Under the heading *contra gulam,* "against gluttony" comes the admonition:

> Considera, o homo, quomodo Adam per gulam perdidit paradisum![22]
>
> (Consider, o man, in what manner Adam, through gluttony, lost Paradise!)

This and similar comments could have conditioned the approach even to our parallel in many of the Lenten homilies taking the pericope as their starting-point.

The Greek examples cited point, however, equally clearly to the typological approach, and one of the Greek Fathers is of primary importance here. Irenaeus, bishop of Lyons in the second century, uses the parallel of the temptations in the context of this theory of recapitulation (*anakephalaiosis*). Johannes Quasten has summed up this doctrine as follows: it implies

> a taking up in Christ of all since the beginning. God rehabilitates the earlier divine plan for the salvation of mankind which was inter-

21. In the sermons of Maximus, see also PL 57, 559 -62. Further, the Genesis-commentary of Claude of Turin, (PL 50, 914f.); the Matthew-commentary of Rupert of Deutz (PL 167, 1548—see also the Matthew commentary, below, note 41); that of Anselm of Laon (PL 162, 1270); Bruno of Asti (on Luke, PL 165, 91); the Quadragesimal sermon of Hildebert of Lavardin (PL 171, 423 -7); the 'Lignum Vitae' of Bonaventure, in: Obras de San Buenaventura, ed. Leon Amoros, etc., Madrid 1945 -9, II, 308.

22. PL 210, 121.

rupted by the Fall of Adam, and gathers up his entire work from the beginning to renew, to restore, to reorganize it in his incarnate Son, who in this way becomes for us a second Adam .... By this recapitulation of the original man, not only Adam personally but the whole human race was renovated and restored .... Christ renewed everything by this recapitulation.[23]

Irenaeus is not of course the only theologian to take up this line, which is in itself a development of the Pauline anthropology of Romans 5:12. But he defines the attitude in a particularly clear form. He does so in his major work, the text known usually as the 'Contra haereses' or 'Adversus haereses' ('Against the Heretics'), a work preserved mainly in a Latin text of the fourth or fifth century (and used here), with fragments of the original Greek extant, as well as versions in some of the Eastern Christian languages. As Köppen (but neither Howard nor Pope) points out, Irenaeus treats the three temptations of Christ separately.[24] He stresses first the point of the forty-day fast, commenting that this overcomes the fact that Adam ate. This point we have of course seen already in the later 'Passio Bartholomaei', and it is found in other Greek writings in a more or less typological sense.[25]

The Latin text of the 'Adversus haereses' reads for the first temptation:

in principio per escam, non esurientem hominem seducit adversarius transgredi praeceptum Dei .... Quae ergo fuit in paradiso repletio hominis per duplicem gustationem, dissoluta est per eam, quae fuit in hoc mundo, indigentiam.[26]

23. Patrology, Utrecht 1950-60, I, 296. Several critics of 'Paradise Regained' refer to Irenaeus, such as Lewalski, Epic, p. 168 and Evans, 'Paradise Lost,' p. 103.
24. Auslegung, p. 81f.
25. Köppen refers to Chrysostom, PseudoChrysostom and Cyril of Alexandria in particular.
26. V, 21 (PG 7, 1180).

(in the beginning the adversary seduced with food the man who was not fasting into breaking the commandment of God . . . Therefore the fact that man in Paradise filled his belly—both of them ate—had to be wiped out by poverty in this world.)

The second temptation refers to pride, *elatio* in the Latin; but here the reference is to the serpent. Christ's humility in the temptation of the tower is set against this pride; and it is this stress on Christ's humility that will be encountered again in this context in vernacular writings:

Elatio itaque sensus, quae fuit in serpente dissoluta est per eam, quae fuit in homine humilitas . . . .[27]

(the pride that was in the serpent had to be wiped out by the humility that was in the man . . . .)

The third temptation, that of the kingdoms, is seen in a general sense as having wiped out once and for all the sins of Adam. Specific sins of the protoplasts at this point are not named, but emphasis appears to be on Adam's disobedience. This victory by Christ is the final definitive one:

et soluta est ea, quae fuerat in Adam praecepti Dei praevaricatio, per praeceptum legis, quod servavit Filius hominis, non transgrediens praeceptum Dei.[28]

(thus the breaking of the commandment by Adam was expiated by the precept of the law, which the Son of Man observed, by not breaking the commandment of God.)

The parallelism, then, is fully worked out—although it will undergo changes in later theology. More important, it is an

27. PG 7, 1180. On the idea that Adam's faults are cancelled out by Christ's virtues, see Pope, 'Paradise Regained,' p. 53f., Howard, Temptations, p. 53. Tropological implications may of course easily be drawn from this attitude, and as both Pope and Howard point out, the interpretations of the 1 John 2: 16 triad become relevant here.

28. PG 7, 1180

independent piece of doctrine, central, incidentally, to Irenaeus' thought.

The parallel is found early in the Latin Church. Köppen refers to Hilary of Poitiers and to Ambrose,[29] both of whom draw a threefold parallel, and both of whom make incidental points of some relevance to later literature. The chief point of interest with Hilary is the caption to this section of his Matthew commentary: *Tentationum Christi idem ordo, qui Adae* (PL 9, 930)—"the temptation of Christ followed the same order as that of Adam." The question of the order is one which arises at various points of exegetical history. It is generally felt that the Matthew order is the exact parallel to the Genesis story. Luke however, is taken as the historical truth, and the assumption is sometimes made that Matthew deliberately changed the order. Thus Haymo of Auxerre (as PseudoHaymo of Halberstadt), comments:

> Matthaeus vero subtilius ordinem tentationum quo diabolus primum hominem in paradiso decepit, consideravit.[30]

> (Matthew, with more subtlety, takes into account the order of the temptations with which the devil deceived the first man.)

This point is repeated in later writings, although there is a school of thought—beginning with Augustine, and echoed in Aquinas—that the order is in any case uncertain.[31] Nevertheless, a work as widespread as the 'Glossa ordinaria' contains the brief comment, as a gloss on this portion of Luke, that

---

29. Auslegung, p. 82f.

30. Homiliae. Domenica prima in quadragesima, PL 118, 200. See Pope, 'Paradise Regained,' p. 3f. for further material on this point.

31. Augustine, De consensu Evangelistarum II, 16 (PL 1093f.) and Aquinas, Summa theologiae 3a, 41, 4. Since the parallel edition of the 'Summa' by the English Dominicans has not yet reached this, I refer to the edition/translation of P. Synave in the Paris edition, Saint Thomas d'Aquin. Somme Théologique. The relevant passage is in the volume 'Vie de Jésus' II, 247ff.

Matthaeus non sequitur ordinem historiae, sed tentationum Adae—"Matthew does not follow the historical order, but that of the temptations of Adam."[32]

Ambrose, in his Luke commentary, in fact follows the order and some of the exegesis of the Hilary Matthew commentary. This lists the three temptations as gluttony (*gula*), lack of moral firmness (*facilitas*) and ambition (*ambitio*).[33] The first point is familiar, and will remain so until Calvin. The final temptation is very close to *superbia*, which is the final sin in the exegesis of Cassian. In Ambrose's Luke commentary too, comes the parallelism of place that is sometimes found in vernacular writing: Köppen cites the concise statement: *in deserto Adam, in deserto Christus*—"Adam [was expelled into] the desert, Christ [conquered in] the desert."[34]

Like the Irenaean interpretation, these early Latin versions are in essence recapitulative, although this is by no means as clear as with the Greek Father. Their placing within generally more extensive commentaries already tends to obscure the doctrinal importance of the parallel.

A full exegesis comparing the temptations point for point in Latin is that of John Cassian in the fifth century. This exegesis is rarely discussed, and yet the 'Collations', in which it appears, was an influential and widely-read book throughout the Middle Ages. Cassian's commentary is the direct precursor of that of Gregory the Great, which is considered to be the standard for the Middle Ages.

32. PL 114, 254
33. Köppen, Auslegung, p. 83f., with references.
34. See ibid. p. 9. For a later echo of this, see the comments on the 'Golden Legend.' Also Lewalski, Epic, p. 176.

Cassian does point to the recapitulation by Christ of the sins of Adam:

> per illum omne genus hominum condemnatur, per istum omne genus hominum liberatur.[35]

> (by the one all men were condemned, by the other all men were freed.)

But the overall tone is not an apologetic one. Cassian's work is something of a transition in detail and in context from the pure recapitulation implicit even in the stress Irenaeus places on the point, to the somewhat off-hand reference to the parallel as a piece of incidental typology in sermons and commentaries—typology indeed, but with a greatly dimished intrinsic importance. Cassian sees the three sins involved as gluttony (*gastrimargia*), vainglory (*cenodoxia*), and pride (*superbia*). He deals with these first of all in the context of Adam, then in that of the Gospel story:

> Gastrimargia namque est, qua interdicti ligni praesumit edulium; cenodoxia, qua dicitur, Aperientur oculi vestri (Genes. iii); superbia qua dicitur, Eritis sicut dii, scientes bonum et malum (Gen. iii). In his ergo tribus vitiis etiam Dominum salvatorem legimus fuisse tentatum. Gastrimargia, cum dicitur ei a diabolo, Dic ut lapides isti panes fiant; cenodoxia, Si Filius Dei es, mitte te deorsum; superbia, cum ostendens illi omnia regna mundi et eorum gloriam, dicit: Haec omnia tibi dabo si cadens adoraveris me (Matth. iv).[36]

> (Gluttony came about in that he presumed to eat of the forbidden tree; vainglory, when it was said that "your eyes shall be opened"; pride, with the words "you shall be as gods, knowing good and evil." With these three sins the Lord our saviour was also tempted, so we read. Gluttony when the devil said to him: "command these stones to become bread," vainglory with "if you are the Son of

35. V, 6; (PL 49, 616). The fifth book of the 'Collations' is entitled, incidentally, 'De octo principalibus vitiis,' and is essentially moral, rather than doctrinal theology.

36. PL 49, 615f. See Paschasius Radbertus (PL 120, 196).

God, cast yourself down;" pride with "showing him all the kingdoms of the world and their glory, he said: I shall give you all this if
you fall down and worship me.")

In spite of the typology here—and Cassian goes on to discuss the
point at some length, referring even to the discrepancy in order
between Luke and Matthew—it might be noted that there is
later a clear tropological comment; Christ should serve as
exemplum, as a model to us, on how to overcome temptation.
This point is not, however, overwhelming.[37]

Both older and more modern scholars have commented
on the connexion between this exegesis and that of Gregory and
of Aquinas—two very influential figures whose commentaries
may be discussed now. In the case of Aquinas, who is perhaps
the closer to Cassian, there are even direct verbal echoes.[38] But
the commentary of Gregory is important, because it is taken up
and repeated in full or in part by very many later exegetes.
Gregory retains the first two sins of gluttony (as *gula*) and
vainglory (as *vana gloria*), but for pride he substitutes avarice:
As Cassian, he treats the Fall of Man first, and then examines
the parallel with Christ:

Antiquus hostis contra primum hominem parentem nostrum, in
tribus se tentationibus erexit, quia hunc, videlicet gula, et vana
gloria, et avaritia tentavit .... Ex gula quippe tentavit, cum cibum
ligni vetiti ostendit, atque ad comedendum suasit. Ex vana gloria
tentavit eum cum diceret: Eritis sicut dii. Ex provectu avaritiae
tentavit, cum diceret: Scientes bonum, et malum. Avaritia enim non
solum pecuniae est, sed etiam altitudinis .... Sed quibus modis
primum hominem stravit, eisdem modis secundo homini tentando
succubuit. Per gulam tentavit, qui dixit: Dic ut lapides isti panes
fiant (Matth. iv, 3). Per vanam gloriam tentavit, cum dixit: Si filius
Dei es, mitte te deorsum. Per sublimitatis avaritiam tentavit ...
dicens: Haec tibi omnia dabo ...

37. PL 49, 618
38. The comment is made by Alardus Gazeus, whose 1722 edition and
notes are reprinted in the Patrologia: see PL 49, 615f. More recently, see

(The old enemy raised himself against the first man, our parent, in three temptations, namely gluttony, vainglory and avarice . . . . He tempted with gluttony in showing him the forbidden fruit and persuading him to eat. He tempted in vainglory when he said "you shall be as gods." He tempted with avarice in saying "knowing good and evil." For avarice does not apply only to wealth, but also to power . . . But in the same manner in which he overcame the first man, in that way he fell when he tried to tempt the second. He tempted him with gluttony, saying "command these stones to become bread." With vainglory when he said "throw yourself down, if you are the Son of God." With avarice for high position when he said "I shall give you all this.")

The first temptation is identical with that of Cassian. The second hinges upon the promise that Adam and Eve would be as gods (which Cassian sees as pride). The third interprets the promise of knowledge as a lure to power. Although Gregory dubs this avarice, he does in fact equate it with pride: *in hoc ergo diabolus parentum nostrum ad superbiam traxit, quando eum ad avaritiam sublimitatis excitavit,* "here the devil drew our first parent into pride, when he led him to avarice for a high position."[39] This part of Cassian's exposition is therefore retained, although the reason behind it is somewhat different.

Gregory offers here a typology that is at least fulfilled. He comments on the victory of Christ, and his references to "our parent" point to the connexion between Adam and mankind, and to Christ's removal of the problem of original sin. Gregory concludes his exegesis with the *sententia*:

Berthold Altaner. Patrology, trans. Hilda C. Graef from the fifth German ed. of 1958, Freiburg in Br./ Edinburgh/London 1960, p. 538.

39. Homilia in Evangelia XVI (PL 76, 1136). Much attention has been paid, of course, to this text: Pope, 'Paradise Regained,' p. 52; Köppen, Auslegung, p. 84; Howard, Temptations, p. 50; Evans, 'Paradise Lost,' p. 103; Brian Murdoch, 'The Fall of Man in the Early Middle High German Biblical Epic,' Göppingen 1972, p. 70f.

eis modis a secundo homine victus est, quibus primum hominem se vicesse gloriabatur . . .[40]

(he was conquered by the second man in the same way in which he boasted of having conquered the first man.)

The Pauline inheritance remains visible in the reference to the "first and second man"—"Adam" signifying "man" in fact and in Christian tradition. Gregory's final words are tropological, however, and the position of the commentary in a homily, as a more or less *ad hoc* piece of typology, means that once again it has not the emphasis that the point has in Irenaeus. It is a fulfilled typology, then, as in Cassian, but the feeling of Christ's having made good the Fall is not strong. The fact that the Fall and the temptations of Christ are treated apart from one another differs too from the integrated treatment in Irenaeus. This is a simple, and somewhat academic parallel.

But Gregory is the most influential of the earlier expositors of the point. His exegesis is repeated in many of the Carolingian commentaries on Matthew and on Genesis.[41] It is found too in the scholastic period in a large number of sentence-collections,[42] and it is found, of course, in homilies.

40. PL 76, 1136. Already Jerome refers to vainglory, in reference to Christ (PL 26, 32), incidentally.

41. Pope, 'Paradise Regained,' p. 52, n. 2 refers to Bede, pseudo-Jerome and Raban on Matthew; Howard, Temptations, p. 50., n. 16 adds the Genesis-commentaries of Raban, Angelom of Luxeuil; we may add the following: Paterius (PL 79, 690) and Rupert of Deutz (PL 168, 1374) on Matthew; an anonymous Irish commentator on Matthew, in: Eine Würzburger Evangelienhandschrift, ed. K. Koeberlin, Augsburg 1891, p. 43, and Druthmar of Stavelot on the same Gospel (PL 106, 1296f.). See also the 'Historia scholastica' of Peter Comestor (PL 198, 1556), and Zachary Chrysopolitanus (PL 186, 104).

42. For the schoolmen, Howard mentions Hugh of St Victor's 'De sacramentis,' and the sentences of Peter Lombard. To these may be added the earlier sentences of Taio of Saragozza (PL 80, 754); the 'Dialogus de

Gregory's exegesis is reproduced in several influential works of the later Middle Ages—such as the 'Homilarium' of Paul the Deacon, and also the 'Glossa ordinaria' (under Matthew), together with its more condensed form, the 'Glossa interlinearis.'[43] It has been pointed out that the 'Glossa ordinaria' (and indeed, the interlinear gloss) was included in the great Bible published in Antwerp in 1634, already in Milton's lifetime.[44]

The key-note of Gregory's exegesis is the designation of the three sins as gluttony, vainglory and avarice. When this pattern is found in vernacular literature, it points to a source that depends at some stage upon Gregory, if Gregory himself is not in fact the source. But the approach need not of course mirror that of Gregory—it might elevate the parallel once again to the importance which it has in Irenaeus, or it might take a purely tropological standpoint.

sacramentis' of Hugh (PL 176, 25); the 'Sententiae Anselmi' and the 'Sententiae divinae paginae,' in: Anselms von Laon systematische Sentenzen, ed. F. Blimetzrieder (BGPM 18/ii-iii) Münster/W. 1919, pp. 60 and 26; the 'Sententiae Berolinenses,' ed. F. Stegmüller, Eine neugefundene Sentenzensammlung, (Recherches de théologie ancienne et médiévale 11, 1939), p. 49; 'Deus de cuius principio . . . tacetur,' ed. H. Weisweiler, Le recueil des sentences 'Deus de cuius . . .' (Recherches de théologie ancienne et médiévale 5, 1933), p. 261; the sentences of Alexander III (Orlando Bandinelli), in: Die Sentenzen Rolands, ed. Ambrosius M. Gietl, Freiburg in Br. 1891, p. 117; 'Ysagoge in theologiam,' ed. A. Landgraf, Ecrits théologiques de l'école d'Abélard, Louvain 1934, p. 111. The schools of Anselm and of Abélard are thus represented fairly fully here.

43. To Pope and Howard we may add: the gloss on Genesis (PL 113, 92) and the interlinear gloss on Matthew and Luke—both mentioning Adam—in: Biblia sacra, ed. Leander a. S. Martino, Antwerp 1634, V, 81 and 743. For Paul the Deacon, see PL 95, 1214. See further the 'Speculum Ecclesiae' of Honorius of Autun (PL 172, 941), mentioned by Edward Schröder, Das 'Anegenge', Strasbourg 1881, p. 65, in the context of one of the vernacular works to be treated later.

44. Lewalski, Epic, p. 170.

In addition to the exegetes who quote Gregory exactly, there are also a number of Latin theological writers who put forward some elements of the triad only, or who give general allusions to the parallel which may or may not derive from this source. There are, further, Latin exegetical writings and sermons which list three sins corresponding more or less to those of Gregory. To take one example, the Cistercian Isaac de Stella, who died towards the end of the twelfth century, refers in a sermon for the first Sunday in Lent (by far the most common place for the parallel in sermons), to gluttony (*gula*), vainglory (*inanis gloria*) and ambition (*ambitio*) as the three sins. The source is probably Gregory, but the *ambitio* recalls Ambrose: it is, however, simply a more logical name for the sin that Gregory somewhat tortuously sees as avarice.[45] Isaac does, incidentally, echo Irenaeus to an extent too, in that he points out how the specific sins were cancelled out by their opposites: *abstinentia vincit gulam, humilitate inanem gloriam, paupertate saeculi ambitionem,* "with abstinence he overcomes gluttony, with humility vainglory, and with the poverty in the world, ambition."[46] Other writers of the later Middle Ages retain the threefold pattern, but vary the sins somewhat. Ralph of Poitiers (Radulphus Ardentis) refers to gluttony, cupidity and vainglory, for example, and Innocent III to gluttony, false boasting and avarice.[47] Gregory's pattern of sins is found, finally, in some

45. PL 194, 1789
46. Ibid.
47. Howard, Temptations, p. 52, n. 20, refers to Ralph (whose comments are in PL 155, 1794), as well as to Isaac. He cites further the sermons of Innocent (see PL 217, 371f.), and also the 'Deflorationes' of Werner of St Blaise and the commentary on 1 John by Martin of Léon. See the sermons of Godfrey of Admont (PL 174, 168); Peter of Celle (PL 202, 684f.); Garnier of Rochefort (PL 205, 662f.); Martin of Léon (PL 208, 690); William of Auvergne, in: Opera omnia, Paris 1674, II, 215f; Wyclif in: Johannis Wyclif Sermones, ed. F.J. Loserth, London 1887-90, I,

Luke commentaries, in Latin and in Greek, even if Adam himself is not mentioned: but these remain the sins which Christ overcame.[48]

The continuity of the exegesis might be shown, for the later period, by the fact that it appears in a slightly modified form in the 'Summa theologiae' of Thomas Aquinas. Aquinas refers to gluttony, vainglory, and cupidity—the last being exactly equivalent to Gregory's avarice—as the sins with which Christ is tempted. For Adam and Eve (and Aquinas follows the Gregorian pattern in placing a full exegesis of the Fall first), he mentions gluttony once again, in the usual context of the pair having eaten the fruit; for the second sin, however, Aquinas echoes Cassian, linking vainglory with the promise made to the pair that their eyes would be opened; the third sin is *extrema superbia*, the "height of pride", a phrase borrowed from Cassian, based on both parts of the final promise—that the pair should be as gods, knowing good and evil.[49] Aquinas combines, in effect, Cassian and Gregory. The three are very similar, and cover, three major figures, much of the Middle Ages.

Attention so far has been on purely theological writings—commentaries, tracts and sermons. But the point is found too in other writings. The typological compendia of the later Middle Ages very often carry the standard exegesis in a brief form.

122 -4. The frequent use of the material in sermons is itself interesting, and leads one to think that a wealth of further material from similar sources might easily be obtained.

48. Bede on Luke is well-known (PL 92, 369). In Greek, see Theophylactus (of Achrida in Bulgaria, PG 123, 746f.) and Theodore Prodromus (PG 133, 1180—a nice tetrastich on the point). Some further Greek commentaries might be noted for the sake of breadth: Anastasius of Sinai (PG 89, 1020); the 'Scholia vetera' (PG 106, 1086); Theophylactus (PG 123, 182); Euthemius Zigabenus (PG 129, 182). All these are post-Gregory.

49. 3a, qu. 41, 4: Synave ed. pp. 222 -49. See Köppen, Auslegung, p. 94f.

Some examples of this are dealt with in another context, below—such as the 'Pictor in carmine,' a typological handbook for artists. Mention might be made here of the 'Speculum humanae salvationis,' a fourteenth-century work that was translated into a number of European languages, and is also relevant to the study of medieval iconography. Three sins are attributed to the devil's tempting of Christ:

> Notandum autem, quod tentator proposuit Christo tria vitia,
> Quae sunt gula, superbia et avaritia.[50]

> (Note that the tempter proposed three sins to Christ, / namely gluttony, pride and avarice.)

Pride has replaced vainglory, but the meanings are in any case similar. The reference to avarice seems to point to Gregory's triad. The work is merely a catalogue of types and antitypes, so there is no special recapitulative stress on the link with the Fall here: only the gluttony gives rise to a reference to Adam, in fact.

The 'Speculum humanae salvationis' appears to have been influenced among other sources, by the 'Legenda aurea,' the 'Golden Legend' of James of Voragine. The Quadragesimal section of this very important work, however (chapter xxxiv) has little of relevance. A later section, on the Passion, cites Ambrose with the brief comment *in deserto Adam, in deserto Christus,* and also cites Gregory by name in a reference to Adam's pride, disobedience and gluttony, contrasting this with

50. See XIII, 39 -40: Speculum humanae salvationis, ed. J. Lutz and P. Perdrizet, Leipzig 1907 -9, I, 28. For the point in the French translation of Jean Mielot (1448), see the same edition, I, 133. Other vernacular editions are listed there, I, 103 -5. The English text has the point: The Miroure of Mans Saluacionne, ed. Alfred Huth, London, 1888, p. 50f. The German version appears not to make the point, however: see Konrad von Helmsdorf. Der Spiegel des menschlichen Heils, ed. Axel Lindqvist (DTM 31) Berlin 1924.

Christ's humility, his following of the divine will, and his suffering.[51] But the passage is not specific.

Mention might be finally made of a curious addendum to the history of the parallel in medieval Latin writings. Ralph Higden voices in his chronicle, the 'Polychronicon,' the notion that the devil overcame Adam and was overcome by Christ on the same day of the year:

> In qua et diabolum temptantem superavit, quo die diabolus primum hominem supplantaverat.

—an early English translation reads:

> þat day he overcome þe devel þat tempted hym, in þe whiche day þe devel hadde overcome and supplaunted Adam þe firste man ...[52]

This may be linked with the more common typological parallel based on the creation of Adam on March 25, the Feast of the Annunciation—hence the "creation" of the second Adam. It will, however, be more relevant in the study of the Middle English 'Stanzaic Life of Christ.'

The development of the exegesis after the close of the Middle Ages is less relevant here, and the Reformers' views have been discussed in detail by Pope. One point, however, is worthy of mention regarding the later views of the parallel. The most constant portion of the exegetical equation, that of the temptation through gluttony, is rejected by Calvin and the Protestants in respect of Christ. Christ is tempted here not to gluttony, but to break his faith in God's providing for him.[53] The Protestants, as Pope points out, follow this interpretation, but it must be stressed here that it is quite unknown to the

51. Jacobus a Voragine. Legenda Aurea, ed. Theodor Graesse, Leipzig 1846, pp. 151-3 and 230.

52. Polychronicon Ranulphi Higden, ed. Churchill Babington and Joseph R. Lumby, London 1865 -86.

53. Discussed fully by Pope, 'Paradise Regained,' p. 56f., and by Lewalski, Epic, p. 178.

Middle Ages, where the notion of gluttony is vital to typological and tropological interpretation alike.

It is perhaps appropriate to sum up briefly the development of the parallel in theological thought. Irenaeus represents the most emphatically typological approach, in which Christ makes good, sin for sin, what Adam did wrong. The Redemption takes place in the desert. Another form of typological interpretation is that of which the exemplary exponents are Cassian, Gregory and Aquinas: here the victory of Christ is real, but the parallel receives no emphasis, and is often swallowed up into sermons and commentaries that are as tropological as they are typological: this is isolated, if fulfilled, typology. And the victory of Christ is often seen as an example in its own right—how mankind is to conquer the devil. This tropological approach links closely with the stress on gluttony as the first sin of Adam and the aim of the first temptation in the desert, and has much to do with the position of the Matthew pericope at the beginning of Lent. Any of these approaches may be reflected in vernacular writings, without the vernacular work in question being connected necessarily or exclusively with one of the exegetical examples chosen here. The aim of this chapter has been threefold: first, to demonstrate the extent to which the temptation equation was known and discussed in pure theology in the Middle Ages; secondly, to give some idea of possible interpretations and approaches to that equation; thirdly to give an idea of general sources, even if this can in most cases go no further than a blanket reference to the "Gregorian type of exegesis," normally the most likely source of the outline of the parallel, or to "a recapitulative approach in the Irenaean sense."

III   VERNACULAR PROSE WRITINGS

The chief source of theological thought in prose monuments of the vernaculars of Western Europe is for most of the Middle Ages the sermon, and the sermon will be the major focal point of this chapter, with other forms of prose writing— limited in any case—mostly of incidental relevance only. One point might be noted, however, about the translations of the Gospel narrative at this period. While the most widely-known Gospel harmony of the Middle Ages, the 'Diatessaron' of Tatian, carries the Matthew narrative of the temptation of Christ,[1] it is possible to find (albeit later) Gospel harmonies in which the Luke order is taken: an example is the compilation known as the 'Pepysian Gospel Harmony' of about 1400, MS. Pepys 2493 in Magdalene College, Cambridge which has what is clearly the Luke text.[2] The point is worthy of mention since before Milton the order of the narrative practically invariably follows Matthew, in sermons as in creative writings of a more specifically literary nature.

Rather more than thirty years ago, G. R. Owst referred to his now-standard study of the relationship between the medieval sermon and these more expressly literary works as "a neglected chapter in the history of English letters."[3] To an

1. See for example the well-known German text with the Latin version, Tatian, ed. Eduard Sievers, 2nd ed, Paderborn 1892, repr. 1966, p. 37f.

2. The Pepysian Gospel Harmony, ed. Margaret Coates (EETS/OS 157) London 1922, p. 10f. There are of course other harmonies in languages as far apart as Persian and Italian, but these two may suffice to show that both sides may be represented.

3. Literature and Pulpit in Medieval England, Oxford 1933, repr. 1961.

extent, the sermon has, in spite of some scholarship on the topic, remained the stepchild of medieval literary criticism, both for English and the continental languages. It is, moreover, still difficult to obtain texts of the medieval sermons—French is a particularly trying case and there may well be material there— and again, the editions available are very frequently antiquated and hard to manage.[4] Yet the sermon is of obvious interest to the student of medieval literature as one of the most obvious means of transmission of a purely theological idea from the Latin sources into the vernacular. It need never be, of course, a unique source: the fact that a given writer heard a point in a sermon does not mean that he had not encountered it in writing as well. But it is reasonable to assume that a good proportion of theological commonplaces were disseminated in this manner in the first instance. This fact, of course, contributes once again to the difficulty that the modern researcher has in establishing accurate sources for a given motif. R. E. Kaske has commented on the medieval writers' knowledge of ideas, pointing out that

> where he chooses to lead, we must follow; we may spend years in
> accumulating and sifting out what he was picked up painlessly in a
> conversation, a sermon, or an evening's casual reading . . . .[5]

But general conclusions may be drawn from the evidence offered by the sermons. The many examples, in Old and Middle English, German, Icelandic and so on where the temptation parallel is made, may stand representative of a body of others,

4. For some comments on the German material (which may serve as an example), see Brian Murdoch, The Production of Concordances from Diplomatic Transcriptions, in: The Computer and Literary Research, ed. Roy Wisbey, Cambridge 1971, pp. 35-44. On the French sermons see Eugène Aubry-Vitet, Les sermonnaires du moyen age (Revue des deux mondes 82, 1869), pp. 811-40.
5. Patristic Exegesis and the Criticism of Medieval Literature, in: Critical Approaches to Medieval Literature, ed. Dorothy Bethurum, New York 1960, p. 31.

perhaps lost, unedited, or otherwise difficult to obtain, in which the idea was treated. Those adduced here must serve to indicate the general popularity of the motif in sermons over the entire Middle Ages— the English material alone here ranges, for example, from Aelfric to Mirk.[6]

The manner in which a given motif is treated in sermons might of course have had a more or less direct effect on the treatment of the same point in more specifically literary genres of vernacular writing. But in this context it must be borne in mind that the sermon is an hermetic genre.[7] The specific requirements of the preacher will shape his material and his attitude towards it, and the range of approaches manifest in the sermons is likely to be fairly limited. The moralizing tone of the homily—for this is of course a pastoral theology—may or may not be reflected in the literary works, even though the poets came across the details of the motif in a sermon.

The fact that there are numerous vernacular sermons dealing with the point in the middle ages is hardly surprising. Much of the Latin evidence, as indicated, is homiletic, especially in the later periods, and the standardizing exegesis of Gregory the Great is found, after all, in a homily, for all that it is adopted into commentaries and scholastic compilations as well. Gregory's sermons served as one of the primary sources for the medieval preacher in any case.[8] The second contributory factor

6. It need hardly be added, of course, that not every sermon collection is relevant, even when it is readily accessible. Thus there is nothing of value to this study in the Quadragesimal sermon in: Old English Homilies, ed. Richard Morris (EETS/OS 29) London 1868, pp. 24-41.

7. There seems to be no satisfactory distinction between "homily" and "sermon." See the entry "Homily" (by J. O'Shea) in: The New Catholic Encyclopaedia, New York 1967, VIII, 113 -15, as well as Rudolf Cruel, Geschichte der deutschen Predigt im Mittelaler, Detmold 1879, repr. Darmstadt 1966, pp. 1-5.

8. Cruel, Predigt, p. 156. Practically every edition of medieval popular sermons mentions the debt owed to Gregory.

to the wide use of the temptation parallel is of course the liturgical position of the pericope. Sermons for Quadragesima Sunday would naturally take Matthew 4 as their text, and it is also found in sermons for Ash Wednesday. The treatment of the Gospel story — and naturally that of Matthew rather than Luke — would call to mind the exegetical equation with Adam, and to this would be added the extra appeal of the protoplasts as the most notoriously unshriven sinners, guilty in the first instance of greed—eating the fruit—rather than fasting. Psychologically, the chief stress on gluttony is plainly comprehensible as the only concrete sin of the schema. Its relevance at the beginning of a period of abstinence is similarly plain. The Lenten period was traditionally a time in which sermons dealt with the chief sins, and Adam figures frequently, both as the first member of the human race, and as its symbolic representative—the two roles of the first man have been difficult to separate since the writings of Paul.[9] It may be seen already that the attitude to the temptation parallel taken in sermons is shaped very firmly by the position in the Church year.

The medieval theory of preaching was codified in some detail during the later portion of the Middle Ages, although the techniques described were known individually from the earliest times.[10] The sermon did employ the fourfold interpretation of Scripture—including the typological sense—but stress is very frequently on the tropological, and the moral also shapes the use of the other senses, which then occasionally have a somewhat fortuitous air when they do appear. One other element in the medieval sermon that might be noted briefly here, however, is the *exemplum* used as a means of expanding and clarifying a point. This particular type of formalized morali-

9. See Robin Scroggs, The Last Adam. A Study in Pauline Anthropology, Philadelphia/Oxford 1966.
10. See Harry Caplan, The Four Senses of Scriptural Interpretation and the Medieval Theory of Preaching (Speculum 4, 1929), pp. 282-90.

zation has in fact received some attention in critical scholarship
in view of its literary importance in the development of other
narrative genres. But—as Owst, for example, points out—it is
difficult to find a precise definition for the concept, which has
ramified connotations for medieval writers: Owst's own definition is that the *exemplum* is a "moralized anecdote."[11] This
may be drawn from practically any source, although as another
scholar has indicated, it should have human characters, in
contradistinction to the in intent similar fable.[12] When the
source is in fact biblical, then the use of the biblical story as an
exemplum, as a simple anecdote with a general moral, is often
capable of being considered equally well as pure tropology—
interpretation according to the *sensus tropologicus*. It is perhaps
safest to say that while a biblical *exemplum* is often tropology
at the same time, the converse is not the case: not all tropological interpretations may be considered *exempla*. The concept
of the *exemplum* is not interpretative: it does not need extra
exposition beyond its intrinsic exemplary nature. As a concrete
example, the very familiar exposition of the protevangelical
verse Genesis 3: 15 *ipsa conteret caput tuum,* "she shall bruise
your head," according to the *sensus tropologicus* sees the verse
as referring to the general opposition of man to the onset of sin.
Man must "bruise the head" of sin—catch it early and crush the
devil's initial *suggestio.* [13] But this is not an *exemplum*—it could
scarcely stand alone as a pattern. Even a biblical *exemplum*
must be immediately comprehensible in analogical terms.

    The medieval *artes praedicandi* provide for the use of the
four senses and for the insertion of *exempla.* Harry Caplan cites,

11. Literature and Pulpit, p. 149.
12. Joseph A. Mosher, The Exemplum in the Early Religious and
Didactic Literature of England, New York 1911, p. 6.
13. This is a medieval commonplace. See Murdoch, Fall of Man,
pp. 140 -54. See further Gregory's Moralia in Job, PL 75, 552, for a
well-known example of this.

for example, Guibert of Nogent's 'Liber quo ordine sermo fieri debeat' (a work added to his Genesis commentary) as saying that any of the four senses may be used in preaching for moral purposes.[14] So too the use of the *exemplum* is advocated: the 'Summa de arte praedicandi' of Alan of Lille, referred to above, advocates their use already in the twelfth century, although it seems that the clear *exempla*—with non-biblical material—are used primarily after the thirteenth. J. A. Mosher, who refers to Alan, gives various other instances of the advocation of the *exemplum* in the theory of preaching.[15]

There are, of course, a number of Quadragesimal sermons having the Matthew-pericope as their basis, which take the entire narrative of the temptation of Christ as an example to man, warning him to take care in the face of ever-present diabolical temptation. This is, however, not really to be considered as an *exemplum*—at least not in the later sense of the word; rather it is generally exemplary, not strictly an hermetic anecdote, although it approaches it closely.

The view of the incident in this generally exemplary sense has been seen in Latin. A Middle High German sermon of about 1170 from the South German homily-book of Priester Konrad sums up the Matthew-narrative in the following terms

> da sûlt ir in die rede an merken daz der laedige valant ûnsern got selben des niht erlie ern wolt in bechorn; des mugen in die armen sundaere zware wol erfurhten. Nu bittet in hiute, den waren gotes sun, daz er in des helfe daz ir mit sim troste dem vil ûbelen valant also an gesigen mûzt . . .[16]

14. Caplan, Senses, p. 282.
15. Exemplum, pp. 10-19.
16. Altdeutsche Predigten, ed. Anton E. Schönbach, Graz 1886-91, repr. Darmstadt 1964, III, 51. See the in other respects too very valuable study by Volker Mertens, Das Predigtbuch des Priesters Konrad, Munich 1971. This study is worthy of note as a particularly clear modern introduction to the medieval German sermon in general.

(You should notice from this how the wicked fiend did not even spare our God, but wanted to tempt him; and the poor sinner certainly has to expect this sort of thing. So beg him today, the Son of the true God, that he might give his help, so that you may overcome the wicked fiend in this way, with his comforting . . .)

This attitude is common over much of the Middle Ages. To take a later example, from an English manuscript of the early fifteenth century, the sermon for the beginning of Lent in MS Royal 18 B xxiii in the British Museum makes a succinct statement on the exemplary nature of Christ's fast:

> Crist 3aue vs ensampull for to faste, for first he fastid hym-selfe, and 3it had he not nede but to 3e(ue) vs ensampull . . .

and on the general repulse of the devil:

> And þer-for when þat he tempteþ vs to do ill, take we ensampull of oure Lorde, and lattes vs answere as he dud, and sey, "Goy, þou fende . . . I will not breke my fast, ne I will no þinge do as þou tempteþ me to do . . .[17]

The Royal sermon does also, in fact, refer to specific sins—including gluttony and lechery—but Adam is not named. In fact, only the first of the temptations of Christ is narrated, and the very fact that gluttony is mentioned might indicate an unconscious allusion to the parallel. Given the Lenten context, however, and the reference to lechery, this must remain mere speculation.

With the references to the sin of gluttony in sermons for the beginning of Lent it is always difficult to tell whether we are dealing with a general admonition, or with the pre-Reformation interpretation of the first temptation of Christ and the Adamic parallel, or whether it stems merely from the fact of Christ's fasting. It is interesting that there are sermons which,

17. Middle English Sermons, ed. Woodbury O. Ross (EETS/OS 209) London 1940, p. 141f.

while they do not make the parallel explicitly, still refer to Adam and Eve and their gluttony at the beginning of Lent.

An early example of this is provided in the sermon for the beginning of Lent of Wulfstan. The sermon as a whole—which does not mention the Matthew pericope—is concerned primarily with drunkenness (*oferdruncen*), and this does not fit the typological pattern. But there is a general reference to Adam and Eve—the loss of paradise by the first man being used as a negative example, how not to behave.[18] Rather clearer cases are found in later sermons—in the 'Speculum Sacerdotale' of the fifteenth century there is a reference to gluttony in the context of Genesis 2: 17 in the sermon for Quadragesima Sunday.[19] The gluttony of Adam and Eve is, of course, a homiletic commonplace outside Quadragesimal sermons, but here we can at least speculate on a typological source or intent. References to this gluttony may be found in early German sermons, in English down to Elizabethan times and beyond, and outside the sermon—one thinks of the 'Parson's Tale'.[20]

The full temptation parallel is found too in sermons, however, at an early stage. An example by a famous preacher is in the sermon for the first Sunday in Lent of Wulfstan's contemporary Aelfric. The source-material, as was recognized in 1894 by Max Förster, is here purely Gregorian.[21] Aelfric follows the pattern set in several commentaries, however, and

18. The Homilies of Wulfstan, ed. Dorothy Bethurum, Oxford 1957, p. 233f.

19. Speculum Sacerdotale, ed. Edward H. Weatherly (EETS/OS 200) London 1936, p. 60.

20. In German, see Murdoch, Fall of Man, p. 178. In English, see: Certaine Sermons or Homilies . . . 1547-1571, ed. Mary E. Rickey and Thomas B. Stroup, Gainesville 1968, II, 96. See also Chaucer. Complete Works, ed. F. N. Robinson, 2nd ed. London 1957, p. 254.

21. In spite of Bloomfield, Deadly Sins, p. 384, referring to Cassian. See Max Förster, Ueber die quellen von AElfrics exegetische 'Homiliae Catholicae' (Anglia 16, 1894), pp. 1-17.

places before the narrative and exposition of the pericope Gregory's familiar description of the manner in which the devil tempts man into sin: Gregory describes this as follows (and incidentally develops the point later in the 'Moralia in Job'):

tribus modis temptatio fit suasione, delectatione, consensu . . .[22]

(temptation is brought about in three ways, by suggestion, delight and consent . . .)

Which is echoed by Aelfric:

On ðreo wisan bið deofles costnung: þaet is on tihtinge, on lustfullunge, on geðafunge.[23]

(the devil tempts in three ways: that is with suggestion, with delight and with consent.)

Aelfric keeps close to his source, however—both elements are in the sermon on the Gospel, this and the temptation parallel. He does not develop the overall common tropological view of the Fall which sees Eve as the second stage—the delight of the flesh responding to the suggestion of the devil.[24] Instead, Aelfric proceeds with the narrative of the temptation in the desert and follows the Gregorian exegesis very closely.

The relevant section mirrors Gregory in word and in structure. We are given first of all the Fall and Man, and only then the Matthew-narrative. The whole is a very literal rendering of Gregory's comments, and abridged only slightly. Even the definition of avarice is there. Since the texts are so close it would be superfluous to cite the Old English in full, and its value is thus chiefly philological as a gloss on Gregory in the

22. PL 76, 1135, discussed extensively by Howard, Temptations, pp. 56 -65.

23. The Homilies of the Anglo-Saxon Church, ed. Benjamin Thorpe, London 1844 -7, I, 174.

24. Gregory, Moralia in Job IV, 27 (PL 75, 661). The idea stems from Philo of Alexandria, perhaps, and is found often with the triple temptation exegesis in Genesis-commentaries in particular.

vernacular.[25] But the fact of this literal rendering is important as such: this is very clearly a channel through which Gregory's influential exegesis was transmitted in the vernacular—not as an academic translation, comparable to Aelfred's 'Boethius', say, but in a sermon.

As far as typology goes, the same comments apply here as in the discussion of Gregory's own homily. This is *ad hoc* typology: Aelfric is not concerned with the typological aspects of the two events in particular. He does, of course, say that:

> se deofol waes þa oferswiðed ðurh Crist on þam ylcum gemetum þe he aer Adam oferswiðde; þaet he gewite fram urum heortum mid þam innfaere gehaeft, mit þam þe he inn-afaren waes and us gehaefte.[26]
>
> (The devil was overcome by Christ in the same way as he earlier overcame Adam; so that he went from our hearts, captured at the entrance with which he had entered and had captured us.)

But this is largely in his source.

Overall, however, the stress is tropological. Christ's motivation for undertaking the temptation at all is to provide an example (*bysen*) for man of patience in the face of suffering.[27] The important point is the fast, and the inclusion of the Gregorian exegesis is accidental, and not entirely consonant with the moralizing of the rest of the sermon.

A third homily from the Old English period is of interest here: the sermon for Quadragesima Sunday from the collection known as the 'Blickling Homilies'. Once again the notion is found that Christ fasted to set an example to all men: this is not restricted to Lent, and to the point is added a general comment on Christ's life as pattern:

> Us is þonne nédþearf þaet we faeston; forþon þe we beoð oft costode from deofle aefter urum fulwihte. Drihten us manode mid

25. Homilies, ed. Thorpe, I, 176 -8.
26. Ibid.
27. Ibid, I, 174.

his faestenne, & mid eallum his daedum, þaet we sceolan him
þeowian, & deofol oferswiþan . . .[28]

(So it is necessary for us to fast; for we are often tempted by the
devil after our baptism. The Lord warned us with his fasting and
with all his deeds, that we should serve him and overcome the devil.)

The exposition of the Matthew-pericope itself is, however, more
detailed. The point is made first, and we have encountered this
in Latin writings, notably those of Ambrose, that the location
of the temptation of Christ is typologically significant:

Rihtlic þaet waes þaet he eode on westen þaer aer Adám for-
wearþ . . .[29]

(It was right that he went into the desert, where Adam fell earlier.)

Before the preacher here goes on to the temptation parallel
proper, he gives —significantly—three reasons for the willingness
of Christ to undergo the temptation. The three, of course,
echoes the three temptations, but the reasons given sum up of
themselves the main ways of treating the parallel. The first
reason is purely historical—Christ wished to battle with the
devil. But secondly, he wanted to redeem Adam—this gives the
lead to a recapitulative interpretation of the parallel itself when
it does come. And finally, to act as an example for man—the
most common homiletic reason:

For þrim þingum Haeland eode on westen; forþon þe he wolde
deofol gelaþian to campe wiþ hine, & Adám gefreolsian of þam
langan wraece, & mannum gecyþan þaet se awyrgda gast aefestgaþ
on þa þe he gesyhþ to Gode higian . . .[30]

(For three things the Saviour went into the desert; because he
wanted to give the devil opportunity to battle with him, and to free
Adam from the long exile, and to show mankind that the wicked
spirit is resentful of those that he sees are on their way to God.)

28. The Blickling Homilies, ed. Richard Morris (EETS/OS 58, 63, 73)
London 1874 -80, I, 27 -9.
29. Ibid. I, 29
30. Ibid. I, 29.

That the sermon should list all these points in this fashion is interesting—particularly that Christ has the idea of Redemption in mind. It is a homiletic commonplace that Christ's battle with the devil is exemplary, but the redemptory motivation is less frequently encountered in the sermons.

The actual parallel appears to be corrupt, however. The preacher begins by announcing three temptations: but only two are actually mentioned. The passage occurs at the top of a MS page, which is in fact clipped. It is possible that more of the wording has been lost than appears to be the case at first sight, although the omission is perhaps a scribal one.[31] At all events, only the second of the temptations—vainglory—and the third, that of the kingdoms, are discussed. Richard Morris' translation in his edition is misleading here in that he inserts a quite unjustified "First" before the narrative of the second temptation—there is no equivalent in the Old English text.[32] But the temptation with vainglory is linked with the Fall of Man, and specifically with the promise of divinity to the pair. This points conclusively to the Gregorian exegesis in some form, although the writer here has integrated the parallel, it seems, rather than giving us the Fall and then the Gospel narrative:

> þaet ane cwaeþ. 'Doð swa swa ic inc bebeode, þonne beo gyt swa swa God.' Nu he þonne costode Godes Sunu þurh idel wuldor, ða he cwaeþ, 'Gif þu sy Godes Sunu, send þe nyþer.'[33]

> (that he said: "Do as I tell you and you shall be as God." And thus he tempted God's Son with vainglory when he said: "If you are the Son of God, throw yourself down.")

This is of course plainly the second temptation, and the Blickling text must be corrupt if for no other reason than that we have only two temptations mentioned. Presumably the mis-

31. See the facsimile of the manuscript: The Blickling Homilies of the John H. Scheide Library, Copenhagen 1960, fols. 15v and 16r.
32. Blickling Homilies, ed. Morris, I, 28.
33. Ibid. I, 29.

sing temptation dealt in the usual fashion with the gluttony of the pair and the abstinence of Christ. This would certainly have been Adamic. The third temptation, however, leaves the Fall of Man, and Adam is not mentioned, nor is the sin involved given a name. The preacher stresses the iniquity of worshipping the devil instead—there is no trace of the Gregorian avarice.

The last temptation seems to be treated in a tropological manner, but there are still typological points raised; the comparison between Christ and David in the battle with Goliath is here—a different form of typology, but typology nevertheless. And the ending of this section is both typological—or at least redemptory—and tropological. The Redemption is stressed first:

Þurh Cristes sige ealle halige waeron gefreolsode . . .[34]

(Through Christs's victory, all holy men were set free . . .)

A victory then, and the use of *gefreolsode* calls to mind the earlier reference to Adam's freedom from exile. But then comes a general-moral conclusion at some length—with emphasis on general patience and so on. The overall tone is again tropological, but the Blickling homily is unusual in giving so many alternative interpretations.

The question of Christ's motivation in allowing the conflict with the devil is raised again in a slightly later sermon, a Lenten homily from MS Bodley 343 in Oxford, from the twelfth century. Some of the ideas encountered already are here again—the fast as an example to man, the references to Moses and to Elias. But here Christ wishes specifically to overcome the devil in the same temptations that the devil used to overcome Adam and Eve. The temptations are, moreover, the Gregorian triad, in an unusual order—gluttony, avarice and vainglory—which looks at first sight like a Luke-commentary, but which is probably an inadvertently rearranged adaption of Gregory on Matthew:

34. Ibid. I, 31.

Bér þá tó him þa ylce costnungae þe há þá ereste men Adam 7 Euam mid forcostode 7 biswáác, 7 his wylles weald on him aehte; þaet waes þurh 3ifernesse, 7 3ytsunge, 7 ydel3ylp. Þa wolde Crist þone awariede deofel ofercumen on þam ylce þrem costunge þe ðe deofel aer þa éreste men mid biswáác . . .[35]

(He bore then to him the same temptations with which he tempted and led astray the first people, Adam and Eve, and overcame them; that was through gluttony, avarice and vainglory. Then Christ wanted to overcome the wicked devil in the same three temptations that the devil had used to lead astray the first people.)

But once again the general tone of the sermon is moral—the usual emphasis on absistence is there, as befits a Lenten sermon. The inclusion of the temptation parallel is unexplained, and the narrative of the Gospel story (following Matthew, incidentally), contains no further reference to the protoplasts. This seems to be little more than a token typological allusion from Gregory—familiar, but now becoming practically formulaic.

Continental allusions to the parallel in sermons follow a similar pattern. There are brief allusions in early works from Germany, Iceland and Norway, some fuller than others. The Old Icelandic/Old Norse texts are brief: the Old Icelandic homily collection called from its current location the 'Stockholm Homily Book' has a sermon for the beginning of Lent which alludes to Adam in general terms,[36] and there is a sermon for the same period in the Old Norwegian Homily Collection (Arnamagnean MS AM 619 Quarto) which speaks of the three sins of gluttony (*girni*), pride (*ofmetnaðe*) and avarice (*fégirni*) in the context of our parallel.[37] Both of these col-

35. Twelfth-Century Homilies in MS Bodley 343, ed. A. O. Belfour (EETS/OS 137: pt. I) London 1909, pp. 98-100.

36. Homilu-Bók, ed. Theodor Wisén, Lund 1872, p. 63.

37. Codex AM 619 Quarto, ed. George T. Flom, Urbana 1929, p. 123f.

lections are from the late twelfth or early thirteenth century.[38] There is also a brief reference to the parallel in some twelfth-century German sermons from a Carinthian manuscript, and in all these cases the brevity of the reference may, one feels, be taken as a sign of familiarity with the exegetical background. The Carinthian MS reads:

> Mit drîn dingen wart der êrste man Adam uberwunden: mit gîtlichen vrâze, mit ubermuot, mit uppige êre. Diu selben dinch wolt der tievel râten unserm herren.[39]

> (The first man, Adam, was overcome with three things, with gluttony, with pride and with vainglory. The same things the devil wanted to offer to our Lord.)

In both of these latter cases the question of source is a problem. The reference to *superbia,* "pride" in both points perhaps to Cassian, but the avarice in the Norse homily and the order in the Austrian seem to indicate that these are again insignificant variations on Gregory—pride being a common enough element in any case.

Another Middle High German sermon, the general tone of which is again moralizing, does make a fairly clear typological parallel for the first of the temptations, gluttony. The sermon, which is again Austrian, and of the twelfth century, refers in this context to the link between the Fall, mankind and Christ as the Redeemer:

> der leidig uiant . . . want im an dem ersten manne, dem herren adam wol gelungen was, daz der uon sinen raten daz uerboten obiz az, dannin er ûz den wûnneclichem paradyse uerstozen wart unt beide im unt allim mankunne der tot braht wart, do was er des giwis, daz

38. See G. Turville-Petre, Origins of Icelandic Literature, Oxford 1953, p. 115f., with reference there to Gregory as one of the sources of these sermons.

39. Altdeutsche Predigten, ed. Adalbert Jeitteles, Innsbruck 1878, p. 50. See Cruel, Predigt, p. 205f.

er den niwen adamen, unsern herren iesum christum, den gotis sůn
unt der maeide sůn alsam betriegen mohte.[40]

(the wicked fiend, because he had succeeded with the first man,
Adam, who had on his advice eaten the forbidden fruit, with the
result that he was ejected from the paradise of delights, bringing
death both to him and to all mankind—because of this the fiend was
confident that he could deceive in the same way the new Adam,
God's son and the Son of the Virgin, our Lord Jesus Christ.)

The designation *der niwe adam* for Christ is interesting, but the
typology is not borne out through the rest of the sermon, which
concludes with some general moralizing on the subject of the
deadly sins.

One of the longest versions of the parallel, comparable to
Aelfric, is in a Quadragesima sermon from the Oberaltaich
collection, a manuscript of the thirteenth century. Once again
this is plainly Gregorian, rendering the familiar exegesis ver-
batim, and in the same context as with Gregory—first the Fall,
and then the Gospel version. Again there is no need to reproduce the passage,[41] but the same comments apply as did to the
Aelfric homily—this is a very clear path from Latin theology to
vernacular literature as such. The conclusion of this sermon
does stress, however, the double implication of Christ's divinity
and his rôle as an example to man; but the point is not
laboured, and what remains is again a very proper admonition
to fast for the Lenten period.[42]

Only one significant variation need be noted for the later
period. The collection by John Mirk known as the 'Festial'
contains a sermon for Quadragesima which has the threefold

40. *Fundgruben für Geschichte deutscher Sprache und Literatur*, ed.
Heinrich Hoffmann, Breslau 1830-7, I, 100f. Cruel, *Predigt*, p. 156f. again
refers to Gregory.

41. *Predigten*, ed. Schönbach, II, 58f. The notes, p. 226f. cite Gregory
and Haymo of Auxerre.

42. *Predigten*, ed. Schönbach, II, 61.

temptation parallel. The difference here, however, is that the reference is consistently to Eve, rather than to Adam. Otherwise the pattern is again Gregorian. The devil came to *Eue in paradyce in lyckenes of an eddyr, forto tempt hur of gloteny, of vayne glory, and of couetyce.*[43] The connexion with the Gospel is made following this, but once again the stress is on man's avoidance of the sins involved, rather than pure typology, which in view of the emphasis upon Eve would be difficult here in any case.

The treatment of the parallel in the sermon is, therefore, by and large predictable, although it is by no means uniform. There are typological insertions, even if the overall tone is usually moral. It should be clear too that the sermons might well have provided sources for vernacular poems, but this rôle must not be overstressed. Elizabeth Pope, referring to the exemplary attitude taken so frequently in sermons seems to be of the opinion that this is reflected very heavily in vernacular literary monuments.[44] These monuments must be examined, however, to ascertain whether or not this is the case. It should be apparent from the following chapters that the sermon is an hermetic genre (and even here there is a certain variation in attitude), but that the literary—the poetic and dramatic monuments—show a good deal more independence still. The Lenten moralizing does shape the vernacular writings to some extent, but the motif is certainly not treated in a homiletic fashion from Aelfric to the close of the Middle Ages: Milton's originality is one of language and style, but not perhaps as much of idea as has been considered.

43. Mirk's Festial, ed. Theodor Erbe (EETS/ES 96) London 1905, p. 83. My attention has been drawn by Michael Benskin to a collection of postills on the feasts, also fairly late, in Trinity College Dublin MS B. 4. 19, where the three temptations are applied to Christ, but where one—gluttony—is linked with Eve: *wha scho sey þe appulle scho was raueschit to ette of hit* (fol. 1v, col. 2).
44. "Paradise Regained,' p. 29.

IV EARLY VERNACULAR POETRY

It is the early Middle Ages—the centuries between 750 and
1200 — that produce the majority of works where the
temptation in the desert is seen as a recapitulation of the first
Fall. This frequently comes about in poetical works that
combine, as it were, 'Paradise Lost' with 'Paradise Regained'
into *summa*-like expositions of divine history, in keeping with
the cyclic view of the teleological pattern and appropriate,
perhaps, to an age of more solid Christianity—of the strengthening of beliefs in areas that have not, perhaps, been Christian-
ized for too long.

Amongst the earliest allusions in vernacular poetry to the
connexion, however, is found in a country where even at the
time of the work, the eighth century, Christianity was a well-
established tradition. The use of the motif in a quatrain by the
Irish poet Blathmac, son of Cú Brettan, who wrote perhaps
around 750, is significant for a variety of reasons. The location
of the point in Ireland is not, of course, unduly surprising: the
capacities for travel (and hence for the assimilation of motifs
from other literatures), the wide learning, and the production of
devotional verse of a high order by Irish monks in the early
Middle Ages is, of course, well-known.[1] So too it must be
remembered that for many years in the early part of the
so-called dark ages, Ireland was the last bastion of Christian
civilisation, the sole carrier of tradition in the barbarian West.[2]
The poems of Blathmac were discovered only recently by James
Carney, who came across them in seventeenth-century tran-

1. See for example: The Cambridge Medieval History, Cambridge
1911 -36, II, 504 -6 and III, 501f., as well as the various studies of
medieval Irish religious writings published by St John D. Seymour in the
'Proceedings of the Royal Irish Academy' between 1921 and 1927.
2. Kenneth Clark, Civilisation, London 1969, p. 7f.

scription in MS G. 50 in the National Library of Ireland, and who has subsequently published them.[3] In a study of Blathmac, Carney has discussed further the nature of the poems as devotional Marian lyrics, and has pointed to the combination of Irish expression and flavour with Christian traditional motifs.[4] Our case may prove an additional example of his judgement.

The form of the reference is brief—a single quatrain. But it embodies several of the notions so far encountered, in a highly concentrated form due, perhaps, both to the familiarity of the points and to the natural form of the Old Irish quatrain, which makes for concentrated, practically gnomic expression:

Dochum ndíthruib ar doíni
du-derces do thromm-aíni
conro-chloe demun i trib
i n-abbad ar senathair.

—which Carney translates as follows:

To the wilderness for men's sake he was led for severe fasting so that he overcame the devil in the dwelling place in which our ancestor died.[5]

That it is "for men's sake" draws the attention. Here, however, the very brevity of the verse works against us: two possibilities present themselves. This might be simply tropological—"for man to use as an example," or it might imply recapitulation. That the latter is perhaps more likely, is borne out not only by the typological tone of the whole quatrain, but also by an earlier quatrain linking the baptism of Christ with the expiation of original sin in all men:

3. The Poems of Blathmac, Son of Cú Brettan, ed. James Carney (ITS 47) Dublin 1964.
4. Poems of Blathmac, Son of Cú Brettan, in: Early Irish Poetry, ed. James Carney, Cork 1965, pp. 45 -57.
5. The Poems, ed. Carney, p. 58f (172, 685 -9).

Manib dúthracht Dé do nim
ar n-ic do phecad Ádaim
ní boi hi Críst ní ba gó
ríseth a les baitsedo.

(Carney: Were it not that God from Heaven wished to save us from
Adam's sin, there was nothing false in Christ that would need
baptizing.)[6]

In our passage, which comes three quatrains later, Christ does
after all overcome where Adam died: again this might be taken
on a purely literal level. Christ overcame the devil in the place
to which Adam was expelled after the Fall. But the contrast in
such a concentrated poetical form is striking of itself. The
linking of the wilderness of the temptations of Christ with the
place of Adam's exile has been seen in Latin writing as a motif
of some antiquity, and it appears too in sermons in the vernacular at an early stage.[7] This again points to an essentially typological rather than tropological approach.

As indicated, however, this type of poetry is not designed
for lengthy exposition, and in this very fact lies much of its
poetic effect. There is much in the very important corpus of
early Irish religious poetry that remains open to interpretation
for just this reason.[8] Blathmac's poetry is, moreover, primarily
Marian, narrating the events in the life of Christ only as they
relate to her: a fuller exposition would have been thematically
and poetically inappropriate here. These lyrics, moreover, have
an air of private devotion, poems not intended for a wide
audience—much like some of the sonnets of Gerard Manley
Hopkins over a millenium later. Accordingly we cannot cite
Blathmac as evidence that the motif had a wide general currency: this we could do only if it were demonstrable that

6. Ibid. p. 58f. (169, 673 -6).
7. Köppen, Auslegung, p. 9.
8. A glance at the existing translation of 'Saltair na Rann' will
confirm this in the context of Adam and Eve: Hull, Poem-Book, pp. 1 -50.
Hull, a notable scholar of Old Irish, admits defeat on some counts.

Blathmac wrote for a large audience, which seems unlikely. And yet the very use of the point bespeaks its familiarity to the Irish religious writers at a very early stage. It is perhaps significant too to note that perhaps the earliest iconographical representation of the temptation pericope is in the 'Book of Kells', a work of Irish inspiration, even if it was not in fact produced in Ireland itself.[9]

Very different in poetic character, but presenting perhaps even greater problems regarding our motif is the poem or group of poems in Old English known as 'Christ and Satan'. Although there is no direct reference to the parallel of the Fall and the temptation in the desert, this is still of great interest to the present study. 'Christ and Satan' is the last poem to be entered in the Junius manuscript, which contains also the 'Genesis', 'Exodus' and 'Daniel', and it seems to be set off from the three biblical poems within that manuscript.[10] The work, previously ascribed, like the others, to Caedmon, falls into three sections, and has been viewed variously as three separate poems, as a tripartite work but with the sections in the wrong order, and as a perfectly logical and homogeneous whole.[11] The three sections of the poem, which was composed probably between 790 and 830, treat of the fall of Lucifer and the angels, of the harrowing of hell, and the temptation of Christ in the desert. The last passage, which is obviously significant here, is not complete: we have only two temptations, that of the stones, and that of the kingdoms, with an apparent lacuna between them. Christ's repulse of Satan at the conclusion is particularly forceful. From the simple "vade" of the Vulgate we get:

9. The point is discussed in the chapter of the present work dealing with the iconography of the motif.

10. The Junius Manuscript, ed. George P. Krapp, New York 1931. See especially the introduction, pp. xxxiii-vi and xviiif.

11. See Krapp's introduction, p. xxxiv, with reference to the studies of Grein and Wülcker in the nineteenth century. C.L. Wrenn, A Study of Old English Literature, London 1967, p. 98 speaks of "a triple group."

Gewit þu, awyrgda, in þaet witescraef,
Satanus seolf; þe is susl weotod
gearo togegnes, nalles godes rice.
Ah ic þe hate þurh þa hehstan miht
þaet ðu hellwarum hyht ne abeode,
ah þe him secgan miht sorga maeste,
þaet ðu gemettes meotod alwihta
cyning moncynnes.[12]

(Go, fiend, to the pit of torment/ you Satan, punishment is pre-
pared for you/ certainly, and not God's kingdom./ And I bid you,
by the highest power/ that you do not promise any hope to the
hell-dwellers,/ rather that you should tell them of the greatest
sorrow/—that you met the almighty creator/ the king of men.)

This continues for another score or so lines, the defeat of the
devil being definite, and the harrowing of hell promised. We can
link the narrative with the work of Christ as a Redeemer,
however, more specifically with the line:

þa þam werigan wearð wracu getenge.[13]

(Then on the accursed one was vengeance taken)

Vengeance for what? —one assumes for the sin of Adam.
Christ's defeat of the devil here wipes out the earlier defeat, to
"avenge . . . supplanted Adam." There is of course no overt
mention of the Fall: but the hexaemeral connexion of the first
portion of the work may suffice for this, playing 'Paradise Lost'
(to some extent, at least), to the 'Paradise Regained' of this
section.[14]

But the order of the three sections is problematic. The
fact that the temptation in the desert follows the harrowing of
hell has caused critics who accept the poem as some sort of
whole to reverse the order of the last two parts. This attitude
has, however, been attacked by Bernard F. Huppé, in an

12. Junius MS, ed. Krapp, p. 157 (vv. 690 -7).
13. Ibid. p. 158 (v. 710).
14. Several critics have linked the 'Christ and Satan' with Milton
more or less casually: Wrenn, Study, p. 98.

analysis of the structure of the work in his study of the overall relationship between doctrine and vernacular poetry. Huppé considers that the poem may be left as it stands, arguing that to "feel that something is wrong structurally with 'Christ and Satan" is to miss the theme of the poem, which is clearly stated at the beginning. This theme is the incommensurate might of God."[15] Huppé is right in considering that the poem is a complete whole, and he is correct, moreover, in his summary of the theme. But his view of the relationship between theme and structure may perhaps be corrected slightly. His determination of the order rests upon a false assumption regarding the intent of the poem. This Huppé sees as essentially tropological: "in repelling the Temptation, Christ showed how mankind should also repel temptation."[16] If Christ were to be taken here as an *exemplum* pure and simple, one might expect overt moralizing of some sort: but 'Christ and Satan' cannot be compared with any of the homiletic treatments of the pericope. Here, as in Blathmac and in many later works, the repulsion of the devil in the desert is climactic historically and typologically: Christ triumphs, and in doing so, makes good the earlier loss.

In this light, one may then consider the structure. Even with the MS. reading, of course, the poem remains effective as it stands—placing the emphasis on the victory on earth. But aesthetically it remains, in this order, unsatisfying. The theme of the poem as a whole, if we may add to Huppé, is that of the incommensurate might of God over the devil; thus we see the might in heaven—God defeats Lucifer,—very properly followed with a similar defeat on earth (in revenge for the Fall of Adam there). The ending of this portion in fact points on to the completion of the work in the harrowing of hell. We end with a vision of hell that is as yet unharrowed, but which has no hope (as is clear from the passage cited above) of being spared from this. The pattern is in some ways less close to Milton than to the

15. Doctrine and Poetry, New York 1959, p. 227.
16. Doctrine and Poetry, p. 231.

poem by Giles Fletcher, not too long before Milton's work, entitled 'Christ's Victorie and Triumph in Heaven, on Earth and over and after Death'. The central part of Fletcher's poem treats of the temptation of Christ, and the anonymous writer of 'Christ and Satan' is interesting as having seen, like Milton and Fletcher, that the temptation is the true victory on earth, and the necessary preliminary to the harrowing of hell. One might almost argue that a central position for the temptation scene highlights it even more clearly than if it were to come last.

The connection between the temptations in the desert and in Eden comes out much more clearly in a recapitulative-typological sense in another early Germanic work, the ninth-century Old Saxon 'Heliand' ('Saviour'), a combination of Gospel harmony and exegesis designed to explain and consolidate the faith of the newly-converted Saxons. This aim in the work distinguishes it sharply, of course, from such works as the Blathmac poems. With the Irish quatrains, there is already implicit a considerable amount of Christian culture. But with the 'Heliand' less may be presumed of the audience, and an exegetical point is likely to be developed in more explicit detail.

The relevant portion of the 'Heliand' begins with a description of the Fall, we are told, in the context of Satan's tempting of Christ:

> huuô he thesa uuerold êrist,
> an them anginnea   irminthioda
> bisuêc mit sundium,   thô he thiu sinhiun tuuê,
> Âdaman endi Êuan,   thurh untreuua
> forlêdda mid luginun,   that liudio barn
> aftar iro hinferdi   hellea sôhtun,
> gumono gêstos.[17]

(. . . how he first of all led astray this world/ at the beginning, all the people,/ with sin, when he the married couple,/ Adam and Eve,

---

17. Heliand and Genesis, ed. Otto Behaghel, 8th ed. Walther Mitzka (ATB 4) Tübingen 1965, p. 38 (XIII, 1034 -9).

wickedly/ led astray with lies, so that the children of men/ **after** their departure went into hell,/ the souls of men.)

Already the causal link with the Fall in terms of original sin is made plain: the importance of what will happen is stressed—the devil tempted Adam and Eve, with far-reaching consequences.

But God decides that the Fall can be made good by recapitulating this incident: Christ is to be sent to bring mankind heaven rather than hell. In the lines following those cited above we hear how:

> Thô uuelda that god mahtig,
> uualdand uuendean   endi uuelda thesum uuerode forgeben
> hôh himilrîki: bethiu he herod hêlagna bodon,
> is sunu senda.[18]

(Then almighty God desired/ the ruling one, to change, and desired to give back to men/ the kingdom of high heaven: so he sent the blessed messenger,/ his own son . . .)

The narrative of the temptation then begins, with reference to Adam once again:

> [Satan] uuelda thô mahtigna
> mid them selbon   sacun   sunu drohtines,
> them he Âdaman   an êrdagun
> darnungo bidrôg,   that he uuarð is drohtine lêð,
> bisuuêc ina mid sundiun   — so uuelda he thô selban dôn
> hêlandean Krist.[19]

(Satan wanted then the mighty one,/ the son of the Lord, with the same guilt/ with which he, in former days/ had craftily led Adam astray, so that he deserted his Lord,/ had led him into sin—this he wanted to do again/ with Christ the Saviour.)

There is, however, no exegesis in context, and the individual temptations are not linked with the Fall of Man. Even so, the context clearly points to a typology of recapitulation: the

18. Ibid. p. 38 (XIII, 1039 -42).
19. Ibid. p. 38 (XIII, 1044 -9).

parallel determinism of God and the devil is interesting: God wishes man to regain heaven, and the devil wishes to fell the heavenly messenger in the same way as he felled Adam. It must be admitted that the conclusion of this portion of the poem is a tropological admonition to the pious to behave as Christ did, but the link remains with the Fall and the specific wiping out of original sin (while neutralizing *the* original sin—English does not have the convenient distinction that German makes between *Ursünde,* "primal sin," and *Erbsünde,* "inherited sin.").

Although the 'Heliand' is fuller here than was Blathmac, we are still unable to postulate a source. E. Sievers, discussing the text, suggests Gregory, as well as Raban on Matthew or Bede on Luke.[20] The latter seems unlikely, but the two former works are quite possible as sources: we have, as Gregory, the Fall of Man first, and then the temptation in the desert. Raban repeats Gregory's exegesis in his Matthew and Genesis commentaries, and is geographically plausible as a source. But the detailed parallelism found in the Gregorian text is omitted, and typology of the parallel is made rather stronger, although with Gregory the typology is fulfilled. Several reasons may be put forward for this. With Blathmac the reason for the brevity was probably the poet's familiarity with the motif anyway, and the overall effect was enigmatic. Here the brevity is due to the opposite reason: the audience would not have been familiar with the exegesis, and to include it at length would have been confusing. It is not the overcoming of specific sins that the poet wants to put across, but the fact of the Redemption as a whole. To cause his audience to begin thinking about gluttony or avarice would have destroyed the evangelistic effect of the work. One recalls the report of Tacitus, several centuries before on the German love of feasting: the Saxons may well not have changed. The whole tone of the 'Heliand' is of course adapted to

20. Zum 'Heliand', (Zeitschrift für deutsches Altertum 19, 1876) pp. 15 -7.

the German audience,[21] and at this stage of their Christianiza-
tion, only the fact of the Redemption is vital: the details of the
typology are immaterial. For the same reason, of course—that
of not antagonizing the audience too much—the evil of the Fall
is played down. The stress on the devil's lies takes the edge off
the responsibility of Adam and Eve, and this stress is quite
common in early Germanic writings. Another Old Saxon
example of this is the so-called 'Genesis B,' preserved for the
most part in Anglo-Saxon, in which there is an emphasis on the
fact that Eve acted in good faith, misled by the lies of the
devil.[22] This contrasts with the attitude expressed in a later
German work, the Vorau 'Genesis', composed in about 1130.
The poet criticizes Adam and Eve, who

> slîuen in ir tracheit. si
> wahte dev uirwizecheit. mir girde si
> ime zûgî. mit geluste er si uei.[23]

(slept in their unwatching negligence. Idle curiosity
awoke them. They approached him (the devil) with greed.
He took them with concupiscence.)

The fullest of the early versions of the parallel in the
vernacular is in fact High German, rather than Low German, as
indeed are two other detailed poetical versions of the point
from the earlier part of the Middle Ages. The earliest, though, is
the 'Evangelienbuch', the rhymed Gospel harmony composed

21. See J. Knight Bostock, A Handbook on Old High German
Literature, Oxford 1955, pp. 141-65. Bostock discusses the source of the
poem, p. 155, and concludes that although one might think that the poet
had used Gregory's homilies, all the points from these are also in Raban
and Bede.

22. Evans, 'Paradise Lost,' pp. 163 -5.

23. Deutsche Gedichte des XI und XII Jahrhunderts, ed. Joseph
Diemer, Vienna 1849, p. 7, 24 -6. I have discussed this elsewhere (Murdoch, Fall of Man, p. 77f.) linking with a sermon by Bernard of Clairvaux.

between 860 and 870 at the monastery of Weissenburg in Alsace. The work is important to German literary history for various reasons — it is the first German text for which we have the author's name, it is one of the first, if not the first work in German to employ end-rhyme, and it is prefaced with a detailed justification on Otfrid's part for writing the work at all.[24] The nature of the 'Evangelienbuch' is best summed up by the title of a study of it by Donald McKenzie: 'Otfrid — Narrator or Commentator'?[25] for Otfrid is both. This was, of course, the case with the 'Heliand' to a certain extent. But there is a difference in that Otfrid is not persuading a basically non-Christian audience of the value of the Christian message — he is working in an atmosphere of established Christianity, but he is appealing to an audience that is not necessarily well instructed in exegetical matters. Accordingly his style tends to be long-winded and over-explanatory, a fact due too in part to the exigencies of the metrical and rhyme patterns that he is using.

Basically then, Otfrid offers in each of his five books (five, he tells us, instead of four, so that the four of the Gospels can neutralize the five sinful senses of man: the work is full of number-symbolism, as well as other technical devices, such as acrostic or telestich verses) a narrative of a portion of the Gospel according to the historical sense, although it is often padded with incidental exegesis. In addition to more or less pure narrative, there are also passages of exegesis as such, headed either *spiritaliter, moraliter,* or *mystice.* The *moraliter* passages are of course tropological. But the others can contain (or combine) interpretations according to any of the senses. The various ways in which Otfrid handles his material has been considered by Klaus Schulz in a work which, despite a somewhat cumbersome title, is nonetheless an excellent scholarly

24. See Bostock, Old High German, pp. 168 -90.
25. Stanford 1946, repr. New York 1967.

analysis,[26] and Schulz takes precisely our passage as an example
of a narrative with exegetical commentary separate from it:
Schulz draws attention to the stress on the Redemption, and
while Otfrid does of course stress this fact – as does the
'Heliand' – at a number of points, it is still significant that it
should be made here, so early in the Gospel Story.

Otfrid's narrative of the temptation in the desert occupies
three cantos in the second book (II, 4 -6), comprising a narrative, a commentary headed *spiritaliter,* and then a further brief
commentary headed *de eodem,* "on the same point." Taken
together, the three passages offer an integrated linking of the
temptations in Eden and in the desert: the Fall of Man is close
even when Otfrid is narrating the Matthew-pericope in the
historical sense. The whole section, a *summa in parvo,* while
clearly of theological interest, is not without literary merit.

'Evangelienbuch' II, 4, then, is a narrative in the *sensus
litteralis,* which can and does contain exegetical material
already. The link with the Fall here is in the first instance
verbal: echoes of the standard vocabulary used to describe the
Fall are heard already as the devil approaches Christ:

Tho sleih there fárari   irfîndan wer er wári[27]

(the adversary crept there   to find out who he might be)

The link is the verb *slichan,* used normally of serpents: the word
can (rarely) mean "to proceed in a stately fashion," but this
would hardly be appropriate here. Another German poem, to
which attention will be devoted shortly, says of the devil at the
time of the Fall, that

der chom geslichen lise . . .[28]

(he came creeping quietly along . . .)

26. Art und Herkunft des variierenden Stils in Otfrids Evangeliendichtung, Munich 1968, pp. 22 -36.
27. Otfrid. Evangelienbuch, ed. Oskar Erdmann, 4th ed. Ludwig
Wolff (ATB 49) Tübingen 1962, p. 60 (II, 4, 5).
28. Anegenge, ed. Dietrich Neuschäfer, Munich 1966, p. 245 (v.

This is then followed with a general reference to the connexion between the Fall and the temptations of Christ. Otfrid — as in the 'Heliand' and elsewhere — stresses that the devil overcame the pair with lies in Eden: the devil muses on how he himself has control over all the gates to the world — how then did this seemingly pure man get in?

> Er tháhta odowila tház   thaz er ther dúriwart wás,
>   er íngang therera wórolti   bisperrit sélbo habeti;
> Er thar niheina stígilla   ni firliaz ouh únfirslagana;
>   then íngang ouh ni ríne,   ni si ékordi thie síne,
> Thier in themo éristen man   mit sinen lúginon giwan,
>   mit spénstin sies gibéitta,   joh zi áltere firléitta.[29]

(He thought perhaps of the fact that he was the doorkeeper,/ and he himself had barred the entrance to the world; / nor did he leave there any little entry-stile unbolted:/ the entrance, moreover, was touched only by his people, / whom he had won in the conquest of the first man by his lies,/ conquered with temptation, and led astray for all time.)

That a Redemption is needed is plain from the manner in which the rule of the devil is stressed, together with the implied reference to original sin. The connexion is not, however, pursued at any length here. There is a detailed discussion of the devil's wonder at who Christ might be, but the passage follows otherwise the Matthew pattern. This, of course, relates to the exposition of the entire incident in the context of the two natures of Christ. Otfrid fuses the two interpretations in his passage, giving first the motivation of the devil — that he wishes to find out (*irfindan*) the nature of Christ, but at the same time (as is evident from the first Otfrid-citation above) having in mind the linking of the temptation in the desert with that in Eden. There is also an occasional tropological aside. Otfrid

2832). The context is also typological. See p. 292 and my own comment in a review of this edition (Modern Language Review 64, 1969), p. 446.

29. Otfrid, ed. Erdmann, p. 60 (II, 4, 7 -12).

comments, for example, of the temptation of the kingdoms, that

Er spénit unsih álle   zi míhilemo fálle
in wórton joh in wérkon . . .[30]

(He [the devil] tricks us all into many a fall,/ in word and in deed . . .)

But these tropological comments are not overwhelming. The temptation scene ends with a stress on the humanity of Christ, a favourite theme of Otfrid apart from considerations of the dual-nature doctrine, and raised at this point too, incidentally, in the 'Heliand'.[31]

The tropological approach is developed further in II, 5, the first of the *spiritaliter* passages. But it is here mixed with a typological exegesis based presumably on Gregory or on one of his followers. The sins to which Adam was tempted are enumerated — pride, gluttony, vainglory and what appears to be avarice — and in spite of a typological comment on Christ's victory over these, the main point is to warn man against these. The real tone of this section, apart from its typological insertions, is set by the opening lines:

Wir scúlun uns zi guate   nu kéren thaz zi múate,
  mit wiu ther díufal so fram   bisueih then ériston man;
Wir scúlun dráhton bi tház,   thaz wir giwárten uns thiu baz,
  joh wir iz giwárilicho   bimíden iogilicho.[32]
(We should, for our own good, now take to heart/ the way in which the wicked devil led astray the first man;/ we must consider this well, so that we may the better defend ourselves,/ and avoid, watchfully, the same fate.)

The typological pattern does get a full treatment: the sins to which Adam is tempted are named first, and, as indicated, seem

30. Ibid., p. 63 (II, 4, 87f.).
31. Johannes Rathofer, Der 'Heliand'. Theologischer Sinn als tektonischer Form, Cologne/Graz 1962, p. 154f.
32. Otfrid, ed. Erdmann, p. 63f. (II, 5, 1 -4).

to be Gregorian.[33] The sin of pride is given, it is true, a more prominent position than it had in Gregory (although he does mention it), and this may be for the simple reason that *superbia* is, after all, the chief of the sins. There are several later German versions of the pericope which follow Otfrid in this stress. The pattern of sins reads:

> Âdaman then álton   bisuéih er mit then wórton,
>   ther júngo joh ther gúato   giréh inan gimúato.
> Spúan er io zi nóti   jénan zi úbarmuati,
>   zi gíri joh zi rúame,   zi suaremo ríchiduame.[34]

(He led astray the old Adam with his words/ but the new, good one took bold revenge./ He successfully led the former into pride,/ greed, [desire for] glory and to dangerous [desire for] riches.)

The Pauline echo of the *deuteros anthropos* (= *ther júngo . . . [Adam]*) seems to indicate recapitulation, and these two lines do indeed point to Christ's victory, but only in the most general of terms. The situation is just as with Gregory, however – we must consider the context. Otfrid describes the Fall of Man as having lost man his homeland (*heimingi*)[35] – a favourite tropological point of this poet, which recurs fairly frequently in the 'Evangelienbuch', based on the topos of the

---

33. Erdmann refers in his notes p. 64 to Bede on Matthew. The edition of Otfrid. Evangelienbuch, ed. Paul Piper, 2nd ed. Freiburg/Br./ Tübingen 1882 -4, I, 163f. refers to Raban on Matthew, citing the Gregorian exegesis. Piper comments that the poet of the Heliand uses the same source, since the vocabulary is similar, but the vocabulary for the Fall and the temptations remains fairly static over much of the Middle Ages in German. The verb *besuuichan* 'tempt', which Otfrid uses, is there in Old Saxon in the 'Heliand', in an updated German form in later Genesis-poems, and even in Middle English, as *beswikan,* in the twelfth-century 'Ormulum'. A.L. Plumhoff, Beiträge zu den Quellen Otfrids (Zeitschrift für deutsche Philologie 31, 1899), p. 484f. speaks of the 'Glossa ordinaria' here, unaware that Otfrid antedates it by several centuries.
34. Otfrid, ed. Erdmann, p. 64 (II, 5, 5 -8).
35. Ibid. p. 64 (II, 5, 10).

lost *patria paradisi.*[36] The poet does, however, give a brief integrated parallel of the two events:

> Thémo álten det er súazi,   thaz er thaz óbaz azi,
>   gispuan thaz ér ouh thaz firlíaz,   thaz drúhtin inan dúan hiaz;
> Gilih quad góton warin,   in thiu sie iz ni firbárin;
>   quad gúat joh úbil wessin,   thes gúates thoh ni míssin.
> Bat thésan ou zi nóti,   thóh er mes ni hórti,
>   (ni dét er iz bi gúate!)   thia stéina duan zi bróte;
> Er síh ouh fon ther hóhi   thes huses nídarliazi;
>   quad, hérduames irfúlti,   in thiu er nan béton wolti.
> In selben wórton er then mán   tho then ériston giwán,
>   so ward er híar (thes was nót!)   fon thésemo firdámnot . . .[37]

(By his sweet blandishments he persuaded the first man to eat/ and made him go against what the Lord had commanded him;/ he said "you will be like gods, if you do not restrain yourselves;/ you will know" — he said — "good and evil, and not lose any advantages."/ He said to the other Adam — although he took no heed — /(with evil intent), "make these stones bread." Also that he should throw himself from the top of the temple./ He said he would fill him with riches, if he would worship him./ In the same words as he used to overcome the first man,/ so was he here — necessarily — damned by the new man.)

The treatment is, then, fairly concise. One wonders if an audience not entirely familiar with the whole of the Gregorian exegesis would really be able to fit the pieces together here? The last portion of this typological passage is at first sight recapitulative once again — and Gregory, it will be remembered, has precisely such a *sententia* at the end. But this is not the end

---

36. See for example the treatment of the Magi, sent home by another route — again based on a common exegesis. Otfrid, ed. Erdmann, p. 39f. (I, 18, *mystice*).

37. Ibid. p. 64 (II, 5, 15 -24). The first line looks like a reference to *delectatio*, and Otfrid may have in mind here the three stages by which man may be tempted — and for which the Fall is used tropologically as a symbol: *suggestio, delectatio, consensus.* See Gregory on this in the Moralia in Job IV, 27, 49 (PL 75, 661).

of the section, just as Gregory does not end his sermon on this
note. Otfrid's conclusion here is again tropological, forming a
framework with the opening lines. The devil must be driven
from us in this way, if we are to reach heaven. The typology of
the parallel is here more or less incidental. Otfrid is interested in
Adam only insofar as it was through his Fall that we lost our
homeland. But that "we" is important. In dogmatic accordance
with the teaching of original sin, man is all one in Adam, and
the overall lesson is that the devil tricked "us" once, but Christ
has shown us how to overcome him – how the devil must be
fon uns firdriban, "driven out by us."[38]

Otfrid's next section, II, 6, develops some of the points
raised here, but although there is still a stress on the unity of
mankind in Adam, and the loss of the paradisaical homeland,
this portion of the 'Evangelienbuch' is perhaps of greater
interest to the notion of recapitulation. The section is a condensed 'Paradise Lost' and 'Paradise Regained', discussing the
Fall in some detail and deploring its consequences.[39] But this
description is followed by a passage on the Redemption, based
this time, however, on the actual sacrifice of Christ:

er gáb . . . ana wanka bi únsih muadun scálka
thaz sin liaba houbit . . .[40]

(he gave, without faltering, for us, miserable wretches,/ his dear
head. . .)

What is interesting is the fact that such a glimpse of the
Redemption should come here. The usual Redemption is, of
course, on the cross, but Otfrid obviously feels that the conquest
of the devil in the wilderness, which is his immediate topic, is vital

38. Otfrid, ed. Erdmann, p. 64 (II, 5, 25).
39. The passage is similar in tone to the description of the Fall in
the eleventh-century Vienna Genesis, again in German. Die Frühmittelhochdeutsche 'Wiener Genesis,' ed. Kathryn Smits, Berlin 1972, pp.
112 -125 (vv. 374 -515).
40. Otfrid, ed. Erdmann, p. 66 (II, 6, 51f.).

to the Redemption, and thus he introduces the full Redemption here as an extra section.

Equally unusual for consideration as a Miltonic forerunner is a somewhat later German work, the so-called 'Anegenge' ('The Beginning'). This was written in what is now Austria in about 1160 -70, and has only recently been re-edited after over a century. The work is not well-known,[41] and is usually written off even in the handbooks for Germanists as a poor compilation from the poet's own notes as a theology student.[42] While the 'Anegenge' is by no means in the front rank of medieval German literature, it is constructed with perhaps a greater literary skill than has been generally acknowledged. The theology of the poem, though based to a large extent on the contemporary commonplaces, might also be considered original in some points of arrangement, particularly in respect of the motif under discussion here.

There are in any case few scholarly studies of the work: that of Heinz Rupp, however, perhaps the only critic to subject the poem to a thoroughgoing literary and structural analysis, draws up a well-balanced structural schema for the work which might be cited here:

Prologue
Creation and Fall of the Angels
The Trinity

Man (Creation, Fall, Adam to Noah)

(Excursus: *de visione Dei*)

Redemption (Debate in heaven, Nativity, Redemption)[43]

41. Watson Kirkconnell, The Celestial Cycle, Toronto 1952, repr. New York 1967, p. 520 confuses it with the contemporary 'Summa Theologiae' (also in Middle High German), and incidentally misspells the name of the work.

42. Helmut de Boor, Die deutsche Literatur von Karl dem Grossen bis zum Beginn der höfischen Dichtung, 2nd ed. Munich 1955, p. 175.

43. Deutsche religiöse Dichtungen des 11. und 12. Jahrhunderts, Freiburg/Br. 1958, p. 276.

This schema shows already the break-down of the work as a kind of *summa,* a point noted also by Rupp. The poet is concerned with the circular nature of the divine plan, and Rupp again notes the close relationship that there is in general here between the Fall and Redemption — the former having the latter implicit in it.[44]

The relation between the sections of the poem dealing with the Fall and with the Redemption is well-balanced in detail. Thus there is a diabolical council which decided to send a messenger from hell to tempt Eve, which is set against the heavenly council — the well-known medieval allegory of the "four daughters of God" — which results in an angelic messenger being sent to Mary. This general mood of recapitulative typology is continued in the description of the temptation of Christ in the desert.

God makes the decision to cease being angry with mankind, and will send

> einen mensch . . .
>> uns ze trôste,
> der mit sîn selbes lîbe erlôste
> allez manchunne . . .[45]

(a man,/ for our comfort,/ who with his own body would save/ all mankind.)

The simple designation *ein mensch,* "a man," points to Christ's humanity, and calls to mind already the *deuteros anthropos* of Pauline typology. This man, moreover, will do penance (*buoze*)[46] for the sins of Adam — will do penance and will win a victory, the victory through humility being, of course, the essential Christian paradox.

---

44. Religiöse Dichtungen, p. 264.
45. Anegenge, ed. Neuschäfer, p. 252f. (vv. 2962 -5). See also the notes (to v. 2307) on *wider vart* as *recapitulatio* in a general sense (p. 287). See also *widerlegen,* v. 2973, p. 253.
46. Ibid. p. 252f. (v. 2985).
47. Ibid. p. 252f. (vv. 2980 -4).

The birth of Christ is narrated very briefly here — some half-dozen lines — and we pass then, very significantly, to the temptations in the desert. The formulation at the opening of the narrative of the pericope is interesting of itself. The connexion with Adam is made again:

> den tievel er sich bechorn lie,
> rehte drî stunde
> mit der selben sunde
> dâ Adâm an geviel
> in des tievels giel.[47]

> (He allowed the devil to tempt him/ three times,/ with the same sin/ with which Adam fell/ into the devil's maw.)

The content is familiar enough. The words, however, suggest another internal-structural link with the Fall over and above that implicit in the context. When Adam and Eve have eaten the fruit in the earlier portion of the work, the poet introduces the strange motif that God gave the pair three chances to repent:

> drî stunt er chot:
> wâ bistû, Adâm ? [48]

> (three times he said/ "where are you, Adam? ")

This is not exegetical, and it seems at least possible that the poet is working out an extra typological point on his own.[49] As far as Christ's penance is concerned, however, the emphasis is first of all on the fasting: Christ's fast wiped out the sins of Adam and Eve — and here some are enumerated: sacrilege, lust, perjury. These sins are not part of the usual temptations parallel, but they do, however, echo a similar attribution elsewhere in the poem, of six sins to Adam. Morton W. Bloomfield has pointed out that a variety of sins may frequently be attributed to Adam, and I have myself speculated that the sins mentioned in the 'Anegenge' may derive from the 'Elucidarium' of Honoré

48. Ibid. p. 168f. (v. 1390f.).
49. Murdoch, Fall of Man, p. 125 discusses the point.

of Autun, with the additional influence of liturgical confessional prayers.[50]

The temptation parallel is integrated, and the sins are taken one at a time. There is, throughout, a clear emphasis on Christ's virtues, however, as the forces which overcome the sins of the first couple. Gluttony is dealt with first, and the devil attempts the temptation with the stones to see whether Christ may be led into this sin:

> zuo der chelgîtecheit
> het er in gerne getriben ![51]

> (He would gladly have led him into gluttony)

But the devil is repulsed, and the poet comments that Christ's abstinence has neutralized the gluttony of Adam:

> mit hunger buozt er duo
> der armen chelgîtecheit.

> (With hunger he atoned for/ the gluttony of the miserable ones)

to which is added an allusion to the importance for the Redemption of mankind:

> ze vertilgen unseriu leit[52]

> (to wipe out our suffering)

The temptation of the temple follows, and although no name is given to the sin that the devil has in mind for Christ here, his humility is set against the vainglory of the first couple:

> dâ mit galt er diemuote
> die uppige guote
> die Êva und Adâm
> dar an heten getan
> daz si gelobt wolden werden
> von den liuten ûf der erden.[53]

51. Anegenge, ed. Neuschäfer, p. 254f. (v. 3022f.).The word used for gluttony is unusual, and means literally "greed of the throat."
52. Ibid. p. 254f. (vv. 3028 -30).
53. Ibid. p. 256f. (vv. 3047 -52).

(with that he made good, with his humility/ the vainglory/ that
Adam and Eve/ had had/ in wanting to be praised/ above all others
on earth.)

This seems to be the Gregorian interpretation of vainglory,
based on the *eritis sicut dii,* a point stressed earlier in the
'Anegenge' in one section dealing with the Fall.[54] Cassian, it
will be remembered, based his *cenodoxia* on the promise that
the pair will have their eyes opened. The third temptation
looks, however, like Cassian's exegesis. Avarice is not named,
and instead the pride alone is stressed. Avarice is, as in Otfrid,
implied as a sin of Adam and Eve:

> duo wolt ern bechorn mit der ubermuote.
> dô vuort er in ûf ein hoehe
> und sprach, swaz er ubersaehe,
> daz er in des gewaltic taete,
> ob er in nidervallende ane baete
> dô hiez ern vurder schaben!
>
> . . . .
>
> dâ buozt er die missetaete
> daz Êva und Adâm
> dar an heten missetân
> daz si wolten gotes rîchtuom.[55]

(Then he wanted to tempt him with pride/ He led him to a high
place/ and said that whatever he saw/ he would place under his
command/ if he fell down and worshipped him./ He said, "be-
gone! ". . . Thus he did penance for the misdeed/ of Adam and Eve/
which they committed/ in that they coveted God's riches.)

The context points to Gregory's exegesis: the idea of riches
indicates the sin of avarice, even if it is not named, possibly
because the concept is somewhat difficult to grasp in any case.
It suffices for the poet to refer to the pride, which Gregory even
uses in the same context. The knowledge of good and evil is
God's realm, and this is what Adam and Eve are presumed to
have coveted.

54. Ibid. p. 246f. (v. 2875f.). The correct text is the diplomatic on
the left-hand page, and the emendation by the editor is unlikely to be
accurate. See my review (Modern Language Review 64, 1969), p. 446.
55. Anegenge, ed. Neuschäfer, p. 256f. (vv. 3058 -71).

The chief difference between this work and the Gregorian (or indeed Cassian's) exegesis is that where both of those treat the Fall and then the temptations of Christ, the 'Anegenge' does not do this. We have of course already had the story of the Fall as such in a previous section: but the effect of taking the parallel point for point here underlines the redemptive work of Christ. In many ways — contextual as well as structural — the 'Anegenge' echoes rather Irenaeus than one of the later exegetes. Certainly the passage is Irenaean in spirit, even if the Greek Father is unlikely to have been the source.[56] There are, as a matter of fact, some brief tropological asides here — Christ's behaviour teaches us in general terms how we may avoid the devil's snares and thus reach our heavenly homeland — the paradise-fatherland topos arises again in the Adamic context. But these points are made well after the discussion of our pericope.[57] More important, the description of the temptations as neutralizing the Fall is followed immediately by a reference to the Crucifixion — the sacrifice that is the final expiation of the sin in Eden — the crown of thorns is set typologically against the crown that Adam and Eve desired in paradise.[58] But the reference to the Crucifixion here is brief, compared with the narrative of the temptations, and this is significant of itself. There is, it is true, the well-drawn parallel between the Fall and the Annunciation, taking up a longish passage prior to our section. But it is still important that the end of the whole work — the completion of the divine plan, and the way in which God makes good the Fall, described in the first part of the work, — puts a very clear stress on the temptation, framed only

56. V. Teuber, Über die vom Dichter des 'Anegenge' benutzten Quellen (Beiträge 24, 1899), pp. 355 -7 is the only critic to discuss specific sources here, although others look at general source possibilities. But Teuber is apparently unaware that there is a connected exegesis behind the point, although he mentions (p. 349) Hugh of St Victor's version in a different context.

57. Anegenge, ed. Neuschäfer, p. 260f. (vv. 3125 -30).

58. Ibid. p. 258f. (vv. 3072 -3101).

by the Nativity and the Crucifixion. The conquest of the devil in the desert is obviously felt to be an important one.

The 'Anegenge', as indicated, is not a great work: there are a number of notorious errors in it, and it is in places very long-winded. But it cannot be denied that as literary representation of the divine plan the work is of the greatest value, especially in typological terms. The historical juxtaposing in the structure of the work of the Fall and the Redemption meets the eye first: the typological parallels within the historical balance then become apparent — the wheels within wheels — and the Fall and Redemption are seen to be depicted throughout in terms of one another. This is a genuine recapitulation of the Fall by the victory of Christ: Milton and the poet of the 'Anegenge' make strange bedfellows, perhaps, but the connexion is still far more viable than might have been expected.

The final large-scale treatment of the pericope in this earlier period is in a poem by a writer known to us *der wilde Man* — the "wild man" — which is probably a surname — "Wildmann" — rather than an appellation.[59] The poem in question, written in the period contemporary with or slightly later than the 'Anegenge', and in the Middle High German dialect of the lower Rhineland, deals with the legend of Saint Veronica, but contains much of the life of Christ. The poet wrote several other poems on religious topics.

The point of the temptation-parallel is not made, then, in such a significant context as in the 'Anegenge', and the approach is in fact somewhat different here from any of the earlier Germanic versions of the equation. One interesting deviation from the norm at the beginning of the pericope is the fact that Christ hides himself on a mountain:

59. Die Gedichte des Wilden Mannes, ed. Bernard Standring (ATB 59) Tübingen 1963, p. x.

> da barch he sich aleine
> uf einim hoen steine.[60]

(He hid himself alone/ upon a high stone)

But the temptation begins in a familiar fashion — the devil (in accordance with the dual-nature interpretation) is perplexed by this man, and wishes to find out more about him — *weder he got ob menschi were*, "whether he were God or man."[61] The parallel with the Fall is then introduced, and the points are taken one at a time, as in the 'Anegenge'. The signal difference here, though, is that the temptation is directed at Eve, rather than at Adam in the first instance. Nevertheless, the first reference is to the sin of gluttony:

> do virsuchte in alse he vir Ewin dethe,
> der he den sconin apil bot.
> he sprach: "nim disen/ sten undi mache brot,
> ob du godis sun bist."
> du wande er in mit valiser list
> undi mit vrasheide bikoren,
> da mit der mennische wart virloren.[62]

(So he tried to do the same as he did with Eve/ to whom he gave the fine apple./ He said: "Make these stones bread/ if you are God's son."/ He had in mind to tempt him with false cunning/ and with gluttony,/ with which mankind was lost.)

The second temptation does not give a name to the sin involved. Instead, there is a stress on the humility of Christ in overcoming it — which again calls to mind the writings of Irenaeus and some later exegetes. The connexion that the German poet draws with the Fall here is interesting, though. The devil tempts Christ on the temple-top, and this is equated with Eve's tempting of Adam into eating the fruit. The idea is a logical one — we have seen the temptation of Eve, now we have the passage from Eve to Adam. This is not, however, in any of the well-known exegetical commentaries, although Eve is occasionally blamed in

60. Ibid. p. 7 (v. 217f.).
61. Ibid. p. 7 (v. 223).
62. Ibid. p. 7f. (vv. 226 -32).

(later) vernacular texts. One might, perhaps, attribute this to the poet's originality in handling the Fall as a gradual sequence of events, while keeping it integrated in this antitype framework. It speaks for the poet's skill.

The third of the temptations from the Gospel is named — avarice (*girheit*) — and this is connected with Adam, specifically with the promise "you shall be as gods." This calls to mind Aquinas and Cassian rather more than Gregory — both stress this part of the devil's promise, rather than the knowledge of good and evil. But Aquinas is too late, and both exegetes refer here to pride, not to avarice. The Gregorian exegesis seems to be behind the passage again at some remove, but the unusual nature of the structure here precludes the establishing of any direct and positive source. Christ of course resists the devil, when Adam had fallen — with disastrous results, the poet inserts, for all Adam's progeny — and the pericope ends as in the Matthew text.

This is perhaps not clearly recapitulative typology. It is rather an *ad hoc* typological parallelism of two historical events. No moral is drawn, and although there are references to original sin, the victory of Christ is by no means conclusive, and the devil leaves to try an easier target, Judas. But the treatment of the point here is interesting for the integration of the Fall into the parallel. There are other literary points about the treatment of the point by *der wilde Mann* — the dramatic appeal of the passage is clear here, and the poet incorporates a great deal of direct speech into his narrative, pointing on, perhaps, to the dramatic treatments. The context of the poem, however, is what really precludes any proper recapitulative typology here. The life of Christ is incidental to the body of the work, the story of Veronica, and there is therefore a very predictable difference between this poem and a *summa*-like work such as the 'Anegenge', or even the Gospel-book of Otfrid, at least devoted exclusively to the life of Christ.

Other early medieval vernacular poems are of less relevance here. There are medieval German poems that deal with the life of Christ, but do no more than mention the Matthew narrative, without naming the sins: the 'Life of Jesus' by Frau Ava might be set beside the much later so-called 'Erlösung', to provide examples from either end of the Middle Ages.[63] The life of Christ is handled too in various of the Marian poems, especially in German, but they do not carry our exegesis. One might search further for examples of the use of the pericope in an allusive form — in medieval writings a pagan will sometimes tempt a Christian warrior with riches, and will be associated with the devil in so doing.[64] These incidents, however, are unlikely to have any connexion with the Fall of Man.

63. The poems of Ava are edited in: Die religiösen Dichtungen des 11. und 12. Jahrhunderts, ed. Friedrich Maurer, Tübingen 1964 -70, I, 369 -513. The 'Erlösung', is edited by the same scholar: Leipzig 1934, repr. Darmstadt 1964.

64. See Rodney W. Fisher, The Role of the Demonic in Selected Middle High German Epics, Diss. Cambridge 1968, p. x and p. 41f. (referring to the 'Rolandslied') and p. 58f. (on a similar point in the 'Orendel').

V LATER VERNACULAR POETRY

The contribution to the present study from the later Middle Ages — and the terms "early" and "later" are of course merely arbitrary divisions of convenience — is on the whole less fruitful than the literature discussed in the previous chapter. The true ancestors of Milton in poetry at least (this does not necessarily apply in other genres) appear to have flourished in the main before 1200. Nevertheless, some of the later work is interesting, even if one has to add that its significance rests fairly frequently more upon the fact that it was well-known as devotional material than upon any real literary merit. This is the case, for example, with the metrical homily and legend collections of early thirteenth century England. These might, indeed, have been treated under the heading of sermons as such, but the classification of these works is a vague one. One collection that we shall examine, the 'Ormulum', consists of metrical *sermones de tempore,* or rather, of moralized paraphrases of the Scripture for given days. Other comparable collections, such as the 'South-English Legendary' and the 'Northern Homily Collection' combine this with the popular tale and with the lives of the saints. The difference in name of these two very similar collections is indicative, and the fact that the 'Legenda aurea' has a strong influence on works of this kind also gives an indication of their nature — metrical amplifications to sermons, adjuncts rather than sermons as such. John Small's comment on the Northern collection may stand for the use and purpose of these collections as a whole:

> The sermons may ... have been intended to be read to the people after the regular services of the Church were concluded; and the singular tales or "narrations", which indicate the rude simplicity of the age, seem to have been introduced more effectually to fix the attention of the audience.[1]

1. English Metrical Homilies from Manuscripts of the Fourteenth Century, ed. John Small, Edinburgh 1872, p. vi.

Small's somewhat disapproving Victorian tone does, however, bring out the nature of the works: they were read to the people, and we may form a picture of a pretty extensive lay audience. Again, however familiar the points of interpretation involved may have been to the composers, they are explained at length to the audience. The works seem to have had considerable currency. From their close connexion with the sermon we expect − and find − a heavy tropological emphasis. On a very basic aesthetic level these are, however, poetical works, implying at least some creativity, be it only in the forming of rhymed couplets. This must justify their inclusion here; that they are well-known, and that they show differing and distinct attitudes to the exegetical connexion of the Fall and the temptations of Christ (including some points not found elsewhere) justifies their inclusion at all.

A start (if perhaps a dull one) may be made with the collection mentioned first, the 'Ormulum,' a vast (and incomplete) collection of metrical sermons according to the ecclesiastical pericope system, integrating narration and commentary much as in Otfrid's 'Evangelienbuch', although with less skill. It was written by Orm, whence the name, in the North-East Midlands, in around 1200. Joseph Mosher has characterized the work in terms that are not flattering, but which are nevertheless accurate:

> ... the homilies are almost entirely lacking in originality ... Orm clings [for his sources] to Beda, Gregory, Josephus, and Isidor ... The borrowed material is treated in a thoroughly hackneyed manner ...[2]

And yet it is perhaps precisely because of Orm's pedantics that the evidence of the 'Ormulum' is of interest, apart from its role in disseminating the motif to a wide audience. The portion for the first Sunday in Lent − in line of course with the pericope − contains our motif, and the approach is predictably tropological. Gregory's exegesis in some form seems to have been the

2. Exemplum, p. 50. It might be noted that Mosher treats all the metrical collections as sermons proper in his study.

source, but there are additions, and the version from Gregory's homily is by no means reproduced exactly.

Christ is tempted first with gluttony, and Orm explains in some detail wherein the gluttony lies. There is then a connexion with Adam:

> . . . 3iff he [Christ] wollde makenn braed
> 7 makenn itt ne mihhte
> þa waere he þurrh þe lust off braed
> I gluterrnesse fallenn,
> 7 waere þa bikahht 7 lahht
> þurrh fanding off þe deofell
> þat illke wise þatt Adam
> Was laht þurrh gluternesse.
>
> . . . .
>
> All swa summ Adam allre firrst
> Biswikenn wass þurrh aete,
> All swa bigann þe deofell firrst
> To fandenn Crist þurrh aete.[3]

This gives rise to a general attack on gluttony, based on the notion that Christ fasted as an example to mankind of how to overcome the lust of the flesh — an idea encountered in several of the prose sermons.

With the second temptation, Orm runs across the problem of the Luke order, and devotes some twenty or thirty lines to pointing this out. Eventually he comes to a conclusion similar to that reached by, say, Haymo of Auxerre — that Matthew is making a deliberate connexion with the Fall.[4] He goes on to give the entire temptation parallel, referring to Matthew as a source throughout, and based in all probability on Gregory in some form: Gregory of course speaks first of the Fall, then of the Gospel story. The passage may be cited at some length to give an idea of Orm's general style in handling the motif:

3. The Ormulum, ed. Robert Holt, Oxford 1878, II, 49f.; these are vv. 11617-11642.

4. PL 118, 199f. The parallel is not an exact one, however.

Maþþew
Onn hiss Goddspelless lare
Uss writeþþ, þatt te Laferrd Crist
Wass fandedd þurrh þe deofell
þatt illke wise þatt Adam
I Paradys wass fandedd,
7 brohht to grund 7 unnderrfot
7 i þe deofless walde.
Forr allre firrst wass Adam þaer
þurrh gluterrnesse wundedd,
7 affterr þatt þurrh idell 3ellp
þatt iss þurrh modi3nesse,
7 allre lattst he wundedd wass
þurrh gredi3nesses waepenn.
7 all þatt illke wise wass
Crist Godess Sune fandedd,
Affterr þatt itt writeþþ uss
Maþþew þe Goddspellwrihhte.
Forr allre firrst he fandedd wass
þurrh fodess gluterrnesse,
þurrh þatt te laþe gast himm badd
Off staness makenn lafess.
7 siþþenn affterr þatt he wass
þurrh modi3nesse fandedd,
þurrh þatt te laþe gast himm badd
Dun laepenn off þe temmple.
Forr 3iff þatt Crist itt haffde don
Hiss mahte forr to shaewenn,
Het haffde don þurrh idell 3ellp
7 all þurrh modi3nesse,
7 allre lattst wass Jesu Crist
þurrh gredi3ness fandedd,
þurrh þatt te laþe gast himm baed
All weorelldrichess ahhte,
Forr þatt he shollde lutenn himm
7 bu3henn till hiss wille.[5]

The repetitive nature of the style is at once clear, but this would
certainly have imprinted the allegory firmly in the mind of the

5. Vv. 11767-11802, Holt II, 54f.

audience. The three sins, then, are as in Gregory: gluttony (*glutermesse*), vain glory (*idell ȝellp*) and avarice (*grediȝnesse*), although they are not yet described in the case of the first Fall.

The parallel is reiterated, however, at some length in the rest of the passage: in the later references the exegesis is integrated — the sins are treated one at a time, — but the entire context is tropological:

> þuss fandeþþ deofell Godess follc
> O þise þrinne wise . . .[6]

Christ overcomes the devil, but although the Adam and Eve parallel is there throughout the passage there is no real sense of recapitulation. The devil is simply defeated — he leaves *Forrschamed off himm sellfenn,*[7] — but he is not crushed completely. The final prayer is that we may all overcome the devil in this way, and in spite of the fact that Christ does win a victory, this can only be seen as tropological — this is again the sermon *exemplum.*

The motif is found again in rather less overdone form in another of the homily-legend collections, in this case the 'Northern Homily Collection.' This collection has not been edited in full. The oldest manuscript, of the early fourteenth century, appears to be the Edinburgh collection edited by John Small in 1872. This is incomplete, containing only the sermons for Advent, Nativity, Epiphany and for Candlemas, at which point it breaks off.[8] The collection exists in a number of other manuscripts, however, in a variety of dialects. Even from the portion edited by Small one may form an idea of the text and its sources — references to Gregory himself are fairly frequent.[9] Indeed, the point at which the comparison of the two temptation scenes is made also contains a reference to that exegete.

6. Vv. 12306f., Holt II, 73.
7. V. 12529, Holt II, 80.
8. Small, Homilies, describes this and some other manuscripts of the work in his introduction, pp. xi-xxii. See further Gordon H. Gerould, The North-English Homily Collection, Diss. B.Litt., Oxford 1902, pp. 5-10.
9. See Gerould, Collection, p. 102f. and Small, Homilies, pp. 46, 3; 45, 16 etc.

Here the reference is fairly brief. I cite it from a manuscript in the Henry E. Huntington Library (San Marino, California), an early fifteenth century text in what appears to be an Irish dialect. The date and the dialect, compared with the Edinburgh manuscript, give a brief indication of the spread of the work:

> Her on spekyth seynt gregory
> And schowyth vs apertly
> þat crist wos temptyd on þat wysse
> þat adam wos in paradyse
> þe fend made our fadyr adam
> With threfold syn fal in blame
> þat is to sey with glotony
> With couetys and with vaynglory.[10]

The order differs in fact from Gregory's exegesis: we should expect *glotony — vaynglory — couetys,* as is the case with other Middle English poems and plays, such as the 'Stanzaic Life of Christ', a work to be considered later in this chapter. It is possible, however, that the rhyme has caused the change. Apart from the order and the names of the last two sins, there are definite similarities of phrase between this and the 'Ormulum', and the 'Northern Homily Collection' is primarily interesting here once again as a means by which the outline of the parallel enters vernacular thought and writing.

The parallel collection to the Northern cycle, the 'South-English Legendary', does not have the point. In the Corpus Christ College manuscript (MS CCCC 145), the fullest version of this work, from the early fourteenth century, the section *de quatragesima* merely links the forty-day fast of Christ with the Lenten fast: Christ is an *ensample* here.[11] There is no compari-

---

10. HM 129, fol. 57b. I am indebted to Michael Benskin, who transcribed this text for me, having noted it in the course of his own studies on Hiberno-English dialects. He tells me that the MS is from north of Dublin, possibly Meath. Mr Benskin's work on the MS is being carried out in collaboration with Angus McIntosh, Forbes Professor of English at the University of Edinburgh, to whom I am also indebted, albeit at second hand, for comments on the provenance of the work.

11. The Early South-English Legendary ... from Corpus Christi Col-

son with Adam, nor is there any re-telling of the episode in the desert.

A rather fuller instance of this attitude is found in another, slightly later Middle English work, the mid-fourteenth century 'Meditations on the Life and Passion of Christ,' a work described by Rosemary Woolf as an extremely good translation-paraphrase of the Latin 'Philomena' of John of Howden. Here the entire pericope is disposed of briefly and tropologically:

> Thou were led in-to wildirnesse,
> Tempted thorw deueles wykednesse.
> Thou wiþstode, þanne fley þat fo;
> Ensample we han to don also:
> Wiþ god ensample and god techyng
> þe peple is lad to lif lastyng . . .[12]

Again Adam is not mentioned, nor the sins with which Christ was tempted. But the attitude, if not the handling, is exactly that of the 'Ormulum.'

Several further examples may be adduced from this period in which the pericope is briefly treated. The late thirteenth-century 'Northern Passion', for example, speaks merely of how Christ fasted to fulfil the *olde lawes*[13] – and this point is in fact even omitted in some of the manuscripts. A German poem

lege Cambridge MS 145, Vol. I, ed. Charlotte d'Evelyn and Anna J. Mill (EETS/OS 235) London 1956, p. 129, vv. 22-4. The Laud text was edited by Carl Horstmann (EETS/OS 87) London 1887.

12. Vv. 199-204 of: Meditations on the Life and Passion of Christ, ed. Charlotte d'Evelyn (EETS/OS 158) London 1921, p. 6. On this text see Rosemary Woolf, The English Religious Lyric in the Middle Ages, Oxford 1968, p. 161, esp. n. 1, which has references to studies comparing John of Howden's work with the 'Meditations', and to editions of the former text. The whole chapter of Woolf's book, "Lyrics of Richard Rolle and the Mystical School" is of interest here.

13. See vv. 10-12: The Northern Passion, Vol. I, ed. Frances A. Foster (EETS/OS 145) London 1913, p. 4. The point is not in the French text which Foster prints in her introductory volume II (EETS/OS 147) London 1916, pp. 102-25. Nor does the parallel Southern Passion, ed. Beatrice Daw Brown (EETS/OS 169) London 1927, have the point.

dealing with the life of Christ that is roughly contemporary with this work has a full treatment of the narrative as such (closest akin, perhaps, to such works as Ava's 'Leben Jesu', the English 'Cursor Mundi' or the German 'Erlösung'), but ends again on an exclusively tropological note, even if the attitude is rather more personally put than in the 'Meditations' and the 'Ormulum'. The poet of 'Christi hort' ('The Treasure of Christ'), one Gundacker von Judenberg, about whom practically nothing is known, concludes his description of the temptations of Christ with the prayer:

> nu hilf, helferiche,
> daz ouch ich gewaltichliche
> der werlt, dem tivel an gesig . . .[14]
>
> (Now help me, you who are so full of help, / that I, too, may with such force / overcome the world and the devil . . .)

Another continental work that falls into this category is the fourteenth-century Franco-Italian 'Ystoire de la Passion,' contained in the MS Bibliothèque Nationale Fr. 821. The Adamic allusion is very brief, although some interesting points are there. Lucifer's decision to tempt Christ is based upon an uncertainty regarding his nature:

> Mes je ne pois trover mie
> Nul peché en le fil Marie
>
> (But I can find no sin / in Mary's son)

He decides therefore to send a devil to tempt Christ in the same way as he tempted Adam and Eve earlier in Eden. The parallel is not, however, pursued in the narrative proper, which is in any case very concise. The only sin actually named is that connected with the temptation of the kingdoms, here given as *covoitise,* "avarice."[15]

14. Vv. 613-5 of: Gundacker von Judenberg. Christi hort, ed. J. Jaksche (DTM 18) Berlin 1910, p. 10. In English, compare the 'Cursor Mundi,' the massive compendium which mentions *glotoni* as the first sin in the temptation story, but has no Adamic references and names none of the other sins. See the edition of Richard Morris (EETS/OS 62) London 1876, volume III, p. 742 of the complete text. See v. 12941 of the Cotton MS.

15. Ystoire de la Passion, ed. Edith A. Wright, Baltimore 1944. The

There are, of course, a number of poetical versions of the life and passion of Christ from this period which contain no reference at all to the parallel, or to the sins involved.[16] Others do, however, contain versions of the Gospel story that are worthy of examination both in respect of the dissemination of the typology, and also in a more purely literary sense. Three of these may be considered, each of them interesting for different reasons, and all from very different geographical origins. The first is an Icelandic devotional poem primarily to the Virgin, written at some time before 1361 by Eystein Asgrimsson, a regular of the monastery of Thykkviboer in Iceland, and entitled 'Lilja' ('The Lily'). The passage in question is not extensive, and the connexion with Adam is not borne out, but it is there nevertheless. The devil wonders at the appearance of Christ, and stressed his manhood (in connexion with the dual-nature doctrine), just as was the case in other early Germanic treatments of the theme such as the 'Heliand' or Otfrid's 'Evangelienbuch':

> þyrstr er hann ok fǫlr af fǫstu,
> firrisk hlátr, enn kann at gráta.[17]

> (He is thirsty, and pale from fasting / does not laugh, and knows how to weep)

and for this reason, as in the familiar soteriological exposition, the devil decides to tempt him. The parallel with Adam is not brought out in detail, but is alluded to in an interesting fashion. The temptation of Christ will be easy compared to that of

lines cited are 193f., p. 31, and the Adamic parallel is found in vv. 205-12 on the same page. The narrative itself in vv. 213-40, p. 31f., the reference to avarice in v. 233, p. 32.

16. For example the fourteenth century French Livre de la Passion, ed. Grace Frank, Paris 1930.

17. Text cited from the revision of Finnur Jónsson's work, Den Norsk-Isländska Skaldediktningen, rev. Ernst A. Kock, Lund 1946-9, II, 219. See stanza 42. There are translations of the work by Eirikr Magnusson, Lilja (The Lily), London/Edinburgh 1870, (see p. 43) and more recently into German by Wolfgang Lange, Christliche Skaldendichtung, Göttingen 1958, p. 64.

Adam and Eve, for they seemed to have been more glorious than this man:

> Mér virðiz, sem miklu haera
> maetum guði er Ádam saeti,
> áðr ek sveik þau Évu baeði
> aerusnauð í myrkr ok dauða.
> Satt er, at faestir sjá við prettum;
> svá mun enn um Jésúm þenna
> því treystumz ek framt at freista;
> forðum hefi ek slaegvitr orðit.[18]

(It seems to me that Adam, / earlier, sat higher with God / before I tricked him and Eve / dishonoured into darkness and death / It is true that few see the trickery / and that's what will happen with this Jesus. / So I shall tempt him / I have been a trickster for a long time.)

The notion of Adam's glory is in itself a medieval common-place, although it is not usually found in this context: it has its roots, perhaps, in Rabbinic thought.[19] That the point should be made here is literarily and theologically effective, however, for this emphasizes the nature of Christ's victory when it does come.

The devil is of course vanquished: the imagery for this is again impressive:

> Vélakrings af vǫfðum strengjum
> vundin opt — ok sneruz á lopti —
> skeytin ǫll ens flaerðar fulla
> fjanda brjóst í gegnum standa.[20]

(All the strong arrows / often from woven strings / swerve aloft / and strike the fiend's own breast.)

This is indeed a victory. But within the framework of the poem as a whole it is not the final victory, and there is no immediate discussion of the Redemption, as there was in some of the other

18. St. 43, Kock, p. 219; Magnusson, p. 45; Lange, p. 64.
19. On the point in general, see my own paper: The Garments of Paradise (Euphorion 61, 1967), pp. 375-82.
20. St. 45, Kock, p. 219; Magnusson, p. 47. Lange, p. 64.

Germanic treatments. The overall effect is not typological in any real sense. Apart from the fact that the parallel is not drawn in particularly full terms, the basically tropological intent – one that is remarkably similar to the slightly earlier 'Christi hort' – comes out in a stanza that is a kind of interpolated prayer in the middle of the narrative. This comes just before the lines quoted above. The poet prays:

Sonr Máriu, sonr enn dýri,
sonr menniligr guðs ok hennar,
kenn þú mér at forðaz fjandann
frǫlkunngan, enn þér at unna![21]

(Son of Mary, dear son / her son and the human son of God / teach me to avoid the fiend / and his craftiness, and to love you)

That Christ's action is an example becomes clear with these lines. The allusion to Adam is entirely unconnected with this (unlike the treatment in the 'Ormulum', where it was integrated tropologically), and may be dismissed, for all its poetical value, as unimportant from the point of view of typology. The 'Lilja' is an example of the incidental use of the familiar comparison – for it must have been familiar for the poet to have introduced it here, and as a monk he would certainly have known some of the commentaries on the point. We may assume that the poet has taken out of the tradition only that small part which serves his purpose, and has modified and perhaps added to the tradition in a way which suits his genre of religious skaldic poem.

A German work of the same century is perhaps closer to the standard exegesis of the temptations in the desert, although the reference to Adam and Eve is again fairly brief, and the work is not without its problems in this context. The anonymous Alemannic poem known as 'Der saelden hort' ('The Treasure of Salvation'), preserved in a manuscript of the late fourteenth century, deals with Christ, John the Baptist and the Magdalene. The poet narrates the temptation in the desert as part of the life of Christ, and cites Matthew as his source – a source which he follows in the first instance fairly closely. The actual narrative is

21. St. 44, Koch, p. 219; Magnusson, p. 45; Lange, p. 64.

followed, however, by a passage of interpretation. The sins with which Christ was tempted are analysed, this time in a tropological sense, — they are used as a general warning in each case. The sins named are *girdi,* "gluttony," *uppige ere,* "vainglory" — which is equated with *hohvart,* "pride," and finally *gitikait,* which must here be the equivalent of avarice.[22] What is interesting here, however, is that the poet names Chrysostom as a source: Heinrich Adrian, editing the text, comments that this must refer to the 'Opus imperfectum in Matthaeum' of Pseudo-Chrysostom, a late sixth century work that was ascribed to Chrysostom throughout the Middle Ages.[23] In fact, however, this seems unlikely. The relevant portion of the 'Opus imperfectum' (PG 56, 663-8) does not make the point, although Chrysostom's own sermon does in fact see greed as the first of the temptations (PG 57, 211). The passage would seem to be based, more simply, on one of the commentaries that follows Gregory, since the pattern is almost exactly as here. Any of the relevant commentaries might have served as a source, and any of them, indeed, might have contained an inserted or marginal reference to Chrysostom as a pseudo-source, which the poet then adopted. Only the inclusion of *hohvart*, "pride," differs from Gregory, and its inclusion here recalls Cassian, for example. But it is an addition, for unlike the 'Anegenge,' avarice is represented here.

The inclusion of pride, however, is not particularly significant. The second of the Adamic temptations, "ye shall be as gods," might be construed as vainglory or as pride, and here we have both sins in the second position, although the context is not Adamic. But German poetry frequently contains general references to gluttony, pride and avarice (or envy) as sins of Adam. Otfrid's 'Evangelienbuch,' it will be remembered, prefaced the Gregorian triad with a reference to pride, and other, later analogues are common. Samuel Singer, who has listed a

22. Der saelden hort, ed. Heinrich Adrian (DTM 26) Berlin 1927, p. 81. See vv. 4521-38.

23. Ibid., p. 81 (as note to v. 4522).

number of relevant places, points for example to a Carinthian sermon of the twelfth century, to the very long 'Renner' of Hugo of Trimberg, as well as to a number of other cases where three sins of this type are mentioned.[24] Several of these are at least chronologically possible as sources for 'Der saelden hort.'

'Der saelden hort' has, finally, a direct reference to the first Fall in this context, although it is a brief one, and fairly inconclusive: the reference is to pride and avarice alone, and comes at the beginning of a tropological passage. Man is beset by

> . . . hohvart und git,
> do mit der tiefel do veriet
> Evun und Adamen.

> (pride and avarice / with which the devil that time betrayed / Eve and Adam . . .)

The sins are repeated twice in a tropological context. It is interesting, however, that in both these latter cases the specific remedies for these temptations are named. The second case makes the moral point clear:

> sus soltu vigentlichen stan
> gegen Sathana berait.
> die hohvart und die gitikait
> mit demût, armût nider stich![25]

> (Thus you should stand armed / and prepared against Satan. / pride and avarice / with humility and poverty strike down!)

We recall the stress on the humility of Jesus in some of the early German works in particular.

Tropology, then, is the keynote of the point as it is

24. Zu Wolframs 'Parzival,' in: Abhandlungen zur germanischen Philologie: Festgabe für Richard Heinzel, Halle/S. 1898, p. 391f., n. 4. The title of this interesting paper tends to conceal the fact that it is largely concerned with the Genesis tradition, and contains a wealth of relevant material.

25. The first passage is vv. 4642, Adrian, p. 83 (with reference in the notes, p. 218, to Gregory as the source). The second is vv. 4764-7, Adrian, p. 85.

treated in 'Der saelden hort.' Adam and Eve are indeed tempted in the same way as Christ, but so are all men − the only significant feature about their case is that they are known to have been defeated. The poet intends and draws no express typological parallel between the two events.

Of the Middle English texts that contain the parallel of the temptations, the fullest is the so-called 'Stanzaic Life of Christ,' a work often noted as containing the analogy, but a work which is less frequently analysed.[26] As a literary monument the work is pedestrian − closest akin, perhaps, to the metrical homilies. But it is of interest nevertheless, and for a variety of reasons: for the dissemination of the material in the vernacular − the poem contains perhaps the closest version of Gregory's exegesis in verse; for the addition of detail and development of the theme; and for the importance − to be discussed in a later chapter − to the study of the drama, specifically the Chester plays. The work itself was composed in Chester in the fourteenth century, and has as its basic sources the 'Legenda aurea' and also the 'Polychronicon' of Ralph Higden, also composed in Chester. The 'Stanzaic Life of Christ' does, however, add material from exegetical commentaries − and our passage is a case in point.

The narrative of the temptation of Christ gives at the outset the name of Gregory as the source − it will be narrated not according to the Bible, but *as sais Gregory / in his 5 Omelie.*[27] The Gregorian interpretation of the story is thus inserted right away. But it is interesting that before the story is told in detail, the entire pericope is summed up in two quatrains. These quatrains echo the last part of Gregory's exegesis, his comment that Satan *eis modis a secundo homine victus est, quibus primum hominem se vicisse gloriabatur,* "was conquered by the second Adam in the same things in which he exulted to

26. Evans ('Paradise Lost'), Howard (Temptations), and Pope ('Paradise Regained') all have (footnote) references to the work. Only Evan goes even slightly beyond this.

27. A Stanzaic Life of Christ, ed. Frances A. Foster (EETS/OS 166) London 1926, p. 176, v. 5242f.

have conquered the first." The tone is that of the typology of recapitulation, and the words (echoed in the Chester play) are a coincidental foreshadowing of Milton:

> When he had fourty daies fast
> After þe time he baptist was,
> the deul temptide hym atte last,
> As the gospelle mynde mas.
>
> but Crist for alle þe deulis cast
> ouer-come hym wel tho in þat cas,
> for he supplauntide long time past
> our forme fadir out of his plas.[28]

The brief allusion to the Gospel in a filler-line brings home the fact that the whole passage uses Gregory rather than Matthew, and shows how important spiritually the interpretative side had become. The fusing of narrative and commentary is of course familiar throughout the Middle Ages, but the naming of sources in this fashion lends an immediacy to the point.

The detailed narrative then follows in a form which parallels the 'Homilia in Evangelium' exactly. Although this is a narrative of Christ's life, the Fall is expounded first. Adam is tempted with gluttony (*glotery*), vainglory (*vaynglorie*) and avarice (*auarise*). Just as in Gregory, the last of these is explained — as it is indeed in the Chester play — with Gregory himself cited again.

> "Auarise," sais sayn Gregory,
> "sovnes not onely in monee
> but in he3enes witerly
> And couetise of gret degre;"
>
> ffor qven mon wilnes gret maistry
> of he3enes or of dignite,
> Gregory in his omely
> sais that couetouse is he."[29]

Avaritia enim non solus pecuniae est, sed etiam altitudinis. Recte enim avaritia dicitur cum supra modum sublimitas ambi-

28. Vv. 5245-52, Foster, p. 176.
29. Vv. 5281-8, Foster, p. 177f.

tur... We could hardly be closer to the Latin with the English stanzas.

Satan, then, tempted Adam, not only in the same way as he did Christ, but also on the same day (*þat ilk day*): the editor of the 'Life' points out (p. 389) that this derives from Higden, ('Polychronicon' iv, 332-6 in the Rolls Series edition) just as the rest derives from Gregory's sermon. The number (5) cited for Gregory's sermon is of course irrelevant unless a manuscript of the sermons of demonstrable West-Midland provenance or four-teenth-century situation were to be found. The fact that a number is given seems to indicate Gregory himself as a source, rather than one of the commentaries that cites (and names) him: the Middle Ages had no qualms about citing at second, third, or fourth hand, but this does not seem to be the case here.

As far as the working-out of the parallel is concerned, Adam is only named in the context of the first temptation – that of gluttony. It is perhaps pertinent to speculate here on why this should be the case – it happens in other versions too. Of course the fact that this is the first temptation is relevant: but fear of unnecessary repetition would scarcely have bothered the author of the 'Stanzaic Life.' One assumes that, quite apart from the Lenten connexion, which focusses of course on that specific sin, gluttony is so much more comprehensible a failing than vainglory or a specialized sort of avarice.

Christ is victorious, but the poet here does not reiterate the typological quatrains from the beginning of the passage. This fact is indicative of attitude: the poet does not see this as the true Redemption – that will come with the Passion, later on. For the moment, we simply have the beginning of the Ministry. So too, of course, Gregory, whose interpretation, typological – fulfilled and typological – as it is, is part simply of a general sermon, and not part of a soteriological schema, as with Irenaeus. In following Gregory so closely, the 'Stanzaic Life of Christ' is middle-of-the-road typology. The reference to this work as a predecessor of Milton – however implicitly this is done – needs a great amount of qualification. The passage ana-

lysed above is, however, not the only relevant portion of this
work. The idea of Adam's three sins is used again later on, but
although the connexion seems to be close, it is not quite as closely
related to the first as seems the case on initial acquaintance. This
time Adam is said to have sinned in pride, gluttony and disobedience:

> Adam synnet in synnes thre,
> pryde, glotery, vnbuxumnesse,
> thurght whiche harmet so was he.[30]

The reasons are as follows: pride, in that he wanted to be as
God; gluttony in eating the fruit; disobedience in breaking the
command. All the sins are commonplace individually, and
Frances Foster, editing the 'Life,' points out that this passage is
based on the 'Golden Legend':

> quoniam primus homo secundum Gregorium peccaverat per super-
> biam, inobedientiam, et gulam, voluit enim assimilari Deo per sci-
> entiae sublimitatem, transgredi praecepti Dei limitem et gustare
> pomi suavitatem; et quoniam curatio habet fieri per contrarium,
> idea iste modus satisfaciendi congruentissimus fuit, quia fuit per
> humilitationem, divinae voluntatis impletionem et afflictionem.[31]

> (whereas the first man — according to Gregory — sinned in pride,
> disobedience and gluttony, in that he wanted to make himself as
> God, by means of the greatest knowledge, he transgressed the
> limiting precept of God, and ate the sweet fruit; and since a cure is
> effected by an opposite, therefore this was the most suitable means
> of making good — by humility, the fulfillment of the divine will,
> and suffering.)

The reference is presumably to a Gregorian interpretation of
Philippians 2: 3, but may be affected by our passage. The
English poem takes up the point of the cure by opposites, and
develops this according to Christ. The notion itself is interesting — the 'Life' refers to *fisik and ... surgery*[32] and one calls to

30. Vv. 6242-4, Foster, p. 212.
31. Text from the edition of Graesse, p. 230 ('De passione Domini').
See Foster, p. 292.
32. V. 6267, Foster, p. 213.

mind the fusion of opposites that is such a central thought in medieval alchemy.[33] More important, perhaps, is the direct connexion with Christ here: this is not in the 'Legenda aurea,' but the English work associates it with the life of Christ, and in doing so refers to the fasting, if not to the temptation:

> ... to hele prouyde he toke mekeness
> and shewet hit, as I preue may,
> and forto hele vnbuxumnesse
> hys fader wille fulfullet ay,
>
> and forto hele glotery
> fourty days he fast in fere,
> thus by contrarius surgery
> he helet these thre synnes her.[34]

Only the fasting is taken then, and that as a counter to gluttony. We have seen this attitude already in some of the sermons and other English texts where the temptation is very briefly handled. But the emphasis on Christ's virtues is also familiar, and his *mekeness* calls to mind the stress in works such as the 'Anegenge' or the 'Veronica' on precisely this humility. It may be that the poet has the temptation typology in mind here. And this is again typology — Christ is neutralizing, making good. The fasting in the desert at least neutralizes the gluttony in the Garden of Eden. This later passage is perhaps more fully typological than the real narrative of the temptation pericope, even though it is linked with it only by one sin — the (medievally) ubiquitous gluttony. Pride is, of course, sometimes part of the temptation equation, but not in the earlier part of the 'Stanzaic Life.' The poem goes on to a full parallel of Christ's work as Redeemer, and it is significant that this passage is part of the poem's treatment of the Passion.

33. See such standard works as those of C. G. Jung, Psychologie und Alchemie, Zurich 1944, and Mysterium coniunctionis, Zurich 1955-7, especially the introduction to the latter, vol. I, 1-4.

34. Vv. 6269-76, Foster, p. 213.

It would be beyond the scope and intent of this study to consider the writings of the Reformation and Renaissance periods in any detail. The parallel of the temptations does of course persist in verse until Milton. It is drawn for example in the 'Umanitá del figliuolo di Dio' of Teofilo Folengo in the sixteenth century, and this will be dealt with in another context later. Of the works more immediately precedent to Milton, one might be mentioned, however: the work entitled 'Christ's Victorie and Triumph in Heaven, and Earth, over, and after Death' by Giles Fletcher, which appeared in 1610, some sixty years before 'Paradise Regained.' The connexions with Milton have been pointed out, and the work has been discussed in some detail by Milton scholars, together with other relevant works from the period,[35] but for the present study what is important is the layout of the poem. The theme is the Redemption. This is the subject of the first section, the 'Victorie in Heaven' — Justice and Mercy discuss the Redemption, and this is decided. More important here is the second poem, the victory of Christ on earth. This covers the temptation in the desert, and although Christ is tempted by a highly allegorized enchantress, the temptations include some that are familiar from the medieval works: vainglory (in the context of the temptation of the temple);[36] what amounts to gluttony (in the presentation of a Bacchic feast);[37] avarice (a true avarice, however, involving *mounts of gold, and flouds of silver*);[38] and ambition.[39] All these Christ overcomes, and his victory is expressed in very brief terms in the antepenultimate stanza of the poem:

> But he her [sc. the enchantress's] charmes dispersed into winde,
> And her of insolence admonished,

35. See Pope, 'Paradise Regained,' p. xii.
36. I have used the edition of Frederick S. Boas: Giles and Phineas Fletcher. Poetical Works, Cambridge 1908-9, repr. Grosse Pointe 1968. The 'Victorie' is in I, 5-87. See on the point in question: Victorie on Earth 37-8, Boas, I, 49.
37. Victorie on Earth 50-52, Boas I, 52f.
38. Victorie on Earth 53, Boas I, 53.
39. Victorie on Earth 56, Boas I, 54.

And all her optique glasses shattered.
So with her Syre to hell shee tooke her flight . . .[40]

The final section of the tripartite poem then deals with the
Passion and the Resurrection. This is not yet a complete view of
the temptation in the desert as Redemption, then, since we have
the last portion of the poem, much of which is also strictly "on
earth." But some things are significant. The title of the second
section — that this is a victory on earth; and also that it is the
first indication of the Redemption of Adam, whose Fall is the
centre of debate in the first part, even if the parallel is not
drawn explicitly in the second.

Two medieval works might be recalled here: the Old
English 'Christ and Satan' — which does not have a Passion, but
a harrowing of hell, but which does have the temptation as its
central portion, its "victory on earth;" and the Middle High
German 'Anegenge', which has the debate in heaven preceding,
and the Passion following a detailed typological parallel of the
temptation of Christ with that of Adam. All three works — the
two medieval texts, and Fletcher's poem, at least show the great
importance of the temptation pericope. The titular divisions of
Fletcher are interesting in that they overcome the problem of a
double victory — the question of what the real victory is — the
temptation or the Passion. Fletcher would seem to say: both.
But as far as man is concerned, as far as Adam and his progeny
are concerned, the victory in the desert is the most important.

Milton is not the main concern of this study, but since
Milton is, in a sense, the crown of the tradition, it might not be
out of place to conclude the discussion of the poetic tradition
with a few comments on the best-known exponent of the point.
We may take up a point raised in the first chapter. The Milton
critic, C. A. Patrides, has denied that 'Paradise Regained' has
any intent of portraying a Redemption. In our terms, he would
not consider it an illustration of recapitulative typology:

> 'Paradise Regained' does not pretend to celebrate the God-man's
> redemption of mankind. In harmony with the common sentiment

40. Victorie on Earth 60, Boas I, 56.

that the encounter in the wilderness marked "the entraunce of
Christ into/ the execution of his office," Milton's epic focuses on the
initial stages of the Saviour's ministry.[41]

Leaving aside the point of whether the citation from John
Udall's 'Combate betwixt Christ and the Deuill' is fairly termed
"common sentiment", the internal evidence of the poem —
especially in connexion with 'Paradise Lost' — does not bear out
this view. As evidence of his interpretation, Patrides cites the
angelic hymn at the close of the poem, where Christ is bidden
to

... enter, and begin to save mankind.[42]

He misses the point that this i s the end of the poem. Paradise,
lost by Adam and Eve, has already been regained — the two
titles show this clearly enough. The worst part has been overcome, the devil has been conquered, the dragon at the gate of
the castle has been killed: now e n t e r and begin to
s a v e . . . . Patrides' emphases are not the only ones possible.
Saving is merely a formality now.

Several passages may be cited for the demonstration of
the recapitulative typology of the piece, even though there is no
parallelism of the two temptations within the narrative proper.
The general typology spans the poem. Thus in the first book:

I, who e're while the happy Garden sung,
By one mans disobedience lost, now sing
Recover'd Paradise to all mankind,
By one mans firm obedience fully tri'd
Through all temptation, and the Tempter foil'd
In all his wiles, defeated and repuls't:
And Eden rais'd in the waste wilderness.[43]

Eden, then, in the wilderness: we recall the linking of the places
of the temptation in medieval writings, and also the setting of
Christ's obedience to recapitulate, to neutralize Adam's failure
to obey. The 'Stanzaic Life of Christ' comes to mind here in

41. Christian Tradition, p. 145f.
42. Paradise Regained iv, 635, Columbia ed., II/2/481.
43. Paradise Regained i, 1-7, Columbia ed., II/2/405.

particular, and there are other passages in Milton which suggest that poem, though it is scarcely likely that Milton knew it.

Christ will attack the devil

Winning by conquest what the first man lost
By fallacy surprised . . .[44]

and man will be raised to grace once again.

Even if the parallelism is not sustained through the entire narrative, there are occasional allusions to the first couple throughout.[45] At the end, however, of the fourth book, the recapitulation again becomes apparent. Christ has

. . . avenged
Supplanted Adam, and by vanquishing
Temptation, has regain'd lost Paradise.

This is the crux: the tempter's "snares are broke," and even the harrowing of hell is promised.[46] Of course the Ministry and the Passion have yet to come, but Milton does not choose to discuss these — and surely not only because it was a theme beyond his skills.[47] The relationship between the two great epics is too close. 'Paradise Lost' tells of the first Fall, not only of man, but also of Lucifer,

Who durst defy th' Omnipotent to arms.[48]

In his choice of subject-matter alone, Milton is in a tradition that begins with Blathmac in the eight century. And from the

44. Paradise Regained i, 154f., Columbia ed., II/2/410.

45. For example: Paradise Regained i, 405; ii, 349 etc — Columbia ed., pp. 419 and 436. And there are of course other typological connexions, some less apparent than others, such as the reference to forty as 4 x 10 in ii, 245 (Columbia ed., p. 433), familiar to medievalists as the product (fulfillment of the old law by the new, ten commandments and four Gospels.

46. Paradise Regained iv, 606-8, Columbia ed., II/2/480f.

47. It will be remembered that Milton's stanzaic 'Passion' breaks off after a few stanzas with the words: *This subject the Author finding to be above the yeers he had, when he wrote it, and nothing satisfi'd with what was begun, left it unfinisht.* See the Columbia ed., I/1/23-25.

48. Paradise Lost i, 49, Columbia ed., II/1/10.

titles and the balance of his two epics he expresses the spirit, if not the letter, of the medieval view of the temptation in the desert as the great recapitulation of the Fall of Man.[49]

49. It is beyond the scope of this study to discuss the works of those critics who take 'Paradise Regained' as the triumphant recapitulation. See for one example the study by Northrop Frye, The Typology of 'Paradise Regained,' in: Milton's Epic Poetry, ed. C. A. Patrides, Harmondsworth 1967, pp. 301-21. Frye concludes that "with the climax of 'paradise Regained' the great wheel of the quest of Christ comes full circle . . ." (p. 320).

VI THE DRAMATIC VERSIONS

The religious drama of the later Middle Ages, dealing as it does with the Fall and also with the events of the life of Christ, frequently in the cyclic form which emphasizes *per se* the nature of the divine plan, offers an opportunity of presenting in vivid form the juxtaposition of the temptations of Christ with those of Adam and Eve. Both the cycle and the non-cycle mysteries, in England and on the continent, contain material that contributes further towards the overall impression of the parallelism of the two events in the Middle Ages, and beyond that into the sixteenth century. The evidence of the drama is important, for this is popular theology in a very proper sense. The dramas are conceived for performance before an at least partly lay audience, untutored – in the formal sense, anyway – in biblical exegesis as such. We may assume that a brief allusion to an exegetical point was well enough known – in all probability from sermon expositions that have in any case a close affinity with the medieval mysteries – for it to have been comprehensible to the audience at large. Fuller allusions, or detailed workings-out of an idea, provide evidence of one of the ways in which theological knowledge of this kind was disseminated at the period.

It must be borne in mind, of course, that the term "dramatic," in the earlier part of this chapter at least, is one of generic convenience. Although it is possible to make some judgements regarding characterization at a fairly basic level, what is of primary interest here once again is the addition of individual detail or the overall attitude to the temptation parallel. Among the most detailed treatments of the allegory before the sixteenth century, for example, is that of the 'Chester Butchers' Play,' which is in effect little more than a lecture adapting Gregory's exegesis, with the figure of Christ and Satan serving as little more than two-dimensional visual aids.

In the Middle Ages proper, there is no actual juxtaposition

of the two temptation scenes, although they occur of course within the same cycle. This does not happen until the works of Gil Vicente in the sixteenth century. Allusions to the motif are made, however, either overtly, or indirectly, in several of the plays taking Matthew as their theme. It is possible, moreover, to find reference to the typological pattern at least implicit in those plays whose subject is the Fall.

Some medieval plays, of course, offer no more than a faithful rendering of the Matthew text, and this contains, naturally, no hint at the parallel, as the nature of the three temptations is not specified there. Examples of this are provided by such works as the very long Middle High German passion of the fourteenth century, the 'Alsfelder Passionsspiel,' or the 'Heidelberger Passionsspiel'.[1] Continental references to the parallel in the context of Matthew are in any case rare.

In contrast to this type, a second dramatic level may be seen in versions where all, or one or two of the sins with which Satan tempted Christ are mentioned, often in the familiar sequence of gluttony, vainglory and avarice, but without explicit reference to the Fall. In cases such as these the question arises as to whether or not the (Gregorian) parallel does in fact lie behind the point? Those exegetical commentaries which describe the sins alone are more often than not expositions of Luke, and the fact that the order in the dramas is invariably Matthew might preclude these as a source. In spite of the fact that a few sermons mention the sins in the context of Christ alone, or linked with 1 John 2: 16, the connexion with the Fall is so well established as to make it likely that an interpretation such as that of Gregory is indeed the source in some form, and that the reference to the Fall of Man has been omitted deliberately. The dramatist might, for example, simply be abbreviating for the sake of clarity. But what seems more probable is that

1. The former has been edited by Richard Froning, Das Drama des Mittelalters, Stuttgart 1891-3, repr. Darmstadt 1964, pp. 607-9: see vv. 1138-97. See for the Heidelberg play the edition of Gustav Milchsack, Tübingen 1880, pp. 12-15: see vv. 257-316.

this is a question of attitude. Those plays in which the sins are mentioned, but not the Fall, tend to be heavily tropological, close to the sermon. The inclusion of any typological overtones would blur the effect, even if Adam's experience is used simply as an example of how not to behave. It is dramatically more logical to emphasize one sense of interpretation, rather than confuse the audience by hinting, even if only vaguely, at a second.

Examples from two of the English cycles may be shown in evidence of this attitude: the 'Weavers' Play' from the Hegge dramas and the 'Locksmiths' from the York mysteries. In the former, the devil refers to the means by which he has tempted Christ:

Ow in gloteny nor in veynglory it doth ryght not a-vayl
Cryst for to tempt it profyteth me ryght nought
I must now be-gynne to haue a newe travayl
In covetyse to tempt hym it cometh now in my thought . . .[2]

Gloteny, veynglory and *covetyse* are of course the three sins of the Gregorian interpretation, and the first of them is mentioned, incidentally, earlier in the play — a quite predictable stress on the most heavily emphasized sin of the trio. The York play is very similar: the devil tries with the three sins of the Hegge play, which are given the same names:

In glotonye þan halde I gude
　　　to witt his will.

. . . .
I schall assaye in vayne-glorie
　　　to garre hym falle

. . . .
I will assaye in couetise
　　　to garre hym fall.[3]

Both plays are tropological in essence, both moralities, in a non-technical sense, rather than mysteries. The basic notion

2. Vv. 144-7: Ludus Coventriae, ed. K. S. Block (EETS/OS 120), London 1922, p. 198.
3. Vv. 47f., 93f., 131f.: The York Plays, ed. Lucy Toulmin Smith, Oxford 1885, repr. New York 1963, pp. 179, 181, 182.

underlying both is the homiletic one that Christ's aim is to show
man how to withstand temptation. Significantly, Jesus himself
voices in both cases the point that the entire pericope is to be
taken as an example. Thus in the N-Town play he comments:

> Now All mankende exaumple take
> by these grete werkys þat þou dost se
> how þat þe devyll of helle so blake
> in synne was besy to tempte me
> Ffor all his maystryes þat he dyd make
> he is ouercom and now doth ffle
> all þis I suffyr ffor mannys sake
> to teche þe how þou xalt rewle the
> Whan þe devylle dothe the Assayle
> loke þou concente nevyr to synne
> For no sleytys ne for no gynne
> and þan þe victory xalt þou wynne
> þe devyl xal lesyn all his travayl.[4]

Man has, admittedly, now the certainty of grace if he withstand
temptation, but there is no victory of Christ here — only the
possibility of one for man. And yet this passage contains a
further hint at the exegetical treatments of the Fall: the as-
sailing of the devil corresponds to the initial *suggestio* of the
devil, following again the exegesis standardized by Gregory, and
man is warned against the final stage, *consentio* in those terms.

The conclusion of the York play is as explicit in its
moralizing: Jesus comments:

> For whan þe fende schall folke se
> And salus þam in sere degre,
> þare myrroure may þei make of me,
>   for to stande still;
> For ouere-come schall þei no3t be,
>   bot yf þay will.[5]

The overall effect calls to mind the familiar link between the
medieval mystery play and the sermon.[6] The very use of *ex-*

4. Vv. 196-208: Block, p. 199f.
5. Vv. 193-8: Smith, p. 184.
6. See for example the recent study by M. D. Anderson, Drama and

aumple in the Hegge play reminds one of the homiletic *exemplum,* and it is this that we are dealing with here – the moralized anecdote, be it biblical or not. Christ's coming has made no difference to mankind yet, for all that we might suspect some sort of typological parallel to the Fall behind the terminology. Only in the Hegge play, at the beginning of our portion, do we suspect in the motivation of Christ something of the redemptory nature of his battle in the desert:

> This suffyr I man for the
> Ffor þi glotenye and metys wrong
> I suffyr for þe þis hyngyr stronge . . .[7]

But in spite of the reference here to gluttony, what lies behind this passage is probably a general admonition against that sin, rather than a conscious link with the Fall. The source is probably a Lenten sermon. The lines are in any case very like those in the last part of the temptation scene, quoted above.

The concentration upon the tropological in the two plays is in one sense dramatically unsatisfactory. In each case, the devil simply returns to hell. In the York play this merely has the effect of rounding off the action, and allowing the moral to be pointed out. In the Hegge Play the devil leaves in a definite state of bewilderment, defeated but unsure why. Critics have noted this point as a not entirely satisfactory one, although it does link with the teachings on the dual nature of Christ.[8] At all events the play shows a conflation of the two exegetical treatments of the narrative of Matthew. One might contrast this outcome, for example, with the triumphant conclusion

> ich bin din her vnd ouch din got![9]

of Christ to Satan in the 'Donaueschinger Passionsspiel.'

It might be noted that the portrayal of the Matthew

Imagery in English Medieval Churches, Cambridge 1963, pp. 51-84. Also Owst, Literature and Pulpit, pp. 471-547.

7. Vv. 74-6: Block, p. 196.

8. Pope, 'Paradise Regained,' p. 40.

9. Ed. Eduard Hartl, Das Drama des Mittelalters, Passionsspiele II, Leipzig 1842, repr. Darmstadt 1966, p. 106 (v. 428).

pericope on stage as an *exemplum* continues beyond the Middle Ages, and may be found — to provide but one example — in the sixteenth century writings of John Bale, in his 'Comedy . . . concernynge the temptacyon of our lorde and sauer Jesus Christ' (1538). Here, in fact, there is mention of the Fall connexion, although it is not extensive. The Tudor play is in its treatment of the subject, essentially medieval: the questions of Protestant theology raised need not concern us here.[10] Christ again undertakes the temptation as a mirror for mankind, and the notion of the *exemplum* is again present: Christ says

> In to thys desart, the holy Ghost hath brought me,
> After my baptyme, of Sathan to be tempted,
> Therby to instruct, of Man the imbecyllyte,
> That after he hath, Gods holy sprete receyued,
> Dyuersely he must, of Sathan be impugned,
> Least he for Gods gyse, shuld fall into a pryde,
> And that in parell, he take me for hys gyde.[11]

In spite of Calvin's rejection of the notion that the devil did not tempt Christ with gluttony, it is on the question of making the stones into bread that the first Fall i s recalled. Christ says

> Thys caused Adam, from innocencye to fall,
> And all hys ofsprynge, made mysreable and mortall.[12]

Again gluttony, then, is the point that appears to have stayed in the dramatist's mind. But the parallel is not continued. Bale as prolocutor sums up the point of the temptation at the close of the play:

> Lete it not greue yow, in thys worlde to be tempted,
> Consyderynge your lorde . . .
> . . . . . .
> For Christes vyctorye, is theirs that do beleue.[13]

---

10. Ibid., p. 58.
11. Sig. D lr. I have used the facsimile edition (London 1909) of the unique Bodleian copy: A brefe Comedy or enterlude concernynge the temptacyon of our lorde and sauer Jsesus Christ . . . by Johan Bale, 1538.
12. Facsimile text sig. D 3r.
13. Sig. E 4r — Sig. E 4v.

A victory, but not a victory that is ultimate, and not one which breaks the power of the devil once and for all. We are faced once again with the dramatized sermon of the Middle Ages.

The major French cyclic 'Mystères' offer a considerable amount of relevant material, not all of which can be considered here, although examples may be taken from the earliest of these texts, the fifteenth century 'Passion de Semur' and from the best-known work, the 'Mystère de la Passion' of Arnoul Greban. As a general point, it is interesting that the close proximity of the drama to the sermon, so clear from the Chester play, is underlined here by the fact that in many cases the prologue or conclusion is spoken as a sermon by a *prescheur*.[14] The 'Passion de Semur' makes no direct comparison between the temptations of Adam and Christ, although during the discussions in hell about the appearance of Christ, Adam himself says

> C'est celluy que nous actendons,
> Le prix de no redempcion.[15]

> (It is the one for whom we have waited / the price of our redemption.)

The temptation narrative does allude to the three sins of the Gregorian pattern, although the third, avarice, here appears as *anvie, invidia*: Lucifer tempts Christ

> ... de glotonnie,
> De vainne gloire et d'anvie

> (by gluttony, vainglory and envy)

The substitution of envy for avarice seems reasonable in the context. The scene itself is brief. One point might be mentioned, however, namely that this scene closes the performance

---

14. See Emile Roy, Le Mystère de la Passion en France, Dijon/Paris 1903, p. 14 on the 'Passion St Geneviève.' Further Grace Frank, The Medieval French Drama, Oxford 1954, p. 180. On the French 'Passions' in general it might be noted that a number do not contain our point (such as the 'Passion d'Amboise' or the 'Provençale Passion.') Many, too exist only in fragmentary form or have not been edited.

15. Roy, Mystère, p. 83 (vv. 4287f.).

of the first day. A *messaiger* bids the company return the next day, and the placing of the scene can perhaps be seen as climactic. Adam's words are echoed here:

> ... demain icy reviendra,
> Et vous verrés sans fiction
> Le prix de no redempcion.[16]

(return tomorrow / and you will see in truth / the price of our redemption.)

The 'Passion d'Arras' of Eustache Mercadé, and the great 'Mystère de la Passion' of Arnoul Greban may be taken together, the latter being closely connected with the former. Both are of the early to mid-fifteenth century, and Greban's work appears to have been extremely popular in its own time.[17] The temptation of Christ takes place in both on the second day, and both, incidentally, expand the material from the two days of the Semur play to four days. There is no direct Adamic allusion.

After a defeat, the devil who has done the tempting, reports to Lucifer:

> au desert me suis transporté
> ou il estoit et l'ay tempté
> de trois pechés par compaignie:
> premierement, de gloutonnie:
> puis l'ay cuidé mettre en la loire
> d'elacion et vaine gloire
> au tiers point, pour le mieulx combatre
> je l'ay cuide faire ydolatre,
> contendant qu'il m'eust adoré ...[18]

16. The first citation is v. 4229f., Roy, p. 84; the second vv. 4293-5, Roy, p. 88. Frank, Medieval French Drama, p. 176 comments on the point of position.

17. On the close connexion, see Roy, Mystère, p. 207. The 'Passion d'Arras' ascribed to Mercadé has been edited by J-M. Richard, Le 'Mystère de la Passion.' Texte du manuscrit 697 de la bibliothèque d'Arras, Arras 1891. The great popularity of Greban's work has been dealt with in detail by Frank, Medieval French Drama, pp. 181-7.

18. Lines 10690-8: Arnoul Greban. Le Mystère de la Passion, ed. Gaston Paris and Gaston Raynaud, Paris 1878, p. 140. It might also be

(I have been to the desert / where he was, and tempted him / with three sins together / — first gluttony, / then I presumed to try him with / pride and vainglory; / thirdly, the better to attack him, / I thought of making him commit idolatry, / telling him he should worship me.)

The pattern differs slightly from those so far encountered. The first two sins are as before — gluttony and vainglory, the latter associated once again with pride, as we have seen several times, in works such as 'Der saelden hort' and other German poems. The difference, however, comes again with the naming of the third temptation, which is now very logically felt to imply idolatry — that Christ should worship the devil. Avarice is not mentioned. The point is rare in exegetical literature, although the connexion with Genesis might once again easily be made — based on the promise *eritis sicut dii* rather than on the *scientes bonum et malum,* and taking it as a desire to be false gods on the part of the first couple. The notion is very closely linked with the temptation to vainglory, and calls to mind the Latin interpretations which take the acceptance of the promise as *superbia* or *extrema superbia* — such as Cassian or later, Aquinas.

Elizabeth Pope has pointed out, however, that the temptation of the kingdoms is seen in its own right as a tropological warning against just this sin,[19] and this might have affected the passage. Investigation of other vernacular works, however, shows that this is indeed part of a definite tradition, whatever the Latin source. The evidence is a very similar point made in a poem by the Italian macaronic poet and parodist Girolamo Folengo, known in the Benedictine order, to which he was readmitted in 1534, as Teofilo Folengo. His work 'La umanitá del figliuolo di Dio' contains a reference to the temptation

noted that the last of the great French mystery cycles, the 'Mystère de la Passion' of Jean Michel, performed at Angers in 1486, has this passage virtually word for word. See Jean Michel. Le Mystère de la Passion, Angers 1486, ed. Omer Jodogne, Gembloux 1959, p. 39 (vv. 3110-9). Satan eventually comes to the decision (v. 3124, p. 40) that Christ is God.

19. 'Paradise Regained,' p. 55, on Bruno of Asti.

equation in the fourth book, where the sins that caused the first Fall are listed as *la gola, la superbia et l'idolatria,*[20] "gluttony, pride and idolatry." The fact that these three sins are used specifically in the context of Adam makes it possible that the earlier French works too are based on an Adamic interpretation, rather than on a commentary of the Gospel alone. In fact, the French Passions are, taken overall, rather like the 'Alsfelder Passionsspiel,' merely representing the story of Christ's temptation without comment of a tropological or typological nature. Folengo too does not develop the point to important lengths. A final continental work may be cited in this connexion. The 'St Galler Passionsspiel,' a German play somewhat earlier than the French Passions, contains an echo of the triple temptation that does not accord particularly closely with Gregory's schema. After the temptation, Satan leaves Christ with the complaint that he has been overcome (*vberwunden*), and he is ashamed (a nice touch) to face his fellow-devils because of this. The sins named, however, are first of all pride and then greed. He has tempted Christ

> bit hoffart vn̄ mit frazheit.

The third sin is not named, but it seems to be idolatry, as in Greban and Michel, rather than avarice: the devil says that he

> hede dich (sc. Christ) dar zů beret
> daz dů mich bedes an
>
> (had you — sc. Christ — advised / to worship me)[21]

Of the English mystery-cycles it is only in the Chester plays where there is a fully worked-out juxtaposing of the temptation episodes, and here the basis is clearly Gregorian. However, the actual action of the butchers' play is short. The devil comments in a prologue on the obvious goodness of Christ, and is bewildered by this. He decides, therefore, to tempt Christ through

20. IV, 66: Teofilo Folengo. Opere Italiane, ed. Umberto Renda, Bari 1911-12, I, 116. There is an expanded version of this, the 'Palermitana,' of 1540, seventeen years later: see Kirkconnell, Celestial Cycle, p. 551.
21. See the edition by Eduard Hartl (ATB 41) Halle/S 1952, p. 65 (**vv**. 190-9). It is of course Matthew 4: 9 in retrospect.

gluttony, and here — as with Bale's play — there is a direct link
with Adam: where Adam was defeated, however, Christ is
victorious:

Deus:
... thou pynes thee, Sathan(as),
To supplante me of my place
By meate, as somtyme Addam was,
Of blesse when he was broughte.
Deceived he was that tyme through thee,
But nowe muste faile thy postie ...[22]

The notion of "supplanted Adam" again recalls Milton. In fact,
the last work in which the phrase appeared, the 'Stanzaic Life
of Christ', is very closely linked with the Chester plays. The
editor of the 'Stanzaic Life' has indicated several points of
contact between the works — and the 'Stanzaic Life' was of
course composed at Chester, and based to a large extent upon
the 'Polychronicon' of the Chester monk Higden.[23] Foster does
not, as it happens, discuss this particular section of the Chester
cycle. But verbal parallels such as these, as well as the overall
treatment of the pericope in terms of the (named) Gregorian
exegesis make a connexion here very likely indeed. The source
of this Chester mystery might very well be the Chester 'Life.'
The analogy with Adam is taken up by the devil himself —

Adam, that God hym selfe wroughte
Through my deceate in balle I broughte ...[24]

— before the second temptation. This contains the same notion
that we have encountered, for example, in the Old Icelandic
'Lilja' — the devil's surprise that this *dossiberde,* this good-for-
nothing, should be a tougher proposition than Adam, crowned

22. I have used the older edition of this text, from the British Museum
MS Additional 10305: The Chester Plays, ed. Thomas Wright, London
1843-7. The lines cited are in I, 203.

23. Stanzaic Life of Christ, ed. Foster, pp. xxviii-xliii. See also John
Edwin Wells, A Manual of the Writings in Middle English, New Haven and
London 1916-41, Suppl. 4, p. 1272.

24. Wright I, 204.

in glory. But the man born of woman defeats Satan, who
retreats to hell:

> Alas! my sleighte nowe am I quitte:
> Adam I founded with a fitte,
> And hym in cumberance sone I knitte,
> Through countise of my crafte.
> Nowe, sone of sorowe he mone be sutte,
> And I punished in hell pitte . . .[25]

But the devil does announce his intention of holding a council
in hell. The defeat is not yet absolute, in spite of reference to
Christ's victory.

The sins themselves are not named in this portion of the
play, although the devil comments before the temptation that
he sees no sin in Christ:

> Averice nor anye envye
> In hym coulde I never espie,
> He hath no goulde in treasurye,
> Nor tempted is by no sight.
> Pryde hath he non nor glotanye,
> Ne nor no liking of lecherye;
> His mouth harde I never lye,
> Nether by daye nor nighte . . .[26]

This does not suggest Gregory, although gluttony and avarice
are there. It may be a modified version of the seven deadly sins,
but it calls to mind similar passages in the 'Anegenge' and in the
'Stanzaic Life of Christ.' The latter — the second major reference — is likely to have been the source. There may also be an
echo here of the Johannine epistle in the three points of
"temptation by sight" (*concupiscentia oculorum*), lechery (*concupiscentia carnis*) and pride (*superbia vitae*). The full Gregorian
exegesis — although as indicated, it is unlikely that Gregory's
work is a direct source here — comes out in a lengthy exposition
of the pericope that has just been performed, delivered by a
doccter (in the earlier British Museum Additional MS) and by
an *expositor* (in the Harleian MS). The speech is too long to

25. Wright I, 206.
26. Wright I, 202.

reproduce in full, and it follows Gregory (or the 'Stanzaic Life')
very closely. An opening passage points to the analogy in
general terms:

> Loe, lordings, Godes rightiousnes,
> As Gregorye maketh mynde exspres,
> Synce our forfather overcomen was
> By three thinges to doe evill;
> Glotanye, vaine glorye, their be towe,
> Covetouse of hignes also,
> By thes three poyntes, boute moe
> Christe hase overcomen the devill.[27]

This is then explained — and we have again the definition of
avarice. In its turn, this is followed by the Matthew exposition,
exactly as in Gregory's sermon — or, more to the point, in a
way that recalls the 'Stanzaic Life' even in vocabulary. Dramatically this is hardly satisfactory. No conclusion is drawn either
way, even if there is a victory on Christ's part. We are left with
more or less isolated typological exegesis, fulfilled rather than
recapitulated, in a badly dramatized form. Emil Mâle once
voiced the opinion that medieval drama as a whole is poor stuff,
interesting only for the link with art — a view since countered,
as noted for example by Pickering.[28] But the closest parallel to
the Chester play is precisely an artistic one — the play calls to
mind nothing more clearly than certain manuscript illustrations
of the pericope. Not, of course, such magnificent productions as
the various manuscripts of the 'Bible moralisée,' such as those
in Paris, in the British Museum or in the Bodleian, where the art
is of primary value. But rather the uninspired line-drawings of
the Munich Selestat manuscript of the 'Speculum humanae
salvationis' reproduced by Lutz and Perdrizet.[29] Just as the

27. Wright I, 206f. For the Harleian text (MS Harley 2124) see the
edition of Hermann Deimling, The Chester Plays I (EETS/ES 62), London
1892, p. 224f.

28. See Pickering, Literatur, pp. 106-11, where he discusses Mâle's
view, and cites Otto Pächt as having pointed out that Mâle himself changed
his standpoint slightly later.

29. Lutz and Perdrizet II, plate 25. The MS in question now bears the
designation Munich Clm 146.

drawings there are merely illustrations, rather than works of art
in their own right, so too the action of the Chester butchers'
play is simply a sketch, a very theological sermon that is very
little dramatized. In many ways, the Chester play is even less
effective in popular terms than either the Hegge or York plays.

A far shorter dramatic illustration of the use of the triple
equation is found in a German Corpus Christi play, the fif-
teenth-century 'Künzelsauer Fronleichnamspiel.' Here, however,
the allusion is in the first instance tropological, recalling the
Hegge 'Weavers' Play' and the York 'Locksmiths' Play.' We hear
that

> Der dewfell in (Christ) versuchen bekone
> Mit fressickait, hoffart vnd geitikait
> Damit er Adam vnd Euam had nider gelait
> Mit treyerlay weise versuchunge.

The passage concludes

> Nu huttent euch, alt vnd junge![30]

> (The devil began to tempt him / with greed, pride and avarice. / He
> had felled Adam and Eve / with three kinds of temptation. / Be-
> ware, young and old!)

In the actual narrative of the temptation — these lines are from
a prologue — the Adamic parallel is not drawn, however.

Far clearer in typological intent (rather than standardized
typological presentation) is a medieval mystery which mentions
only one part of the threefold parallel, but makes the victory of
Christ as clear and as important as does Milton. Although found
on English soil, this is not an English work, but the Cornish
'Ordinalia', possibly of the late fourteenth century. The recent
study of this work by Robert Longsworth has demonstrated
admirably the independence of the Cornish plays, and given some
indication of their value for study;[31] they are still worthy,
perhaps, of more attention than has been paid to them.

As far as the parallelism of the temptations is concerned,
only gluttony is mentioned. What is plainly a foreign word is

30. Ed. Peter K. Liebenow, Berlin 1969, p. 107 (vv. 2527-31).
31. 'Ordinalia,' pp. 2-22.

employed for this, moreover, and even though the history of
the Cornish language is particularly badly documented before
the time of Henry VIII,[32] this word sticks out. It might be that
this would indicate an outside source — the English words in the
'Ordinalia' are one of the grounds on which the idea of these
plays' dependence on the English cycles was based. But the idea
is less clear-cut than this: of course the Cornish play depends on
a source here. The very aim of this study is to show how
widespread the notion of the parallel temptation was in the
Middle Ages. But this does not of course reflect upon the
originality of the writer: originality in the Middle Ages is not of
detail, even of theme. Originality is of *handling* received ideas,
and here handling of the temptation of Christ differs strongly
from the English — and continental — mysteries, although
Adam is not mentioned.

The devil, then, tempts Christ through greed (I cite Norris' text with his translation):

> my a vyn mos th'y tempye
> mar a callaf y tenne
> the wuel glotny war nep tw

(I will go to tempt him, / If I can draw him / to do gluttony on any
side)[33]

But already a new note is struck. The devil follows this comment with the very odd remark that he in all probability will
not be able to tempt Christ:

32. Ibid. p. 8, citing Henry Jenner's Handbook of the Cornish Language, London 1904.
33. The Ancient Cornish Drama, ed. and transl. Edwin Norris, London
1859, repr. London/New York 1968, I, 226 (vv. 50-2 of the 'Passion'
section). The translations given are those of Norris. A new translation of
the play has appeared recently without the Cornish text by Markham
Harris, the Cornish 'Ordinalia,' Washington 1969. See the detailed review
of this by Neville Denny (Medium Aevum 40, 1971), pp. 305-9. This
justifies to a large extent the continued use of Norris' edition, and it is
retained here in view of the fact that it is still the only readily available
Cornish text.

sur awos ol ow gallos
byth ny allaf yn ow ros
  the wul pegh vyth y cachye
den yw the pup the weles
saw y ober ha'y thyskes
  pup ol a wra tremene

(Surely, notwithstanding all my power, / I shall never be able, in my net, / To catch him doing any sin. / He is a man for all to see; / Without his work and his teaching / everyone will die.)[34]

The placing of such despond in the mouth of the devil contrasts greatly with the confidence he shows in, say, the 'Lilja.' That the devil realizes that he is doomed to failure expresses surely the notion of the circular nature of the divine plan of Fall and Redemption — a circle that everyone is aware of, even the devil, and certainly the writer of the lines.

 Already at the beginning of the pericope Christ gives a reason for his fasting that seems to point to a breaking of the devil's power rather than to a merely exemplary act:

penys a reys˙ragh y terros
ma fo leheys ˙mvr a y gallos
dre ow fynys ˙ dev vgens nos
thy'm devythys˙a wel the vos

(Penance is necessary, that his arrogance / May be diminished, the greatness of his power / By my pains, forty nights / To me completed appear to be)[35]

Norris' translation is less than clear, and one assumes that this reflects the Cornish text. Even so, the concept of conquering the power of the devil is apparent, as is the idea that this is a decisive struggle between Christ and Satan, not merely an exhibition bout.

 It is at the end of this portion of the Cornish play, however, that the real glory of Christ's victory here is established. The other two temptations follow the Matthew text fairly closely, but the devil at the conclusion, rather than

34. Norris I, 226 (vv. 53-8).
35. Ibid. p. 224 (vv. 43-6).

merely leaving in bewilderment, as in the Hegge play, or be-
moaning his defeat and returning to hell to recover, as in the
Chester play, admits a greater loss:

go vy vyth pan yth thotho
pan of fyfthys thyworto
    ter-gwyth hythew
ha'n maystri bras ol a'm bo
my re'n collas quyt dretho
    may canaf trew

(Woe is me, that I went to him, / That I am vanquished by him / Three
times to day; / And all the great power that was mine, / I have lost it
quite through him, / That I may sing "alas! ")[36]

The scene ends then with the glory of Christ as such. God
himself caps the devil's comments, sending the angels to mini-
ster to Christ, in expansion of Matthew 4: 11. God's comments
are echoed then by Michael and by Gabriel, who proclaims
Christ king of heaven and the world.

    That this represents an attitude to the temptations more
in line with the recapitulation notions of Irenaeus than with the
purely exegetical *ad hoc* typology of Gregory is borne out at
the end of the Cornish cycle. The power of the Crucifixion and
of the Resurrection is not of course diminished — these, too, are
seen as victories over the devil. But it is significant that the
Resurrection — the last third of the Cornish cycle, ends with an
acclaiming of Christ as king that is very similar to the close of
the temptation scene:

    Ihc
me yv myghtern re wruk cas
ol rag dry adam ha'y has
    a tebel scuth
myghtern of a lowene
ha'n victory eth gyne
    yn arvow ruth

36. Ibid. p. 232 (vv. 145-50).

(I am a King, I have suffered / All, to bring Adam and his seed /
From evil plight. / The King I am of joy / And the victory goes with
me / In arms red)[37]

Christ goes on to refer to the Crucifixion as the suffering
undergone for man, but the lines just cited seem to point to his
whole activity rather than to the final sacrifice alone.

Attention has so far been focussed upon the dramatic
versions of the temptation of Christ in the desert. It is possible,
however, to find allusion to the temptation of Christ and to its
successful resistance in those plays whose subject is the Fall of
Man.

That the Redemption should be hinted at at the time of
the Fall is not surprising, as it is in accordance with the notion
of a divine plan that has that Redemption already implicit in
the Fall. This idea is common in the Middle Ages, both in
poetry — such as the 'Anegenge,' or the Middle High German
'Vorau Genesis,' or indeed the earlier Irish 'Saltair na Rann,'
and in the drama.[38]

With some exceptions, it has been seen that the normal
mode of reference to the Fall is to apply it to Adam exclusively — particularly in this context: Adam is the type of Christ,
and Eve, as the type of the Virgin in most cases, is passed over
in silence.[39] Eve has a more dominant role in one medieval
dramatic version of the temptation, however, and this may be
relevant to the comparison between the two temptation scenes
in Genesis and in Matthew. The work in question is the Anglo-
Norman mystery of the twelfth century — an early dramatic

37.   Norris II, 190. These are vv. 2517-22 of the 'Resurrection' play.

38.   See on this point J. R. Margeson, The Origins of English Tragedy,
Oxford 1967, p. 9. On the 'Vorau Genesis,' see Murdoch, Fall of Man,
p. 147. On 'Saltair na Rann' see Brian Murdoch, An Early Irish Adam and
Eve. 'Saltair na Rann' and the Genesis Tradition (Medieval Studies 1973,
in press).

39.   The numerous references of convenience to "Adam's Fall" in the
Middle Ages contrast with the iconographical position, where Eve is
normally present, even if her temptation is sometimes placed together with
that of Adam, telescoping the sequence of events.

text — known as the 'Mystère d'Adam.'[40] Here the devil tempts
Eve, but only after he has already tried to tempt Adam, and has
failed. This prior temptation of Adam is important. All the
elements of the ultimate temptation are there — the devil's
promises regarding the effect of the fruit, and so on, culmi-
nating in the call to pride and vainglory:

> Tu regneras en majesté,
> Od deu poez partir poësté.

> (You shall reign in majesty, / you may share God's power.)

But Adam resists, and in doing so employs terms not unlike
those with which Christ finally repels the devil:

> Fui teu de ci! tu es sathan.[41]

> (Go away from here — you are Satan!)

The devil thus turns his attention to Eve, and the temptation
succeeds.

The notion of a prior temptation of Adam is not original
to the 'Mystère d'Adam.' It appears before this time, in the
ninth-century Anglo-Saxon / Old Saxon 'Genesis B' — and the
connexion between the two works is, incidentally, not restricted to this point, as has been discussed in a stimulating
article by Rosemary Woolf.[42] In the Anglo-Saxon poem we
have the same pattern — Adam repulses Satan (here disguised as
an angel), and Eve falls. The point is not found as such in
theological writings. It appears to be an externalization of the
interpretation — according to the *sensus litteralis* — that the
devil decided to approach Eve precisely because he was afraid of
resistance to his blandishments from Adam.[43] The effect as far

40. Ed. Paul Studer, Manchester 1918, repr. 1949. On the dating see
Studer's introduction, p. lvi.

41. Studer, p. 11 (vv. 193-5).

42. The Fall of Man in 'Genesis B' and the 'Mystère d'Adam,' in:
Studies... in Honor of Arthur G. Brodeur, ed. Stanley B. Greenfield,
Eugene/Oreg. 1963, pp. 187-99.

43. See for a theological example of the notion the Genesis-sermon of
the Greek PseudoChrysostom (PG 56, 531). See too the 'Passion de
Semur' vv 576-85, Roy, Mystère, p. 13. It is worth noting, too, that the

as the present context is concerned is interesting: it establishes Adam in this case as a confirmative type, and places the whole of the recapitulation typology upon the connexion with Eve (normally, of course, a type of Mary). It may be too that this is a case of inverse typology. The familiar exegesis of Matthew 4 and the equally familiar typological connexion of Adam and Christ in general terms gives rise, then, to a situation where Adam actually does prefigure Christ in a sense identical with the way David does, say, in killing Goliath. This is not Irenaean, of course. Christ and Adam are now exactly parallel, and there is no recapitulation. In some ways, this is clearer as typology, but the contrast of the Fall and Redemption is weakened, with a confusing typological view of Eve as a by-product.

One further idea, shared incidentally by the 'Mystère d'Adam' and 'Genesis B' once again, is of interest here. This is the notion of a diabolical council plotting the temptation of Adam and Eve or, indeed, of Christ. The whole motif of the infernal debate is highly ramified, and links together several familiar legends of the Middle Ages: the various strands of the idea are difficult to disentangle, although there has been some attempt to do so. Once again the fact that Milton has councils in hell plotting both the Fall of Man and the temptation in the

actual temptation of Eve by the devil in the 'Mystère d'Adam' is very similar in tone to the blandishments of Satan to Christ in some of the French Passions. Thus Satan addresses Christ in Jean Michel's play as follows: *Tu es si beau, si cler, si net, / si fort, de si grande stature / tu es si belle creature*... "You are so handsome, so fair, so fine, / so strong, of so noble mien, / you are so splendid..." (Jodogne, p. 36, vv. 2812-4). This recalls the words to Eve in the 'Mystère d'Adam:' *Tu es fieblette et tendre chose.../ Tu es trop tendre et il trop dur; / Mais neporquant tu es plus sage*... "you are a delicate and tender creature .../ you are too tender and [Adam] is too hard; / but you are wiser, nevertheless" (Studer, p. 12f., vv. 227-33).

The motif is found too in art. See the illustration of Satan's tempting in the Junius MS (for 'Genesis B'), where Adam refuses and Eve accepts the fruit. Reproduced in S. Humphreys Gurteen, The Epic of the Fall of Man, New York/London 1896, p. 210.

desert has led to a certain amount of study.[44] Milton also has, of course, a council in heaven, and in all these cases he proves himself once again heir to an extensive medieval tradition.

The fullest study of the diabolical council so far has been that of Olin Moore, who points to a Classical and a Christian tradition. The former has at its base Claudian's 'In Rufinum' and the 'De raptu Proserpinae' (and Moore himself points out that these owe themselves a debt to the council of the gods in the tenth book of the 'Aeneid' and in the Homeric hymn to Demeter. And what, in any case, is Pluto — god or devil? This is already an indication of the complexity of the motif). The Christian base — and this is of course of greater interest here — is the apocryphal (but very widespread) 'Gospel of Nicodemus', dating in its full form from the fifth century:[45] here the devils discuss the coming harrowing of hell, wondering what action to take. Moore goes on to discuss the motif in Boccaccio's 'Filocolo,' the 'Merlin' of Robert de Boron, Sannazaro's 'De partu Virginis,' Vida's 'Christiad' and the 'Gerusalemme liberata' of Tasso. None of these cases, however, refers either to a diabolical council at the time of the Fall, nor to one planning the temptation of Christ. Most of these (exclusively poetic) versions are connected with the motif of the harrowing of hell, although some refer to the anxiety shown by the devils in hell about

44. Olin Moore, The Infernal Council (Modern Philology 16, 1918/9), pp. 196-93; Alan McKillop, Illustrative Notes on 'Genesis B' (Journal of English and Germanic Philology 20, 1921), pp. 28; Evans 'Paradise Lost,' pp. 143-67; Woolf, Mystery Plays, p. 220.

45. See Richard P. Wülcker, Das 'Evangelium Nicodemi' in der abendländischen Litteratur, Paderborn 1872. An example of the point demonstrating the distance covered is seen in the 'Slovo o Lazarevom voskresenii' ('Tale of the Resurrection of Lazarus'). The Old Church Slavonic text is in: Pamyatniki starinnoi russkoi literatury, ed. G. Kushelevym-Bezborodko, St. Petersburg 1863, pp. 11-12. There is a translation in: Medieval Russia's Epics, Chronicles and Tales, ed. Serge A. Zenkovsky, New York ap63, pp. 130-6. On the specific relationship between the 'Evangelium Nicodemi' and some of the works under discussion here, see Roy, Mystère, p. 214f.

reports of the appearance of Christ on earth.

Moore does not consider two works which contain the diabolical council and which are relevant to the present study. The first is the 'Ystoire de la Passion,' which has been discussed already in an earlier chapter, and which not only has a description of the council prior to the temptation of Christ, but follows this with a brief reference to Lucifer's earlier temptation of Adam.[46] The second is the Middle English religious poem known as the 'þe Deuelis Perlament' or the 'Parlamentum of Feendis,' from the Lambeth Palace MS 853, written about 1430. Here the devils consult at various points — the birth of Christ, as a preliminary of the temptation in the desert, and later before the harrowing. The sending of Satan is the result of the discussion before the temptation. There is no mention of Adam at all, until the harrowing scene, but the defeated Satan does speak of the manner in which he has been overcome:

> For if y tempte him in wraþþe or pryde,
> Wiþ pacience and mekenes ne sconfiteþ me.
> If y tempte him to letcherie, y muste me hide,
> He voideþ me of wiþ chastitee.
> In glotenie & enuye wole he not abide,
> But is euere in mesure and in charitee;
> In couetise & auarise wole he not ride,
> But is euere in largenes and in pouerte.[47]

This again is not the Gregorian exegesis, and it does call to mind the list of sins in the 'Stanzaic Life of Christ.' Christ's countering of the sins with virtues recalls the same work, as well as others, such as the 'Veronica' or the 'Anegenge.'

That two early medieval works ('Genesis B' and the 'Mystère d'Adam') should have the diabolical council plot the Fall of Man is, however, significant. I have indicated elsewhere[48] that there seems to be a tradition of this in Western

46. Wright, p. 30f. ('Ystoire,' vv. 179-212).
47. Hymns to the Virgin and Christ, ed. Frederick J. Furnivall (EETS/OS 24) London 1868, p. 46 ('Parlamentum,' vv. 153-60). See v. 229f. of the same work, Furnivall, p. 50.
48. Brian Murdoch, The Fall of Man. A Middle High German Analogue

Europe over many centuries, as it appears too in the 'Ane-genge' — a work where originality of detail is neither expected nor found. I have suggested further that the use of the motif in the 'Anegenge' is placed as a deliberate parallel to the very well-known notion of the heavenly debate of the 'four daughters of God"[49] which is dealt with at some length in the German poem, which also, incidentally, has a kind of celestial debate between the three *personae* of the Trinity, seen according to the Abelardian Trinity formula. This sort of parallelism runs through the 'Anegenge' — the devil's temptation of Eve is set against the Annunciation, and so on. Verbal echoes also link the Fall and the Redemption in a variety of ways, and the juxtaposing of the celestial and infernal debates is literarily effective. If there is a full tradition of a diabolical council, then it might well have been influenced in any case by the celestial ones: and one thinks too of the pagan European tradition of the council of the Gods, in the 'Volospá.'[50] The fluctuation between the two types of council is an interesting comment on the early concepts of good and evil in the world.

The idea of the council in hell prior to the Fall appears to be common in later medieval drama: Carl Klimke, for example, refers to a standard preliminary scene in which Satan and Lucifer discuss the temptation, and Satan is sent as a messenger. This may have appeared in the lost Regensburg play performed in 1194, and is certainly there in later German examples.[51]

of 'Genesis B' (Review of English Studies NS 19, 1968), pp. 288-9. See Murdoch, Fall of Man, p. 25f. For a later German illustration, see Hans Sachs, 'Tragedia von schöpfung, fal und außtreibung Ade' (1548) in: Hans Sachs. Werke, ed. Adelbert von Keller, I, Stuttgart 1870, repr. Hildesheim 1964, pp. 30-4.

49. See Hope Traver, The Four Daughters of God, Bryn Mawr 1907.

50. Volospá, v. 22f. *þá gengo Reginöll a rök-stóla / ginnheilög goð, ok um þat gaettosk* ... "Then all the powers, the most high Gods, assembled to their judgment-seats and took council together." See also vv. 35f., 62f., 70f. Edition and translation by Gudbrand Vigfússon and F. York Powell, Corpus Boreale, Oxford 1883, repr. New York 1965, I, 192-6.

51. Das volkstümliche Paradiesspiel, Breslau 1902, pp. 5 and 23.

The 'Nicodemus-Gospel,' of course, has the council at least in the context of Christ, and this combined with the council plotting the Fall might well have led to the idea of a council to plot the temptation in the desert. In addition to the 'Deuelis Perlament,' the idea appears in several of the medieval mysteries.[52] A variety of devils are named — Lucifer and Satan are the major figures, of course, but we also meet Belial, Beelzebub, Ashtaroth and others. The presence of all these devils has of course dramatic possibilities, too, particularly for comic relief. The usual pattern is the sending of Satan as the messenger to earth, just as in the case of the first Fall.

It is appropriate to conclude this survey of the dramatic evidence with a later work, a highly sophisticated mystery play that bridges, to an extent, the gap between the Middle Ages and Milton. The *auto* of the Portuguese goldsmith and court poet Gil Vicente, entitled 'Breve sumário da história de Deus' might be seen as a kind of culmination of very many of the medieval motifs discussed. It is also a masterpiece in its own right which has been, one feels, unduly neglected by students of the drama and of Milton alike, for it forms a precise and concentrated *summa* of the divine plan, linking the Fall and the temptation-Redemption over a century before Milton did the same thing. Compared to Vicente's *auto,* Bale's 'Comedy or enterlude,'

---

52. Many medieval plays have a council of devils at the time of the temptation of Christ: the Hegge Play, vv. 1-65, Block, pp. 193-5; the Chester Play, Wright, p. 206; Passion de Semur, vv. 555-9, Roy, Mystère, p. 13; Greban, Mystère, vv. 10451-563, Paris, pp. 136-8; Jean Michel's Mystère, pp. 36-9; the Alsfelder Passionsspiel, vv. 1047-1137, Froning, Drama, pp. 603-6. The point is there too (as is the debate of the daughters of God) in the Maastricht Passion Play, ed. J. Zacher, Mittelniederländisches Osterspiel (Zeitschrift für deutsches Altertum 2, 1842), p. 324 (vv. 656-73). Here however, the temptation itself is brief and non-Adamic. Other medieval dramas — some earlier than those mentioned above — have a council of devils at the time of the harrowing. See: La Passion Provençale du manuscrit Didot, ed. William P. Shepard, Paris 1928, pp. 72-7 (vv. 1712-1806) and: La Passion du Palatinus, ed. Grace Frank, Paris 1922, pp. 48-53 (vv. 1235-1385).

almost a decade younger, seems pallid. And yet both are rooted in medieval tradition.

The 'Breve sumário' was first performed in 1527, in Almeirim, before King João III of Portugal and his wife Catarina. That it is known in two early editions – the 'Copilação' and a Madrid text – is perhaps significant of itself.[53]

At the very beginning of the play, in the argument, spoken by an angel, the implicit connexion of the Fall and the Redemption is made clear: we shall hear

> ... porque o tenor
> da ressurreição de Nosso Senhor
> tem as raízes naquele pomar,
> ao pé daquela árvore, que ouvistes contar
> onde Adão se fêz pecador ...[54]

(... why the manner of the Resurrection of our lord has its roots in the same orchard, at the root of the same tree where, as you have heard tell, Adam became a sinner.)

We see then a council of devils, who plot the Fall – Lucifer, Satan and Belial. Satan is sent as the messenger from hell (*por embaixador*) and is told by Lucifer to take the guise of a serpent, to fool Eve: *Faze-te cobra, por dissimular.*[55] There is no prior attack on Adam. Lucifer advises to go directly to Eve, because she, as a woman, will be easier to persuade:

53. For a list of the texts, see Paul Teyssier, La langue de Gil Vicente, Paris 1959, p. 12f. The text from the 'Copilação' is reproduced in: Gil Vicente. Obras completas, ed. Álvaro Júlio da Costa Pimpão, Porto 1962, pp. 108-20. There is a facsimile of the Madrid text in: Carolina Michaëlis de Vasconcellos, Autos Portugueses de Gil Vicente, Madrid 1922, unpaginated. The former text is from Lisbon (1562), the latter Madrid (1557-80).

54. I have used the slightly normalized text edited by João de Almeido Lucas, Gil Vicente. Breve sumário da história de Deus, Lisbon 1943. This passage is on p. 41, vv. 5-9. The lines are not in the interesting summary of the work by Jack H. Parker, Gil Vicente, New York 1967, pp. 66-9.

55. Vv. 61 and 82, Lucas, p. 43f.

e vai-te a Eva, porque é mulher,
e dize que coma, não haja temor . . .[56]

(Go to Eve, for she is a woman, / and tell her to eat without fear.)

This is a theological commonplace, of course. Isidore, for example derives *mulier* from *mollis* "soft, moveable"[57] and there are creative versions of the Fall-narrative both in Latin and in vernacular languages where the express point is made that Eve should be approached first: in Avitus' 'Poemata' the serpent expresses a fear of Adam,[58] and in the Old Irish 'Saltair na Rann' of the late tenth century the devil advises the serpent to go first to Eve.[59]

Thus the Fall of Man is accomplished: we hear of the success of the enterprise from Satan himself:

Já são derrubados
Adão e Eva, os primeiros casados . . .[60]

(Now they are overthrown, Adam and Eve, the first couple . . .)

There is, however, a note of optimism after the Fall in that the allegorical figure of the world, *Mundo* will show some mercy to Adam and Eve — for God's mercy is stressed immediately after the Fall, when an angel speaks of *Deus cui proprium est miserere.*[61] The first couple then offer a prayer to the glory of God.

Vicente then takes us rapidly through a large part of Old Testament history: following Adam and Eve we see Abel, and then Job, who resists the temptation of the devil, declaring his faith in the Redemption, according to Job 19: 25:

Eu creo mui bem que o meu Redentor
vive . . .[62]

(I well believe that my redeemer lives)

56. V. 63f., Lucas, p. 43.
57. Etymologiae xi, 2, 18 (PL 82, 47).
58. Poemata II, 140-4 in the edition of Rudolph Peiper, Berlin 1883, p. 216.
59. Vv. 1151-6, Stokes, p. 17; Hull, Poem-Book, p. 24.
60. Vv. 135f., Lucas, p. 46.
61. V. 181, Lucas, p. 47.
62. Vv. 478f., Lucas, p. 57.

This contrasts with the first temptation, then. Adam and Eve are defeated, Job for all he is made a leper and consigned to purgatory, resists Satan. These then are the two forms of typology — the recapitulative, and the comparative: Adam contrasts with the temptation, Job compares with it. Both Old Testament incidents point onward to the final scenes, where we see Christ himself in conflict with the devil.

Moses, Abraham, David and Isaiah follow (calling to mind the sequence of prophets in the 'Mystère d'Adam,' who also predict the coming of the Messiah[63]), and these are followed by St. John, who visits the souls in purgatory. It might be noted that there are conversations throughout the work between the devils in hell and the souls, and that the diabolical council is therefore a running motif throughout the work.

The final scene, however, is that of the temptation of Christ. Once again there is a diabolical council, and Satan is again sent. In spite of some anxiety on the part of the demons, he can surely be conquered — *Enfim êle é homem,*[64] "for after all he is a man." The dual-nature doctrine is integrated here in a subordinate but effective manner. Thus the scene begins, with Satan disguised as a hermit. The temptations follow the Matthew pattern, and Christ is of course victorious. Only after the temptation of the kingdoms does Christ, just as in Matthew, show that he recognizes his tempter:

Retro, retro, mal-aventurado,
falso, enorme, cruel Satanás![65]

(Back, back, miserable one, false, monstrous cruel Satan . . .)

63. See Studer's introduction to the 'Mystère d'Adam' for a discussion of the medieval 'Processus prophetarum' (pp. xxvii-xxix). This feature of medieval drama has a long and involved history of its own.
64. V. 916, p. 72.
65. Vv. 992f., Lucas, p. 75. Álvaro da Costa Pimpão's reading of *cível* for *cruel* in the text of the 'Copilação' (p. 120 of his edition) makes little sense. The Madrid text is quite clear. On a literary level, the build-up of the epithets in angry crescendo is satisfying, especially when compared with the Bible text.

The devil has been defeated, and there is confusion in hell, a parallel to the rejoicing that followed the first success. Essentially this is the close of the *auto*. In the last few moments the image of Christ crucified is displayed, and the last scene is indeed the harrowing of hell:

> Aqui tocam as trombetas e charamelas, e aparece ũa figura de Cristo na resurreição, en entra no limbo . . .[66]

> (Now sound the trumpets and the oboes and there appears a figure of Christ Resurrected, and he enters hell . . .)

But the play is not, as J. H. Parker and others have maintained, a "harrowing of hell."[67] The same arguments apply here as did with 'Paradise Regained.' The reference to events after the temptation in the desert is merely a rounding-off of the victory. The real work is done in resisting the devil: this is a victory on earth, and the victories in heaven and over death are of no interest to living man — to Vicente's audience, to Milton's readers, if you like. The theatrical conventions are different here from those in the Cornish play, but even so the two works may be compared. The latter does, after all, take the edge off the victory in the desert by having a very full Resurrection (unlike Vicente and Milton, but like Fletcher), even if it is linked with the earlier scene pretty closely. What is important here, though, is the striking structural pattern of three temptations and three cases — Adam, Job and Christ — where the devil tempts man. The three pivotal events complement one another. Adam's Fall is absolute: the *ante legem* Fall that is the historical reason for the Redemption, and must be recapitulated in the Irenaean sense. Job is a *sub lege* type, a confirmative case, but with tropological overtones. The greatest moralizing work of the Middle Ages, Gregory's 'Moralia,' is of course based on the book of Job. This is how to resist. Then the *sub gratia* antitype, fulfilling and neutralizing the two types treated first. It is the temptation in the desert that counts, not the harrowing of hell. The Old English 'Christ and Satan' might be set against this as a

66. Final stage direction, Lucas, p. 77.
67. Gil Vicente, p. 68.

contrasting work where the harrowing is as important, at least, as the scene in the desert. Nearer to Gil Vicente's own time, of course, one thinks of Fletcher's poem.

The literary implications are significant: Gil Vicente has made a unified mystery play (if we may call it that — for there are figures there that might belong in the morality rather) which compromises 'Paradise Lost' and 'Paradise Regained' — giving us the translation into another genre of Milton's epics. It is interesting that Job — that other "brief epic" should form the third part of the trio.

And still the play stands at the end of the Middle Ages, linked to it with motifs such as the diabolical councils, which point, equally, onwards to Milton.[68] There is no trace of the exegesis linking the two temptations as such, no reference to gluttony, vainglory or avarice. But the juxtaposition is enough: Vicente has seen, as Milton was to, the implications of the parallel, the spirit, not the letter.

68. It might be noted that Gil Vicente did write an *auto* dealing with a debate in heaven, and one that parallels the Justice and Mercy debate in the 'Anegenge', and much later in Fletcher's 'Victorie' poem — the victory in heaven. See Vicente: Auto de Deus Padre e Justiça e Misericordia, ed. I. S. Révah, Deux Autos méconnus de Gil Vicente, Lisbon 1948, pp. 51-87.

VII MEDIEVAL ICONOGRAPHY

In order to gain a reasonably complete view of a medieval theme or motif, the investigation of that theme in pictorial representation is of course vital. Medieval iconography is another of the ways in which a point may be popularized, another of the mediatory channels between theologian and layman, when the theme is a religious one. The closest literary genre is the drama, in that the play would command a wider audience than a poem, and the public pictorial representations, if we may call them that, carvings, murals, stained glass, would have an equally wide "audience." One has of course to make a distinction between this type of art and the more restricted field of manuscript illustration. But even here an illustration in a manuscript might have served to impress a cleric writing in the vernacular just as much as the accompanying Latin text. Later in the Middle Ages there is another shift, already with the advent of the blockbook, and by the time of the Renaissance the illustrated text is again public property.

As far as the "public" and "private" types of pictorial representation of the present theme are concerned, one further obvious but significant point needs to be made. The estimation of an attitude will be far easier if we are dealing with an illustration to an accompanying text (even if that text is abbreviated) than it is with independent forms such as stained glass or sculpture. Some of the material to be dealt with in this chapter might, indeed, have been looked at under other headings — it is not always easy to decide with a given work whether the text or the iconography is of the greater value. Some works mentioned already, too, must be mentioned again, such as the 'Speculum humanae salvationis' — but this is the attendant hazard of electing to divide a study into generic groups. An iconographic survey is, finally, more liable to be incomplete than its literary counterpart.

The portrayal of the Fall of Man in Christian art is of some antiquity, but the temptations of Christ do not appear at all as an iconographical subject until the early part of the Middle Ages, a state of affairs that is generally attributed to the fact that the pericope has no direct sepulchral or liturgical reference. One of the first instances of the depiction of the temptations appears to be in the 'Book of Kells,' written in about 800, with mainland evidence appearing somewhat later than this.[1] Once the iconography becomes established, however, it remains fairly constant over much of the Middle Ages. A single example may be mentioned from a later period as illustration of the portrayal of the temptation of Christ, though without any allusion at all to that of Adam. This is the Italian version of the 'Meditationes vitae Christi' of PseudoBonaventure (MS Bibliothèque Nationale Ital. 115), which contains illustrations of all three scenes. The iconographic cycle, as indeed the work itself, appears to have been widespread in the later Middle Ages.[2] Again, too, the Matthew order seems to be standard. Elizabeth Pope refers to the originally twelfth-century Greek

1. See Gertrud Schiller, Ikonographie der christlichen Kunst, 2nd ed., Gütersloh 1962, I, 153-5. Further, Louis Réau, Iconographie de l'art chrétien, Paris 1955 -9, II/2, 306f.
2. Meditations on the Life of Christ, trans. Isa Ragusa and Rosalie B. Green, Princeton 1961, pp. 120 -2. The 'Meditationes vitae Christi' of PseudoBonaventura, a work of the late thirteenth century, of which this is an Italian translation, was widespread in its own right, and might have been adduced here for literary as well as iconographic reasons as a point of dissemination of the exposition of the Gospel narrative. The work does not, however, contain any reference to Adam and Eve, although the sins to which Christ was tempted are given as gluttony, vainglory and avarice once again. The work leans heavily on Bernard of Clairvaux, and discusses too the question of the dual nature of Christ, and the failure on the part of the devil to determine whether Christ is God or man, a point that has been noted in literary texts. There is also a strong tropological emphasis. The relevant chapter of the work is XVII, and Ragusa and Green refer to the Latin text in the twelfth volume of: Bonaventure. Opera, Venice 1761. They note too a Celtic version of the work: Smaointe Beatha Chríóst, ed. Cainneach Ó. Maonaigh, Dublin 1944, with a bibliography of other versions. This may serve as an indication of the geographical extent to which the work was known.

compilation known as the 'Guide for Painters,' which states specifically that the order of temptations in Matthew is to serve as the basis for artists, rather than Luke's. This seems to have been followed not only by Byzantine iconographers, but also very widely in the West,[3] although there is one notable exception − or quasi-exception − to the rule which will be discussed in due course. In the Renaissance, of course, artists once again began to feel free to alter the approach as they wished.

The iconographic parallel of Adam and Christ as such is as well known in art as in theology. In its most concentrated form, the typology appears in art as in literature in the linking of the Fall with the Passion, specifically with the Crucifixion, thus giving a concise pictorial underlining to the fulfillment of the divine plan. One thinks in particular of the totally integrated iconography of the "living cross,"[4] or of the medieval commonplace which depicts a skull at the foot of the cross, playing on the name *Golgotha* in Matthew 27:33. A notable iconographical instance of this notion is the illustration for the Friday hours of the Compassion (terce) in the early fifteenth century book of hours made for Catherine of Cleves, where the tree that will make the cross grows from Adam's coffin.[5] The to the modern eye somewhat abhorrent representation of the Crucifixion in which the blood from Christ's side flows into the open mouth of the skull of Adam is nevertheless an immensely concentrated allusion not only to the two ends of the divine plan, but also to the general redemption of mankind, by means of the eucharist, from the death to which it was condemned at the time of the Fall. Both the "living cross" and the connexion of Calvary with the grave of Adam may be linked with the very widespread Adam-legends of the Middle Ages, coupled (as they very often are, in a quite inextricable fashion) with the legends

3. 'Paradise Regained,' p. 9. Note 25f. has detailed reference to examples.

4. Hellmuth Bethe, Astkreuz, in: Reallexikon zur deutschen Kunstgeschichte, ed. Otto Schmitt, Stuttgart 1937ff., I, 1152 -61.

5. See the facsimile of this very fine manuscript ed. by John Plummer, The Hours of Catherine of Cleves, New York 1966, no. 82.

of the Holy Rood itself. There are many literary analogues to these points.[6]

The parallel of the temptation in the desert as the anti-type to the Fall is less common in medieval art. As was the case with literary monuments, however, a certain amount of material may be found, both in implicit and explicit form. As far as the veiled allusion to the typology is concerned, Gertrud Schiller has pointed out how the medieval artist frequently places a tree between Christ and the devil in representations of the Matthew story, which is so prominent that it cannot be dismissed as merely gratuitous decoration.[7] Examples are found both in sculpture and in miniature painting. A well-known example for the former is the carving of the first temptation by Gilbert for the cathedral of Autun from the early twelfth century, a piece imitated slightly later at Saulieu in Burgundy.[8] Although the first temptation is — in art as in literature — the one most frequently treated for comparison between the Old and the New Testaments, it is worth noting that implicit typology of this kind is sometimes stronger in the context of the third temptation, that of the kingdoms. An instance of this is af-

6. See Oswald Erich, Adam-Christus, in: Schmitt, Reallexikon I, 157-67. Adam's skull is supposed to have been carried to Golgotha by the Flood: see the Ethiopian and Syriac Adambooks edited respectively by S. C. Malan, The Book of Adam and Eve, London 1882, p. 161, and E. A. Wallis Budge, The Book of the Cave of Treasures, London 1927, pp. 105-10 and 126f. For a vernacular example, see the 'Saltair na Rann,' vv. 2226-2236, Stokes, p. 32, and Hull, Poem-Book, p. 50, with a slightly later analogue in the 'Lebor Gabála Érenn' ("The Book of the Taking of Ireland"), ed. and transl. by R. A. Stewart Macalister (ITS 34) Dublin 1938ff., I, 97 and 239f. From Ireland too comes an early vernacular liturgical-typological reference to the skull-motif in the works of Blathmac, who tells how the blood of Christ baptized Adam: Carney, p. 20f., strophe 57.

On the literary connexions, see Esther C. Quinn, The Quest of Seth for the Oil of Life, Chicago 1962, with a useful bibliography.

7. Ikonographie, I, 154. See p. 402f. for illustrations of the point.

8. Wolfram von den Steinen, Homo Caelestis. Das Wort der Kunst im Mittelalter, Berne/Munich 1965, II, 290a-b with commentary on I, 294.

forded by the 'St. Albans Psalter' (now in Hildesheim), which is roughly contemporary with the Autun carvings. The illustration of the first temptation has a tree, it is true: but it is the highly stylized and quite different tree of the third temptation which mirrors exactly the tree of knowledge in the Fall-picture.[9] It is at least possible that this is intentional, that the artist intended the culmination of the pericope to be linked with the Fall – in a typological parallelism rather than as a moral connexion resting on the familiar homiletic admonitions against the sin of gluttony.

It might, incidentally, be noted that there is throughout the entire Middle Ages an iconographical emphasis on the first temptation – quite simply because it is the first, one presumes, although Elizabeth Pope cites a nineteenth-century study of Christian iconography by Heinrich Detzel as saying that Western artists tended to concentrate on the final scene of a series.[10] In many depictions of the incident, however, particularly in the 'Biblia pauperum' and similar texts, the entire pericope is – as is often the case with the Fall –syncopated, telescoped into one picture, with the temptation of the stones in the foreground, dominating, and the others in the background. The plates appended to Pope's study, incidentally, are almost all of the first temptation – and these illustrations are all later than the Middle Ages.

There are, however, direct parallels between the two temptations in medieval art, and Elizabeth Pope, again, draws attention to one such case (although commenting on its unusual nature) on the cathedral at Santiago in Spain. The instance is important, however, for the intent is apparently typological once more: the rebuttal of Satan by Christ is placed against the

9. Otto Pächt, C. R. Dodwell and Francis Wormald, The St Albans Psalter, London 1960. The Fall is on plate 17, the first temptation of Christ on 22b, and the third on 23b. See also plates 107-8 for other parallels: of interest is the temptation initial of the French Odbert-Psalter of c. 1000.
10. 'Paradise Regained,' p. 9, n. 26.

Fall, emphasizing Adam's loss and Christ's victory.[11] But the straightforward contrast between the temptations, treated in much the same way as they were by Gregory the Great, is common enough in the Middle Ages, a point not dealt with by Pope, although she makes useful reference to some of the (later) Matthew iconography.

In a study of the 'Biblia pauperum' in the Middle Ages, Gerhard Schmidt provides a particularly clear and concise survey of those works, both technical-theological and artistic, relevant to the typology of medieval iconography, and many of the works he discusses are relevant in the present context: his list may serve as a starting-point for discussion here.[12] Thus as early examples of pictorial typology he refers to the great cross of the abbot Suger of St. Denis, and to the Klosterneuburg altar of Nicholas of Verdun. The former, which apparently contained a large number of typological parallels, is of course lost, and the Klosterneuburg enamels do not have our typology, although Eve's taking of the fruit is set against the Deposition.[13] More important, however, is a technical work, the set of instructions for artists, composed in England in the twelfth century, probably by Adam of Dore, and known as the 'Pictor in carmine,' a work whose influence for the history of typological iconography cannot, according to Schmidt, be overestimated.[14] This collection of types with their New Testament antitypes lists the incidents in the New Testament, and follows these with a series

11. Ibid., p. 51.

12. Die Armenbibeln des XIV Jahrhunderts, Graz/Cologne 1959, pp. 88-99. For further details of typological expression in medieval iconography see the standard work of Henrik Cornell, Biblia Pauperum, Stockholm 1925, especially pp. 120-210, which contains, however, a wealth of material, not all of it relevant here.

13. Cornell, Biblia, p. 142f. For earlier altar decorations along these lines, see pp. 125-7.

14. Armenbibeln, p. 91. See Cornell, Biblia, p. 131f. On the authorship of the 'Pictor,' see M. R. James, 'Pictor in carmine' (Archaeologia 94, 1951) p. 150. The textual quotations given below are all from James' text given in 'Archaeologia.'

of Old Testament types for each case. Under the heading (xxx) *Temptatio domini de gula,* "The temptation of the Lord by gluttony," the author begins:

> Temptat Euam diabolus de gula per serpentem dicens In quacumque die comederitis . . .
>
> (The devil tempted Eve with gluttony through the serpent when he said: "on the day that you shall eat . . .")

Amongst the other types here is the gluttony of Esau (Genesis 25: 29-34), which will be of importance again later. Under (xxxi) *Temptatio domini de uana gloria,* "The temptation of the Lord with vainglory," we find:

> Temptat Euam diabolus de uana gloria per serpentem dicens Eritis sicut dii . . .
>
> (The devil tempted Eve with vainglory through the serpent when he said: "you shall be as gods . . .")

and for the final temptation, that of avarice: (xxxii) *Temptatio domini de auaritia:*

> Temptat Euam diabolus de auaritia per serpentem dicens Scientes bonum et malum . . .
>
> (The devil tempted Eve with avarice through the serpent when he said: "Knowing good and evil . . .")

In each case, five further types are adduced.[15]

This, then, is an abbreviated (and integrated) version of the Gregorian exegetical parallel, in an adapted form appropriate to its context in a manual of reference for artists. The ultimate interpretation of the parallel always remains open. What is of significance, however, is the fact that while the outline is basically as in Gregory's homily, in this case the stress is entirely upon Eve. This (perfectly logical) approach has been encountered already in works such as the 'Veronica' and much later in Mirk's 'Festial.' But it is rare in iconography, where Adam is normally placed at least in the foreground, even when Eve is there too,

The 'Pictor in carmine' has considerable influence in later

15. James, p. 154f.

iconography. Two notable sets of painted glass windows derive from it, the interrelated typological sets in Peterborough and Canterbury cathedrals, both slightly later than the text. Other works deriving from the 'Pictor,' such as the illuminated manuscript MS Eton 177 are less relevant here as they do not contain our typology.[16] Among further works of typological reference closely connected with the 'Pictor' are the 'Concordantiae Veteri et Novi Testamenti' and the 'Rota in medio rotae,' both of the thirteenth century.[17]

The clearest association of written text and iconography is found in the later medieval works known under the generic title of 'Biblia pauperum' (a name which has been the object of some debate). These illustrated collections of incidents from the life of Christ placed with their Old Testament types are widely known after the middle of the thirteenth century, and are disseminated over a long period of time, both as manuscripts, then later as blockbooks, with texts both in Latin and in the vernacular.[18] The 'Biblia pauperum,' for all it is associated generally with the later Middle Ages, has in fact a claim to being the oldest of the pictorial-typological manuscript monuments (since the earliest text seems to antedate the Eton MS based on the 'Pictor in carmine'): it originates in the mid-thirteenth century, then, but has as its closest forbear the equally Christo-

16. For the series in the Peterborough and Canterbury windows, see Cornell, Biblia, p. 132f. Cornell points, p. 130, to various other groupings of English typological monuments. The Eton MS 177 (*Figurae Bibliorum*) mentioned by Schmidt in this context is not, for example, relevant. Cornell, p. 133f.

17. Schmidt, Armenbibeln, p. 92f.

18. Cornell's work is indispensable for a full survey: he distinguishes, for example, six groupings, and illustrates these fully. He also prints a list of significant manuscripts. Schmidt's more up-to-date work is perhaps more easily assimilated and clear. Two introductions might also be mentioned as these are necessarily short and both plain: that of W. L. Schreiber in: Biblia Pauperum, a facsimile of a late text ed. Paul Heitz, Strasbourg 1903; and that of Elizabeth Soltész in: Biblia Pauperum, a facsimile of the very fine blockbook now in the library of Esztergom cathedral in Hungary, Budapest 1967.

logical enamels of the Klosterneuburg altar, for all that that monument is somewhat earlier.[19] The main development of the 'Biblia pauperum' is in the German-speaking areas, with texts in Latin, High and Low German, and a mixture of German and Latin predominating. The works fall, iconographically and textually, into several groups, but the basic pattern is more or less consistent, and the variations (which have been analysed fully by Schmidt and others) are not of interest in our context. Basically the 'Biblia pauperum' consists of a series of from thirty to over sixty New Testament scenes – incidents occurring *sub gratia* – flanked left and right, or at least coupled with Old Testament scenes. The two Old Testament types are most commonly one each of the period before the giving of the Mosaic law (*ante legem*) and of the Mosaic period (*sub lege*). This is not always the case, however, and in the grouping that contains the temptation in the desert, both types are *ante legem*: the Fall of Man (usually right) and the selling of Esau's birthright (left). The depiction of the temptation usually has that of the stones in the foreground, frequently with the other two in the background: I have encountered none where the first temptation is not featured in the prominent place. There is no longer a tree between Christ and the devil, but this is no longer necessary, as the parallel has become explicit. Its omission here strengthens the case for an implicit parallel in the earlier works.

For all that the 'Biblia pauperum' is essentially a Christological-typological work, and for all that the parallel is *prima facie* recapitulative, the effect is by and large tropological once again. The dominance of the first temptation – though this may be accidental – coupled with the types chosen, has the effect of an admonition against gluttony once more, rather than of any sense of recapitulation in the full form. The chief purely typological link comes in the placing of the Annunciation between the curse on the serpent (referring here to the protevangelical na-

19. Schmidt, *Armenbibeln*, p. 97.

ture of Genesis 3: 15) and the incident of Gideon and the fleece (Judges 6: 36-8).[20]

The Latin text of the 'Biblia pauperum' for the temptations in the desert is once again an abridged form of the standard exegesis of the commentaries. There are some variations of wording, but the stress on gluttony is — with some exceptions — clear. For the most part, there is just a brief textual reference to this sin. I cite (with resolved abbreviations) the Latin text of the Munich MS Clm 8201, fol. 83[r], which Cornell reproduces, and which dates from 1414. The text is however, typical, even though the form of this manuscript is perhaps less familiar than others:

> Legitur in Genesi iii quod adam et eua decepti fuerunt per serpentem qui eos de gula temptauit dicens. Eritis sicut dii etc. quod bene figurabat temptationem quam diabolus Christo exhibuit cum temptauit dicens. Dic ut lapides isti panes fiant.[21]

> (We read in Genesis 3 that Adam and Eve were deceived by the serpent who tempted them with gluttony, saying "you shall be as gods, etc." Which well prefigured the temptation which the devil showed Christ when he said: "make these stones bread . . .")

The vernacular versions imitate this almost exactly, and they are as brief: to give just one example of this, consider the text of the beautifully cut blockbook 'Biblia pauperum' made in Nuremberg by Hans Spoerer in 1471, just one year after the first of the blockbook 'Biblias' in Germany from Nördlingen in 1470. The text here reads:

20. See Cornell, Biblia, pp. 11 -53, and the more concise listing by Schmidt, Armenbibeln, pp. 122 -4.

21. Cornell, Biblia, plate 32. See the earlier text reproduced in Schmidt, Armenbibeln, plate 11a, and the corresponding pages in the facsimiles of Heitz and Soltész.

The text ends here with the customary *titulus: Serpens vicit Adam vetitam dum suggerat escam.* ("The serpent conquered Adam, suggesting he eat what was forbidden"). The corresponding *titulus* for Christ is *Christum temptavit Sathanas nec eum superavit.* ("Satan tempted Christ, but did not overcome him"): see Cornell, p. 25 and 199f.

> Man list am puch der geschopfft iij. Das Adam vnnd Eua betrogen
> sein worden durch die schlangen die sye durch die fraßheit versuchet
> etc. das hat bezeichnet die versuchung die than hat der teufel
> cristo.[22]

The passage needs no translation as it is exactly as in the Latin,
without the biblical quotations. There are of course variants in
the Latin texts, but there are none significant here. Of greater
interest perhaps, is the type of 'Biblia pauperum' that Cornell
designates the German narrative version, which contains a
lengthy expansion of the brief point found in most of the
'Biblias'. This is of significance partly because it is in the
vernacular, (and it might have been included under the heading
of vernacular prose texts): but this text shows for the full
typology of the Fall and temptation a variation over Gregory
that echoes other German texts in particular. Cornell comments
on this type that they contain much that should not be in the
'Biblia pauperum', in that they do not have a full relationship
between illustration and text. The earliest seems to be the
fourteenth-century Munich MS Cgm 20, and the narrative 'Biblia pauperum' divides in any case into three sub-types.[23] The
variations here are again not relevant to our study, but it might
be interesting to look at the full text from the Graz Landes-
archiv codex 3, which Cornell prints in full: this dates from the
late fifteenth century, but follows closely a Heidelberg form
(Heidelberg University library Pal. germ. 148) of circa 1400.[24]
The text reads as follows:

> Moyses schreibt in dem ersten puch der gescheph, das da haisset
> Genesis, das got nach dem vnd er den menschen satzt in das paradeis
> vnd im auch gepot das er der frucht nicht azz ab dem paum. Als in
> dann dy slang, das was der tewfel, sagt, sy westen gutts vnd ubels
> davon, vnd wider ried das das got gepoten het, dy selb slang als man
> list het aines menschen haup vnd antliz vnd nam das haup vnd leget
> das in dem paums zwisel vnd liez das ander teil enhalb des paums

22. Biblia Pauperum. Deutsche Ausgabe von 1471, ed. R. Ehwald,
Weimar 1906, plate 10.

23. Cornell, Biblia, pp. 66-8.

24. The MSS are described on pp. 104f. of Cornell's work.

das es Eua icht sehe vnd sich verstund vnd also petrog er sey, wann
het sy in recht gesechen so hiet sy es verstanden. Auch ward Adam
petrogen durch Euam, als das sy zu prachen gottes gepot vnd vber
furen, darum wir all not leiden. Die versuchung Ade vnd Eue pracht
auch vnseren herren zu der versuchung, da in der tewfel versuchet
vnd sprach: Pistu gotts sun, so sprich das dy Stain zu prot werden.
Da wolt er in geuelt haben mit der frasheit. Zu dem anderen
versucht er in mit hochfart, da er sprach, das er sich ab dem tempel
liez, wann es war geschriben das in die Engel scholten aufhalten, das
im nit wurd. Zu dem dritten mal furt er in auff den pergk vnd pott
im alle reich vnd sprach. Ist das du pist nyderuallen vnd pist mich
anpetten so gib ich dir das alles. Got der herr antwurt vnd sprach:
Gee sathanas es stet geschriben das du alain solt an petten den got
vnd nicht versuch den. Vnd da wolt er in versucht haben in der
geitikait.[25]

(Moses writes in the first book of the Creation, i.e. Genesis, that
God took the man and placed him in Paradise and then told him not
to eat of the fruit of the tree. Then the snake — that was the devil —
says that they would know good and evil from this, and advised
contrary to God's command; the same snake, one reads, had a
human head and face, and laid its head between the branches of the
tree and put the rest of itself round the tree obscuring Eve's view,
who then made an error of judgement and thus he deceived her —
for had she been able to see properly she would have understood.
Adam was then deceived by Eve so that they broke God's command
and went astray, from which we all suffer. The temptation of Adam
and Eve caused the temptation too of our Lord, when the devil
tempted him and said: "if you are the son of God, speak that these
stones become bread." There he wanted to fell him with gluttony.
Next he tempted him with pride, saying; that (Christ) should let
himself fall from the temple, since it was written that angels would
support him, so that nothing happened to him. Thirdly he took him
to the mountain and offered him all the kingdoms and said: "if you
worship me I shall give you all this." "The Lord God answered and
said: Go, Satan, it is written that you should worship only God and
not tempt him. And in that he wanted to tempt him with avarice.)

25. Cornell, Biblia, p. 327. I have not attempted to normalize the text
in any way, and problems remain (such as the first *vnd* in the third clause,
and much of the later syntax).

There is, plainly, a great deal of interesting material in this somewhat naive and eccentric text. For the Genesis tradition too there are some unusual motifs here. The description of the Fall of Man of course mirrors the standard iconography (as shown in the 'Biblia pauperum') in the description of the snake with a human head. This motif, found in the 'Historia scholastica' of Peter Comestor, where it is attributed (spuriously) to Bede, becomes commonplace in iconography after the thirteenth century: but it is rarely mentioned at such length in prose writing. The quasi-justification of Eve is also unusual, although one recalls again the treatment of her Fall in works like the 'Heliand' or 'Genesis B.'

For the present context, too, various points emerge. The causal connexion between the two temptations is significant, especially as it follows a reference to the results of the Fall in the allusion to the inheritance of original sin. This points, of course, far more than does the usual 'Biblia pauperum' text, to recapitulative typology. Otherwise the pattern follows Gregory — narrative of Fall and then the Gospel story. The difference lies in the designation of the second temptation as *hochfart*, "pride," instead of vainglory. But this is really a minor variation — we have seen that there are other works (specifically German) which are not connected with the Cassian interpretation (linking pride with the final temptation), but which equate vainglory with pride in any case. This must be the case here, and we are still very close to the Gregorian pattern. That we are, however, textually at some remove from the original is indicated in the awkwardness of the position of the last temptation, tacked on as a sort of afterthought after the real rebuttal of Satan has already taken place.

In placing the 'Biblia pauperum' in the general context of medieval typology, Gerhard Schmidt draws attention not only to earlier works, but also to some later ones that show the influence of the 'Biblia pauperum' itself. In the specific context of the temptation scenes he refers to the 'Concordantiae caritatis' of Ulrich of Lichtenfeld, compiled between 1351 and

1358, and also to the similar works of Christian of Lilienfeld.[26]

One further point might be raised in the general connexion of the 'Biblia pauperum' — the question, to which Elizabeth Pope devotes an entire chapter, of the devil's disguise in the Gospel narrative.[27] Pope discusses various possibilities, with literary and iconographical reference, and states that the devil appears in his own form in art and literature before the fourteenth century. Most of her examples of the disguised devil come from well after this. But there is a medieval tradition that the devil did not do the tempting in his own shape. This may well have arisen by analogy with the descriptions of the Fall of Adam and Eve, where Satan is taken from the times of the deutero-canonical writings and in the New Testament to be identical with the serpent, or where in biblical-apocryphal and vernacular literature he is disguised as an angel of light, as in 2 Corinthians 11: 4.[28] Iconographically there is at least a tradition extending into the fourteenth century that the devil adopted the habit of a monk or friar. Although later texts still show the devil in his own form, one might cite the example of the 'Biblia pauperum' of the fourteenth century from Salzburg (and now codex VII 43a in the Benedictine monastery of St Peter there), where the devil on fol. 138[v], below, is — for all his obvious malevolence — fully disguised as a friar.[29] There are several later cases: the German blockbook of Spoerer of 1471 has a very urbane and cunning looking devil, horned, but still dressed as a friar. So striking in this portrayal that one might almost suspect an early anticipation of the anti-clerical satires

26. Armenbibeln, pp. 93 -7, especially p. 94.
27. 'Paradise Regained,' pp. 42 -50. See also L. W. Cushman, The Devil and the Vice, London 1900, p. 23.
28. See for example Woolf, Fall of Man, pp. 191 -4.
29. Cornell, Biblia, plate 15: see p. 85. The devil is also dressed as a friar in the Paris MS of the PseudoBonaventuran 'Meditations,' ed. Ragusa and Green, pp. 121 -2. The editors comment p. 425f. on the unusual nature of this portrayal, and point out that in the case of the first temptation (on fol. 68v, p. 120) the devil is named as Lucifer. See finally Jean Michel's 'Mystère de la Passion,' Jodogne, p. 35.

(and woodcuts) of the sixteenth century. Another late example is found in the roof-bosses of Norwich cathedral (1509),
again with a squat devil, but dressed as a monk.[30] The Spoerer
blockbook devil contrasts with both of these cases in showing
Christ and the devil as being of equal stature — a perhaps
accidental iconographical parallel to Milton, where Satan is far
from obvious, even if he is not clever enough. The urbaneness of
the Spoerer picture contrasts with Christ's holiness. The reason
for the lack of disguise in many of the later blockbooks,
however, is easily attributable to plain delight in the drawing of
devils, which could well overcome the logic of the pericope: the
Ezstergom blockbook has a particularly devilish Satan, as have
many of the 'Biblia pauperum' manuscripts shown by Cornell
and Schmidt.

But there are earlier instances of the disguise. One such is
a manuscript of the 'Speculum humanae salvationis,' and here
the point is not surprising in view of the text, where the devil
appears *in forma hominis,* "in the shape of a man." This is how
he is portrayed in the Selestat manuscript of the mid-fourteenth
century, for example.[31] Nor is the 'Speculum' unique in de-
scribing the disguise. The Middle English 'Ormulum' states —
already in the thirteenth century, — that the devil came

Inn aness wheress heowe . . .[32]

(In the shape of a man)

There are, therefore, both literary and artistic indications of the
disguise in the Middle Ages, although as Pope surmizes, the

30. Anderson, Drama and Imagery, plate 12b. This is a transept boss.
Anderson also refers to the connexion of such bosses with the 'Biblia
pauperum' and the 'Speculum humanae salvationis,' p. 10f. It might be
noted here that Anderson's fascinating book shows very well how incomplete a survey such as the present study is likely to be: page 7 — "A
precious scrap of evidence might be found in any village church." One
must be aware of the dangers of almost any sort of generalization,
recognizing the impossibility of complete representation.
31. Lutz and Perdrizet, Speculum-edition II, plate 24.
32. V. 11601, Holt II, 48.

tradition may not be a strong one before the fifteenth or sixteenth centuries.

Some more attention may be paid here to the 'Speculum humanae salvationis' itself, and the illustrations which customarily accompany that text, even though the text itself has been discussed in an earlier chapter already. Although the text of the 'Speculum' refers to the Fall in the context of the temptations of Christ in the desert, the manuscripts of this typological catalogue do not depict the Fall, as the 'Biblia pauperum' does. It is, in fact, of the greatest interest to contrast the 'Speculum humanae salvationis' on the one hand with the iconographical derivatives of the 'Pictor in carmine' and the 'Biblia pauperum' on the other. The last-named – the 'Biblia' itself and monuments such as the English glass, restrict them selves to what might be thought of as negative Old Testament types – those capable of fulfillment (the Esau type) and that capable, at least, of recapitulation in Irenaeus' sense (even though the effect in the last analysis of the 'Biblia pauperum' might in fact be rather tropological than typological in any sense). In both of the types, the devil is victorious, and Christ makes this good.

The 'Speculum humanae salvationis' – and we may take the Selestat manuscript as typical in the matter – has a firm emphasis on confirmative Old Testament types – consistently positive against the consistently negative types of the other works. Thus the Selestat manuscript shows three illustrations to accompany the telescoped picture of the three temptations of Christ: these are the victory of Daniel over Bel and the dragon (Daniel 14: 1 -40), David's victory over Goliath (1 Kings 17: 49) and finally the incident of David's killing a bear and a lion (1 Kings 17: 34).[33]

This clear division of types into the fulfilled and the more strictly confirmative becomes the more significant when it is

33. Lutz and Perdrizet, Speculum-edition II, plates 24 -5: see I, 201. Further, see the Mulhouse glass, ibid. II, plate 105. Cornell, Biblia, pp. 161 -8 discusses the relationship between the 'Speculum' and the 'Biblia pauperum.'

recalled that the 'Pictor in carmine' does not distinguish in its listings between the different forms of typology.[34] There seems then to be a careful pattern in the selecting of illustrative typology in the iconographical monuments, and that the different aspects of this sense of Scripture were perhaps more readily apparent in the Middle Ages.

One might of course note one further intrinsic difference in the various types at this point, since it is well illustrated by these iconographical evidences. The temptations of Eve and of Esau have a certain literal reality − they involve actual gluttony: this is not the case with the illustrations of the 'Speculum,' as the parallels there are all allegorically typological. They require actual interpretation before the parallel becomes apparent − they cannot just be set side by side. We have also another nuance in attitude. The stress in the works which show the negative types is on the one actual sin of gluttony. The positive effect of the 'Speculum' selection emphasizes rather the victory aspects, although not in a recapitulative sense. One cannot, it seems, have the two types in combination.

Perhaps less widely known than the 'Biblia pauperum' or the 'Speculum' is the iconographically impressive 'Bible moralisée,' made probably for Louis IX in the thirteenth century: as Cornell notes, the fact that there are some five thousand miniatures in the work has precluded its having been of any wider influence.[35] It has been relatively little studied. It has not been edited as such, but there is a sumptuous four-volume facsimile compiled by Count A. de Laborde, combining three manuscripts: from Oxford (Bodleian MS Bodley 270 B), London (British Museum MS Harley 1527) and Paris (Bibliothèque Nationale MS BN Lat. 11560). This text is well able to serve as a basis for investigation.

The terminology of all these works is confusing. What we have here is essentially a 'Biblia picturata,' a lavishly illustrated picture-Bible, illustration taking precedence over the still inter-

34. ,James, 'Pictor,' p. 154.
35. Biblia, p. 144.

esting text, with eight typologically grouped roundels on a folio-side. The 'Bible moralisée' of Macé de la Charité, based on the 'Aurora' of Peter Riga is neither at issue nor relevant here.[36]

The Genesis text of the Fall, for which Laborde uses the Bodleian manuscript, does not show the temptations of Christ. The parallel is, however, made quite clear in the Gospel portion, for which the Harleian manuscript is used (and will be examined here). Fol. 18[v] of that manuscript devotes six of its eight roundels to the typological comparison between the two Satanic temptations.[37] Here, however, is a divergence from the patterns so far encountered. The text in the margin is almost all that of Matthew (with some discrepancies which will be noted) and de Laborde designates it as such. But the order is that of Luke. The roundels have to be read downwards, first the left-hand column, then the right: if this were not the case, the roundels for John 1: 35f., which complete the set on this folio, would make no sense. The manner in which the temptations parallel is carried out here is worthy of detailed attention. The first roundel shows the temptations of the stones, with the Matthew text, *Tunc ductus est Jesus in desertum* . . . – Matthew 4: 1 -4. There is no tree in the Christ scene, and the devil is in his own shape. A haloed figure is seen above the clouds. This is followed by a roundel showing the entire Fall of Adam and Eve in a syncopated form typical in the Middle Ages. The serpent, with a woman's face, as was common after the thirteenth century, rises out of the mouth of Hell, and offers the fruit to Adam. Eve already has the fruit, and she has just passed some to Adam, who thus has fruit in each hand. This covers then the temptation of Adam by Eve, indicating that the devil tempted Adam in his own right. The text is brief, but it makes the Gregorian exegesis clear:

36. See Kirkconnell, Celestial Cycle, p. 526f. (but note that this text has very little in common with 'Saltair na Rann,' in fact.)

37. A. de Laborde, La Bible moralisée illustrée, Paris 1911 -21. The Fall is in vol. I, plate 7, the Gospel passage (from which I cite here) in III, plate 489.

Hoc significat quod diabolus adam in paradiso ... primum de gula
temptauit cum de ligno uetito comedere persuasit ...

(This signifies how the devil tempted Adam in Paradise, first with
gluttony, when he persuaded him to eat of the forbidden tree.)

S i g n i f i e s , it should be noted, not p r e f i g u r e s, the verb
of the 'Biblia pauperum.' This is an interesting aside on the
nature of typology, for the Gospel is very clearly the starting
point, and the notion of fulfilling something that has happened
does not seem possible here, although it is brought out (strik-
ingly) later on.

It is in the next roundel where the change takes place.
One would expect, of course, the temptation of the temple
now, but instead, we have the kingdoms. Even the Latin text is
confused. It begins with the Luke text: *Et duxit illum diabolus
in montem excelsum* ... (Luke 4: 5) but changes in mid-verse
to Matthew, in spite of the order, covering Matthew 4: 8 to 4:
10. The accompanying roundel must have presented a problem.
The entire Fall has, after all, already been shown, and the first
roundel depicts what is in effect the final scene. Accordingly,
the second roundel has a perhaps somewhat inappropriate scene
which more or less repeats the temptations of Adam and Eve,
but which is closer iconographically to the scenes of the temptation of Christ. The devil is depicted as proffering the fruit to
Adam and Eve, but this time he is in the same form as he is in
the Christ roundels – namely his own shape. This is presumably
intended to make it quite clear that this is the work of the devil,
not of the serpent-woman as such (since there is nothing in the
written text to tell us this). The increased affinity with the
scenes of the temptation of Christ is presumably also in the
artist's mind here: there is even a haloed figure above the scene,
just as in the first roundel, showing the stones temptation. The
text, however, follows the Gregorian exegesis – out of order, of
course, as is the Matthew narrative:

Hoc significat quod diabolus primum hominem temptauit per
auaritiam quando dixit. Scientes bonum et malum ...

(This signifies how the devil tempted the first man with avarice,
saying "knowing good and evil.")

The third temptation of Christ, then, is the temple-scene, once
more with the Matthew text. The corresponding Fall scene is
difficult to place, however. The devil — in his own shape
again — shows Adam and Eve the fruit. This seems to be an
early stage in the temptation of the pair, and in fact, apart from
the devil's shape, the text fits here — this is the devil's promise
that the pair shall be as gods:

> Hoc significat quod diabolus temptauit adam de uana gloria dicens
> eritis sicut dii . . .

> (This signifies how the devil tempted Adam with vainglory, saying
> "you shall be as gods")

The exegesis throughout is that of Gregory, but there are
several important differences between this work and the exposition as it stands in the homily on the Gospel and is repeated in
all the commentaries. The parallel is, as we have seen with some
of the literary works, integrated. Where Gregory has the two
temptations separate, the 'Bible moralisée' treats the parallels as
they come. The alteration of the order is of course the other
difference, and a surprising anticipation of Milton. One can only
speculate on the reasons behind this: perhaps the scribe — or
the artist — considered the temptation with vainglory to be the
most important, a justifiable, but at this time remarkably independent piece of originality.[38]

There is one final feature about the 'Bible moralisée' that
deserves mention, since it points very clearly to the recapitulative side of the typology. The Latin text actually notes a causal
link in the Irenaean sense. After each of the Latin glosses
accompanying the Fall-roundels — merely brief comments on
the Fall in terms of the Gregorian exegesis — comes the line:

> vnde necessum fuit ut eodem uinceretur

> (thus it was necessary to overcome that same [sin])

The 'Bible moralisée' adds to the pure typology of Gregory's

---

38. See Pope, 'Paradise Regained,' p. 68f and pp. 80 -107 on Milton's
placing of the temptations.

exegesis, expanding the general comment he makes about the devil (*a secundo homine victus est,* "he was conquered by the new man") and giving it a broader sense. Christ does not just overcome the devil: the debt of the old sin is paid, and the Fall is neutralized. This is Gregory made recapitulative.

VIII SOME CONCLUDING REMARKS

Conclusions in a work of this nature are very often superfluous; almost invariably they are conclusive only in the sense of a rounding-off of the material as a whole — not in the sense of offering general truths drawn from the evidence presented. There is little need here for a mere regrouping of the works discussed, or for a restatement in simple terms of what has gone before, and for this reason the title of this last chapter is deliberately tentative. But some broad generalizations about the works mentioned may nevertheless still be made.

The aim of the study has been literary in the first instance, and it is hoped that it has shown a fairly wide diversity of literature which would give, in its turn, an indication of the chronological, national, and generic range of the pre-Miltonic treatments of the temptation parallel. Other studies have, after all, tended to proceed directly from Gregory the Great to Milton, or move sideways to less directly relevant works, ignoring the obvious midway stage of the medieval tradition — for a tradition this certainly is.

In some ways, the extent of the conclusions that might be drawn will be limited. A study that is essentially thematic can often tell us little about the audience of the vernacular works it treats. Indeed, we are often better able to make judgements on the underlying intent of a given poet if we have prior knowledge of his audience — as was the case with the Old Saxon 'Heliand.' We are not even able in every case where the point is made briefly to postulate a familiarity on the part of the audience with the entire outline of the motif, although this is sometimes possible. Conversely, of course, the very extent of the vernacular use of the motif (as well as the iconographical representations) tells us that a large number of people would probably have been exposed to the ideas at some stage in the Middle Ages. Medieval drama and medieval church ornamentation is of chief importance here. It is of course more frequently that we can point to the familiarity of a given poet with the motif in its pure theological form. But again, we can often say little about the actual source of a work. We have established that the exegesis of Gregory the Great was the most influential in providing the details of the parallel. This, however, tells us little about the Middle Ages that was not very familiar in any case. Gregory and his predecessor Augustine shaped the thought of the Christian Middle Ages in a way that can scarcely be overestimated.

It is, however, misleading to leave the question of source at that. The pursuit of the exact source for a point — a literary-historical game so beloved of the German scholars in particular in the later nineteenth century — is in any case of a secondary importance. Many writers may indeed have taken over Gregory's exegesis, although we can rarely say that it is or is not taken from a text of Gregory himself: but little more than the details need to have been incorporated into the vernacular work.[1] What is important is the question of attitude taken to the motif: it is very significant that a number of pre-Miltonic versions of the parallel stress it beyond what I have termed the *ad hoc* typology of Gregory's sermon.

The dramatic side of the Gospel narrative will of course have contributed towards the appeal of the point, as indeed it did to Milton,[2] and the nature of the debate may have echoed even the riddle scenes that are so much a feature of heroic poetry in general. A confrontation between God and the devil on earth has more potential and is more conducive to literary representation at least than the sacrifice on the cross, with its more complex overtones. And the plain argument between Christ and Satan must have suggested the equally dramatic confrontations of God, man and the devil at the Fall, and indeed the battle in heaven between God and Lucifer, — the Old English 'Christ and Satan' illustrates this. We may establish then

1. See the similar conclusions reached by Bernd Naumann, Dichter und Publikum in deutscher und lateinischer Bibelepik, Nuremberg 1968, pp. 106 -111.
2. See Lewalski, Epic, p. 166.

an originality in our medieval writers: not of course an indi-
viduality as regards detail – this is rare even in the Latin
writings, – but of approach. Elizabeth Pope comments that

> there is nothing about the tradition more remarkable than the way
> its authorities keep within a limited circle of clearly defined themes
> or ideas. They are like children who have been given a certain
> number of blocks to play with: they select, and discard, and arrange
> in different patterns: but they are always the same blocks.[3]

The analogy is a nice one, but its tone is not entirely fair. The
medieval poet might in any case have agreed, but would point
out that God supplied the blocks anyway. An artist can take
limited material and arrange it in a totally artistic and satisfying
manner. There is such a thing as religious art, and after all,
Milton is in a sense also using the same blocks – ad maiorem Dei
gloriam – as his lesser-known medieval forbears.

Our poets do not necessarily show any local indivi-
duality – and this points to the universality of the Christian
Middle Ages once again. There are small variations of individual
detail that are the product of the poet's environment – Gil
Vicente sees the temptation of the kingdoms as comprising
primarily the Portuguese cities and principalities, and there are
Germanic-warrior overtones in the 'Heliand,' of course. But
otherwise the point transcends local considerations: it is a true
universal.

Various types of approach emerge, which can, admittedly, be associated with similar forms in the pure theological literature. It is interesting in any case that there should be
just such a diversity in the vernacular works as there is in the
Latin and Greek texts. The different approaches may be reviewed briefly: the *exemplum* treatment, with Adam and Eve as
more or less incidental extra examples – the 'Ormulum,' the
Hegge plays and the York plays are examples of this approach,
and it is only to be expected in works that are themselves
sermons, be they versified or dramatized. There is *ad hoc*
typology in a context not stressing the notion of the Redemp-

3. 'Paradise Regained,' p. xv.

tion which is also represented in the vernacular: the 'Veronica' of "der wilde Mann," the "Stanzaic Life of Christ,' the Chester Play. There are brief allusions to the point that seem genuinely typological — Blathmac is an early example. And finally there are treatments that are fully recapitulative, usually part of a *summa*, or at least of a directly Christological work: the 'Ane-genge,' the 'Evangelienbuch' of Otfrid, Gil Vicente's *auto,* as well as less directly related texts such as the 'Christ and Satan' or the Cornish mystery play. Milton's true predecessors are in themselves very diversified, and they are in the main (apart from the dramatic treatments) surprisingly early.

On a wider scale than that of literary criticism alone, the tradition and its various treatments in literature — regardless of whether we consider peripherally influenced works such as the German 'Roland' or indeed 'Sir Gawain and the Green Knight' — afford another example of the confidence of the Middle Ages in the wholeness of the divine plan. The parallelism of Adam and Christ is in any case the symbolic representation of the two poles of human history — its Fall and its Redemp-tion. The polarity of these concepts provided the basis for theological dogma and supplied a topic for imaginative crea-tivity for centuries, and our point is an important individual representation of this polarity. It culminates in Milton, but Milton is an end as well as a crown. Frederick W. Dillistone, in a particularly neatly conceived study of the Fall has pointed out that Milton, with 'Paradise Lost'

> rose to the heights in expressing the Fall in terms of the Ptolemaic world-picture at the very time when that picture was being severely threatened ... by Copernicus and Galileo ... The poem coincided with the end of a theocentric, theonomous universe.[4]

We might say the same of 'Paradise Regained' — that it stands at the end of a tradition. For the Fall in terms of the Ptolemaic world-picture is as relevant to our typology as to 'Paradise Lost.'

4. The Fall: Christian Truth and Literary Symbol, in: Comparative Literature: Matter and Method, ed. A. O. Aldridge, Urbana/Chicago/London 1969, p. 149f.

Indeed, it is more relevant: it comprises both poles, the Fall and the Redemption, the stable facts of history in the stable Ptolemaic universe. The breaking of that stability would come, but the poems treated here express the stability, they do not question it. My introduction cited two writers from the end of the tradition: Gil Vicente and Milton himself. We have seen other writers in the same tradition reaching back to the eight century, and Christian theological writers whose thought reaches back to the second. For the medieval mind, though, the beginning is in the divine plan itself, a plan of history which incorporated coevally from the beginning of time the notions of the Fall and Redemption of Man. And it is an appropriate thought that that Redemption of man should take place in man's terms — that the Old Enemy should be defeated in fact in a manner entirely comprehensible to man, and in a way that parallels exactly the first Fall. Milton may have the last word: the Passion and Resurrection of the God-Man are events almost beyond human comprehension and human art. But the victory in the desert is achieved in human terms, and it is as fitting that this victory be sung as any other.

BIBLIOGRAPHY

The bibliography is divided into two parts, covering primary and secondary material. The first is arranged according to the same divisions as those used in the body of the text (chapters II - VII), works being placed under the most appropriate heading. Only those texts actually cited are included here. Within each group the division is according to language. In the case of Latin prose writings, the major source — Migne's 'Patrologia Latina' — is frequently inaccurate as regards ascription. I have made tacit correction according to the hand-list of P. Glorieux in these cases. The secondary literature is alphabetically arranged, and here some works have been included that were consulted, but not necessarily cited. Very standard works of reference, such as the major dictionaries, have not been listed.

PRIMARY SOURCES

Chapter II Scripture and Exegesis

Bible and Apocrypha

Bible. Bibliorum Sacrorum iuxta Vulgatam Clementinam nova editio, ed. Aloisius Gramatica, Vatican 1959.

Bible (New Testament). Novum Testamentum Graece, ed. Alexander Souter, Oxford 1910.

Bible (New Testament). The New Testament Octapla, ed. Luther A. Weigle, Edinburgh/New York/Toronto 1962.

Apocalypsis Mosis (Greek, 1st cent. BC), transl. L. S. A. Wells. In: Apocrypha and Pseudepigrapha of the Old Testament, ed. R. H. Charles, Oxford 1913, II, 123-54.

Passio Bartholomaei (Greek, 5th -6th cent. AD with early Latin text). In: Acta Apostolorum Apocrypha, ed. Richard Adalbert Lipsius and Maximilian Bonnet, Leipzig 1891 -1903, II/i, 128 -50.

Vita Adae et Evae (Latin, 4th cent. AD), ed. Wilhelm Meyer (Abhandlungen der Bayrischen Akademie der Wissenschaften in München, philos.-philol. Cl 14/iii, 1878), pp. 185 -250. English translation by L. S. A. Wells. See above, Apocalypsis Mosis.

English Texts

The Miroure of Mans Saluacionne, a 15th Century translation into English of the Speculum humanae salvationis, ed. Alfred H. Huth, London 1888.

Ralph Higden. Polychronicon. For the English version of this work see below under the Latin text.

French Texts

Le Miroir de la salvation humaine, transl. Jean Mielot (15th cent.). See below under the Latin version of the Speculum humanae salvationis.

German Texts

Konrad von Helmsdorf. Der Spiegel des menschlichen Heils, ed. Axel Lindqvist (DTM 31) Berlin 1924. (14th cent. translation of the Speculum humanae salvationis).

Greek Texts

Anastasius of Sinai (d. c. 700). Anagogica... in Hexaemeron, PG 89, 851 -1078.

John Chrysostom (c. 347 -407). Homiliae in Matthaeum, PG 57, 21 -472.

PseudoChrysostom. In Genesim, PG 56, 517 -38.

PseudoChrysostom. Opus imperfectus in Matthaeum, PG 56, 611 -946.

Euthemius Zigabenus (12th cent.). Commentarius in Matthaeum, PG 129, 111 -764.

Irenaeus of Lyons (c. 130-c. 202). Adversus haereses, PG 7, 434 -1224.

Scholia vetera in Matthaeum (? 10th cent.), PG 106, 1077 -1174.

Scholia vetera in Lucam (? 10th cent.), PG 106, 1177 -1218.

Theodore Prodromus (12th cent.). Tetrasticha in Novum Testamentum, PG 133, 1177 -96.

Theodoret of Cyrrhus (c. 393 -457). Quaestiones in Genesin, PG 80, 77 -226.

Theophylactus of Achrida (12th cent.). Enarratio in Evangelium Matthaei, PG 123, 143 -488.

Judaic Texts

Moses Maimonides (1135-1204). The Guide of the Perplexed, transl. Shlomo Pines, with an introduction by Leo Strauss. Chicago 1963.

Pirkê de Rabbi Eliezer (anon. 8th-9th cent.AD), transl. Gerald Friedlander, London 1916.

Talmud (Babylonian Talmud, Babli, 6th cent. BC — 500 AD), ed. and transl. I. Epstein, London 1935-52. See the tractate Aboth in the volume Seder nezikin VIII, 1935. There is a further translation by R. Travers Herford in: Apocrypha and Pseudepigrapha of the Old Testament, ed. R. H. Charles, Oxford 1913, II.

Latin Texts

Alexander III (Pope, Orlando Bandinelli, d. 1181). Sententiae, ed. Ambrosius M. Gietl, Die Sentenzen Rolands, Freiburg/Br. 1891.

Alan of Lille (ab or de Insulis, c. 1128-1203). Summa de arte praedicatoria, PL 210, 109-98.

Aurelius Augustine of Hippo (354-430). De consensu Evangelistarum, PL 15, 1527-1850.

Aquinas: see Thomas Aquinas

Aurelius Augustine of Hippo (354-430). De Genesi ad litteram, ed. Carolus Schenkl (Corpus scriptorum ecclesiasticorum Latinorum 28/iii/2, pp. 1-456) Vienna 1894.

Aurelius Augustine of Hippo (354-430). De consensu Evangelistarum, PL 34, 1041-230.

Bede the Venerable (c. 672-735). Hexaemeron, PL 91, 9-190.

Bede the Venerable (c. 672-735). In Matthaei Evangelium expositio, PL 92, 9-132.

Bede the Venerable (c. 672-735). In Lucae Evangelium expositio, PL 92, 301-634.

Bonaventure (1221-1274). Lignum vitae, in: Obras de San Buenaventura, ed. Leon Amoros, Bernado Aperribay, Miguel Oromi and Miguel Oltra (Bibliotheca de autores Cristianos) Madrid 1945-9, II, 281-356.

PseudoBonaventure. Meditationes vitae Christ. See under chapter VII, iconography.

Bruno of Asti (Segni, 1044-1123). Commentaria in Lucam, PL 165, 333-452.

John Cassian (c. 360-435). Collationes patrum, PL 49, 477-1328.

Claude of Turin (PseudoEucherius of Lyons, d. c. 830). Commentarii in Genesim, PL 50, 893-1048.

PseudoChrysostom (Latin, 5th cent.). Homilia de lapsu, PL 95, 1208-10.

Deus de cuius principio etc. See below, Sententiae.

Christian Druthmar of Stavelot (Corvey, fl. c. 860). Expositio in Matthaeum, PL 106, 1261-1504.

Garnier of Rochefort (late 12th cent.). Sermones, PL 205, 559-828.

Glossa interlinearis: see following entry.

Glossa ordinaria (12th cent.). On Genesis, PL 113, 67-182; on Matthew,

PL 114, 63-178; on Luke, PL 114, 243-356. From this is derived the Glossa interlinearis, which is included with the Glossa ordinaria in: Biblia Sacra cum Glossa ordinaria, ed. Leander a S. Martino, Antwerp 1634.

Godfrey of Admont (d. 1165). Homiliae dominicales, PL 174, 21-386.

Gregory the Greàt (c. 540-604). Homiliae in Evangelia, PL 76, 1075-1314.

Gregory the Great (c. 540-604). Moralia in Job, PL 75, 199-PL 76, 782.

Haymo of Auxerre (PseudoHaymo of Halberstadt, fl. c. 840-865). Homilia de tempore, PL 118, 11-746.

Ralph Higden (14th cent.). Polychronicon, ed. Churchill Babington and Joseph Rawson Lumby, Polychronicon Ranulphi Higden monachi Cestrensis with the English translations of John Trevisa and of an unknown writer of the 15th century (Rolls Series 41/1-9) London 1865-86.

Hilary of Poitiers (c. 315-368). Commentarius in Matthaeum, PL 9, 917-1047.

Hildebert of Lavardin (Le Mans, 1056-1133). Sermones de tempore, PL 171, 339-606.

Honoré of Autun (d. c. 1152). Elucidarium, PL 171, 1109-76.

Hugh of St Victor (c. 1096-1141). De sacramentis legis naturalis et scriptae dialogus, PL 176, 17-42.

Hugh of St Victor (c. 1096-1141). De sacramentis Christianae fidei, PL 176, 173-613.

Innocent III (Pope, Lothar of Segni, d. 1216). Sermones de tempore, PL 217, 309-450.

Isaac de Stella (d. 1169). Sermones, PL 194, 1689-1876.

James of Voragine (Jacobus a Voragine, fl. c. 1270). Legenda aurea, ed. Th. Graesse, Dresden/Leipzig 1846.

Jerome (c. 342-420). Commentarius in Evangelium Matthaei, PL 26, 15-228.

PseudoJerome (? Irish, 7-8th cent.). Expositio quattuor Evangeliorum, PL 30, 531-644.

Legenda aurea: see James of Voragine, above.

Maximus of Turin (c. 380- c. 470). Homiliae, PL 57, 221-530.

Maximus of Turin (c. 380- c. 470). Sermones, PL 57, 529-886.

Martin of Léon (d. 1203). Sermones de tempore, PL 208, 27-1359.

Paschasius Radbertus (c. 785- c. 850). Expositio in Evangelium Matthaei, PL 120, 31-453.

Paterius (d. 606). De expositione Veteris ac Novi Testamenti, PL 79, 677-1136.

Paul the Deacon (Warnfrid, c. 720– c. 800). Homiliae de tempore, PL 95, 1159-1458.

Peter of Celle (d. 1187). Sermones, PL 202, 637-926.

Peter Comestor (Manducator, d. 1179/98). Historia scholastica, PL 198, 1049-1722.

Raban Maurus (776/84-856). Commentaria in Genesim, PL 107, 439-670.

Raban Maurus (776/84-856). Commentaria in Matthaeum, PL 107, 727-1156.

Ralph of Poitiers (Ardentis, fl. c. 1100). Homiliae in Epistolas et Evangelia dominicalia, PL 155, 1665-2118.

Rupert of Deutz (c. 1070-1129/35). In Genesim, PL 167, 199-566.

Rupert of Deutz (c. 1070-1129/35). In IV Evangelistarum, PL 167, 1535-70.

Rupert of Deutz (c. 1070-1129/35). Commentarius in Matthaeum, PL 168, 1307-1634.

Sententiae Anselmi (11th or 12th cent.), ed. F. Bliemetzrieder, Anselms von Laon systematische Sentenzen I. Texte (BGPM 18/ii-iii, pp. 47-153) Münster/W. 1919. The Sententiae divinae paginae are in this volume, pp. 1-46.

Sententiae Berolinenses (12th cent.), ed. Friedrich Stegmüller, Eine neugefundene Sentenzensammlung aus der Schule des Anselm von Laon (Recherches de théologie ancienne et médiévale 11, 1939), pp. 33-61.

Sententiae. Deus de cuius principio et fine tacetur (12th cent.), ed. Heinrich Weisweiler, Le recueil des sentences 'Deus de cuius principio et fine tacetur' et son remaniement (Recherches de théologie ancienne et médiévale 5, 1933), pp. 245-74.

Sententiae divinae paginae: see Sententiae Anselmi, above.

Speculum humanae salvationis (14th cent.). ed. J. Lutz and P. Perdrizet, Leipzig 1907-9 (including the French text of Jean Mielot, 1448).

Thomas Aquinas (1226-74). Summa theologica, various editors in: Saint Thomas d'Aquin, Somme théologique, Paris 1940ff. The volumes used here (Vie de Jésus) are edited by P. Synave.

Taio of Saragozza (fl. c. 625). Sententiae, PL 80, 727-990.

Quintus Septimius Florens Terullian (c. 160– c. 220). De ieiunio adversus Psychicos (Corpus Christianorum, series Latina 2, pp. 1255-77) Turnhout 1954.

Werner of St Blasien (d. 1126). Deflorationes, PL 157, 721-1256.

William of Auvergne (d. 1249). Sermones, in: Guiliemi Alverni . . . opera omnia, Paris 1674, II, 1-476.

Würzburg Matthew-Commentary (Irish, c. 750-800), ed. Karl Koeberlin, Eine Würzburger Evangelienhandschrift, Mp. th. f. 61. S. VIII (Programm zu dem Jahresbericht der königlichen Anstalt bei St Anna in Augsburg 1890/1, pp. 19-49) Augsburg 1891.

John Wyclif (c. 1328-84). Sermones, ed. F. J. Loserth, London 1887-90. See especially the Sermones super Evangelia dominicalia, in vol. I (1887).

Ysagoge in theologiam (12th cent.), ed. Arthur Landgraf, Ecrits théologiques de l'école d'Abélard (Spicilegium sacrum Lovaniense 14, pp. 61-285), Louvain 1934.

Zacharias Chrysopolitanus (d. c. 1157). In unum ex quattuor, PL 186, 9-620.

Chapter III   Vernacular Prose Writings

English Texts

Aelfric. Homilies, in: The Homilies of the Anglo-Saxon Church, ed. Benjamin Thorpe, London 1844-6. Vol. I = The 'Sermones catholici' or 'Homilies' of Aelfric.

The Blickling Homilies, ed. Richard Morris (EETS/OS 58, 63, 73) London 1874-80.

The Blickling Homilies (MS). The Blickling Homilies of the John H. Scheide Library, Titusville, Pa., ed. Rudolph Willard (Early English MSS in Facsimile 10) Copenhagen 1960.

Bodley MS 343. Twelfth-Century Homilies in MS. Bodley 343. I. Text, ed. A. O. Belfour (EETS/OS 137) London 1909.

Chaucer. The Pardoner's Tale, in: The Complete Works of Geoffrey Chaucer, ed. F. N. Robinson, 2nd ed. London 1957, pp. 229-65.

John Mirk. Festial, ed. Theodor Erbe, Mirk's 'Festial.' A Collection of Homilies by Johannes Mirkus (John Mirk) I. (EETS/ES 96) London 1905.

Richard Morris, Old English Homilies and Homiletic Treatises (EETS/OS 29) London 1868.

Pepysian Gospel Harmony, ed. Margery Goates (EETS/OS 157) London 1922.

Mary Ellen Rickey and Thomas B. Stroup (editors), Certaine Sermons or Homilies appointed to be read in Churches in the Time of Queen Elizabeth I (1547-1571), Gainesville 1968 (= facsimile of edition of 1623).

Royal MS 18B xxiii. Middle English Sermons from British Museum MS

Royal 18B xxiii, ed. Woodbury O. Ross (EETS/OS 209) London 1940.

Speculum sacerdotale, ed. Edward H. Weatherly (EETS/OS 200) London 1936.

Trinity College Dublin: MS B. 4. 19 (or: 201) 'On the Feasts.'

Wulfstan. Homilies, ed. Dorothy Bethurum, Oxford 1957.

German Texts

Heinrich Hoffmann von Fallersleben (ed.), Fundgruben für Geschichte deutscher Sprache und Litteratur, Breslau 1830-7. See vol. I, 59-126, 'Predigten.'

Adalbert Jeitteles (ed.), Altdeutsche Predigten aus dem Benediktinerstifte St Pauli in Kärnten, Innsbruck 1878.

Konrad the Priest: see below, A. Schönbach. For the group Y sermons, see the bibliography of secondary sources, V. Mertens.

Oberaltaich sermons: see below, A. Schönbach.

Anton E. Schönbach, Altdeutsche Predigten, Graz 1886-9.

Tatian (Greek, 2nd cent.). Diatessaron. See the Old High German and Latin versions edited by Eduard Sievers, Tatian, 2nd ed. Paderborn 1892, repr. Darmstadt 1961.

Greek Texts

Tatian: see above, German texts.

Latin Texts

Tatian: see above, German texts.

Scandinavian Texts

Norwegian Homily-Book, ed. George T. Flom, Codex AM 619 Quarto (University of Illinois Studies in Language and Literature 14/44) Urbana 1929.

Stockholm Homily-Book, ed. Theodor Wisén, Homilu-bók isländska homilier efter en handskrift från tolfte århundradet, Lund, 1872.

Chapter IV Early Vernacular Poetry

English Texts

Christ and Satan, ed. George Philipp Krapp, The Junius Manuscript (The Anglo-Saxon Poetic Records) London/New York 1931, pp. 133-58.

German Texts

Anegenge. Das Anegenge. Textkritische Studien. Diplomatischer Abdruck. Kritische Ausgabe. Anmerkungen zum Text, ed. Dietrich Neuschäfer (Medium Aevum 8) Munich 1966.

Ava. Das Leben Jesu, in: Die religiösen Dichtungen des 11. und 12. Jahrhunderts, ed. Friedrich Maurer, Tübingen 1964-70, II, 398-491.

Erlösung, ed. Friedrich Maurer (Deutsche Literatur in Entwicklungsreihen, geistliche Dichtung 5) Leipzig 1934, repr. Darmstadt 1964.

Otfrid of Weissenburg. Evangelienbuch, ed. Oskar Erdmann, 4th ed. by Ludwig Wolff (ATB 49) Tübingen 1962. See also the edition of Paul Piper, 2nd ed. Freiburg/Br./Tübingen 1882-4.

Vienna Genesis. Die frühmittelhochdeutsche Wiener Genesis, ed. Kathryn Smits (Philologische Studien und Quellen 59) Berlin 1972.

Vorau Genesis, ed. Joseph Diemer, Deutsche Gedichte des XI und XII Jahrhunderts, Vienna 1849, pp. 1-30.

Der wilde Mann. Veronica, ed. Bernard Standring, Die Gedichte des wilden Mannes (ATB 59) Tübingen 1963, pp. 1-21.

Irish Texts

Blathmac. The Poems of Blathmac, Son of Cú Brettan, ed. James Carney (ITS 47) Dublin 1964.

Old Saxon Texts

Heliand, ed. Otto Behaghel, Heliand und Genesis, 8th ed. by Walther Mitzka (ATB 4) Tübingen 1965.

Chapter V   Later Vernacular Poetry

English Texts

Cursor mundi, ed. Richard Morris (EETS/OS 57, 59, 62, 68, 99) London 1874-8.

Giles Fletcher. Christ's Victorie, and Triumph in Heaven, and Earth, over, and after Death, in: Giles and Phineas Fletcher. Poetical Works, ed. Frederick S. Boas, Cambridge 1908-9, repr. Grosse Point 1968, I, 5-87.

Meditations on the Life and Passion of Christ, ed. Charlotte d'Evelyn (EETS/OS 158) London 1921.

John Milton. Paradise Lost, in: The Works of John Milton, ed. Frank Allen Patterson (The Columbia Edition) New York 1931-8, II/1-2. Paradise Regained is in vol. II/2.

John Milton. Paradise Regained: see preceding entry.
Northern Homily Collection, ed. John Small, English Metrical Homilies from Manuscripts of the Fourteenth Century, Edinburgh 1872.
Northern Homily Collection. Henry E. Huntington MS HM 129.
The Northern Passion, ed. Frances A. Foster (EETS/OS 145, 147) London 1913-16. The second volume contains a French text.
The Ormulum, ed. Robert Holt, notes by R. M. White, Oxford 1878.
The South English Legendary, edited from MS Laud 108 in the Bodleian Library, ed. Carl Horstmann (EETS/OS 87) London 1887.
The South English Legendary, edited from Corpus Christi College Cambridge MS 145 and British Museum MS Harl. 2277, etc., ed. Charlotte d'Evelyn and Anna J. Mill (EETS/OS 235, 236, 244) London 1956-9.
The Southern Passion, ed. Beatrice Daw Brown (EETS/OS 169) London 1927.
Stanzaic Life of Christ, ed. Frances A. Foster (EETS/OS 166) London 1926.

French Texts
Le livre de la Passion, ed. Grace Frank (Classiques français du moyen age 64) Paris, 1930.
Northern Passion: see above, English texts.
Ystoire de la Passion BN Ms. fr. 821, ed. Edith Armstrong Wright (Johns Hopkins Studies in Romance Literatures and Languages 45) Baltimore, 1944.

German Texts
Gundacker von Judenberg. Christi hort, ed. J. Jaksche (DTM 18) Berlin 1910.
Der saelden hort, ed. Heinrich Adrian (DTM 26) Berlin 1927.

Scandinavian Texts
Eystein Asgrimsson. Lilja, in: Finnur Jónsson, Den norsk-isländska skaldediktningen, rev. ed. Ernst A. Kock, Lund 1946-9, II, 212-28. German translation by Wolfgang Lange, Christliche Skaldendichtung, Göttingen 1958, pp. 56-72. English translation by Eirikr Magnusson, Lilja. The Lily . . . by Eystein Asgrimsson, London 1870.

Chapter VI The Dramatic Versions

Cornish Texts

Ordinalia. The Ancient Cornish Drama, ed., transl. Edwin Norris, London 1859, repr. London/New York 1968. Translation only by Markham Harris, The Cornish 'Ordinalia,' Washington 1969.

Dutch Texts

Maastricht Passion Play. Julius Zacher, Mittelniederländisches Osterspiel (Zeitschrift für deutsches Altertum 2, 1842), pp. 302-50.

English Texts

John Bale. A brefe Comedy or enterlude concernynge the temptacyon of our lord and sauer Jesus Christ, 1538. Facsimile ed., London 1909.

Chester Plays, ed. Thomas Wright (Shakespeare Society 17, 35), London 1843-7. Also ed. H. Deimling (EETS/ES 62, vol. I only) London 1892.

Hegge Plays. Ludus Coventriae or the Plaie called Corpus Christi, ed. K. S. Block (EETS/ES 120) London 1922.

Parlamentum of Feendis. In: Hymns to the Virgin and Christ, The Parliament of Devils and Other Religious Poems, ed. Frederick J. Furnivall (EETS/OS 24) London 1868, pp. 157-82.

York Plays, ed. Lucy Toulmin Smith, Oxford 1885, repr. New York 1963.

French Texts

Arnoul Greban. Mystère de la Passion, ed. Gaston Paris and Gaston Raynaud, Paris 1878.

Eustache Mercadé. Mystère de la Passion. Texte du manuscrit 697 de la bibliothèque d'Arras, ed. J-M. Richard, Arras 1891.

Jean Michel. Mystère de la Passion (Angers 1486), ed. Omer Jodogne, Gembloux 1959.

Mystère d'Adam, ed. Paul Studer (Modern Language Texts, French Series Medieval) Manchester 1918, repr. 1949.

Passion d'Amboise, ed. E. Picot, Fragments inédits du 'Mystère de la Passion' (Romania 19, 1890), pp. 264-82.

Passion du Palatinus, ed. Grace Frank (Classiques français du moyen age 30) Paris 1922.

Passion Provençale, ed. William P. Shepard, La Passion Provençale du manuscrit Didot (Société des anciens textes français) Paris 1928.

Passion de Semur, ed. Emile Roy, Le 'Mystère de la Passion' en France du XIVe au XVIe siècle (Revue Bourguignonne 13/3-4) Dijon/Paris 1903.

German Texts

Alsfelder Passionsspiel, ed. Richard Froning, Das Drama des Mittelalters (Deutsche Nationalliteratur 14/1-3) Stuttgart 1891-3, repr. Darmstadt 1964, pp. 547-859.

Donaueschinger Passionsspiel, ed. Eduart Hartl, Das Drama des Mittelalters. Passionsspiele II, (Deutsche Literatur in Entwicklungsreihen, Drama des Mittelalters 4) Leipzig 1942, repr. Darmstadt 1966.

Heidelberger Passionsspiel, ed. Gustav Milchsack (Bibliothek des litterarischen Vereins in Stuttgart 150) Tübingen 1880.

Künzelsauer Fronleichnamspiel, ed. Peter K. Liebenow (Ausgaben deutscher Literatur des XV bis XVIII Jahrhunderts. Drama 2) Berlin 1969.

Hans Sachs. Tragedia von schöpfung, fal und außtreibung Ade, ed. Adelbert von Keller in: Hans Sachs. Werke I (Bibliothek des litterarischen Vereins in Stuttgart 102) Stuttgart 1870, repr. Hildesheim 1964, pp. 19-52.

St Galler Passionsspiel, ed. Eduard Hartl, Das Benediktbeurer und das St Galler Passionsspiel (ATB 41), Halle/S. 1952.

Irish Texts

Saltair na Rann, ed. Whitley Stokes (Anecdota Oxoniensia, Modern and Medieval Series 1/3) Oxford 1883. Translation in: Eleanor Hull, The Poem-Book of the Gael, London 1912, pp. 1-50. New translation and edition in preparation by D. Greene (Dublin).

Italian Texts

Teofilo Folengo. La umanitá del figliuolo di Dio, in: Opere Italiane, ed. Umberto Renda, Bari 1911-12, I.

Latin Texts

Avitus of Vienne (d. c. 523). Poemata, ed. Rudolf Peiper (Monumenta Germaniae historica, auct. antiq. 6/2) Berlin 1883, pp. 197-294
Isidore of Seville (c. 560-636). Etymologiae, PL 82, 9-728.

Portuguese Texts

Gil Vicente. Breve sumário da história de Deus, ed. João de Almeida Lucas (Clássicos Portugueses trechos escolhidos, século XVI, teatro) Lisbon 1943. Also in: Obras completas, ed. Álvaro Júlio da Costa Pimpão, new ed. Porto 1962, pp. 108-20. Facsimile edition of Madrid text in: Autos Portugueses de Gil Vicente . . . edición facsimil, ed. Carolina Michaëlis de Vasconcellos, Madrid 1922.

Gil Vicente. Auto de Deus padre e justiça e misericordia, ed. L. S. Révah, Deux autos méconnus de Gil Vicente, Lisbon 1948, pp. 51-87.

Scandinavian Texts
Volospá, ed. Gudbrand Vigfússon and F. York Powell, Corpus poeticum boreale, Oxford 1883, repr. New York 1965, I, 192-6.

Slavonic Texts
Slovo o Lazarevom voskresenii, ed. G. Kushelevym-Bezborodko, Pamyatniki starinnoi Russkoi literatury, St. Petersburg 1883, pp. 11-12. Transl. Serge A. Zenkovsky, Medieval Russia's Epics, Chronicles and Tales, New York 1963, pp. 129-36.

Chapter VII Medieval Iconography

Literary material
The Book of Adam and Eve (Ethiopian), ed. S. G. Malan, London 1882.
The Book of the Cave of Treasures (Syriac), ed. E. A. Wallis Budge, London 1927.
Lebor Gabála Érenn. The Book of the Taking of Ireland I, ed. R. A. Stewart Macalister (ITS 34) Dublin 1938.

Iconographic material
Bible moralisée, ed. Alexandre de Laborde, Paris 1911-21.
Biblia pauperum. Deutsche Ausgabe von 1471, ed. R. Ehwald, Weimar 1906.
Biblia pauperum, ed. Paul Heitz, with an introduction by W. L. Schreiber, Strasbourg 1903.
Biblia pauperum. Facsimile Edition of the Forty-Leaf Blockbook in the Library of Esztergom Cathedral, ed. Elizabeth Soltész, Budapest 1967.
Biblia pauperum: see the bibliography of secondary sources under Hendrik Cornell, Gertrud Schiller, Gerhard Schmidt.
PseudoBonaventure. Meditations on the Life of Christ. An Illustrated Manuscript of the 14th Century, Paris, Bibliothèque Nationale MS Ital. 115, transl. and ed. Isa Ragusa and Rosalie B. Green (Princeton Monographs in Art and Archaeology 35) Princeton 1961.
The Hours of Catherine of Cleves, ed. John Plummer, New York 1966.
Pictor in carmine, ed. M. R. James (Archaeologia 94, 1951), pp. 141-66.
St Albans Psalter, ed. Otto Pächt, C. R. Dodwell and Francis Wormald (Studies of the Warburg Institute 25) London 1960.
Speculum humanae salvationis: see bibliography to chapter II, above.

SECONDARY SOURCES

C. Abbetmeyer, Old English Poetical Motives Derived from the Doctrine of Sin (Diss. Minnesota 1900) Minneapolis/New York 1903.

Berthold Altaner, Patrology, transl. Hilda C. Graef from 5th ed., Freiburg/Br./Edinburgh/London 1960.

M. D. Anderson, The Imagery of British Churches, London 1955.

M. D. Anderson, Drama and Imagery in English Medieval Churches, Cambridge 1963.

Matthew Arnold, On the Study of Celtic Literature, London 1867.

Eugène Aubrey-Vitet, Les sermonnaires du moyen age (Revue des deux mondes 82, 1869), pp. 811-40.

Erich Auerbach, Figura. In: Scenes from the Drama of European Literature, transl. Ralph Manheim, New York 1959, pp. 9-76.

Erich Auerbach, Typologische Motive in der mittelalterlichen Literatur (Schriften und Vorträge des Petrarca-Instituts / Köln 2) Krefeld 1964.

Erich Auerbach, Mimesis. Dargestellte Wirklichkeit in der abendländischen Literatur, 3rd ed. Munich 1964.

Wolfgang Babilas, Tradition und Interpretation. Gedanken zur philologischen Methode (Langue et parole 1) Munich 1961.

Matthias Becker, Bild-Symbol-Glaube, Essen 1965.

Paul E. Beichner, The Allegorical Interpretation of Medieval Literature (PMLA 82, 1967), pp. 33-8.

Aubrey F. G. Bell, Gil Vicente (Hispanic Notes and Monographs, Portuguese Series 1) Oxford 1921.

Gustav Adolf Benrath, Wyclifs Bibelkommentar (Arbeiten zur Kirchengeschichte 36) Berlin 1966.

Michael Benskin, An Argument for an Interpolation in the Old English 'Later Genesis' (Neuphilologische Mitteilungen 72, 1971), pp. 224-45.

Michael Benskin and Brian Murdoch, Review of: J. M. Evans, 'Paradise Lost' and the Genesis Tradition (Neuphilologische Mitteilungen — in press).

Hellmuth Bethe, Astkreuz. In: Reallexikon zur deutschen Kunstgeschichte, ed. Otto Schmitt etc., Stuttgart 1937ff., I, 1152-61.

Robert Blomme, La doctrine du péché dans les écoles théologiques de la première moitié du 12. siècle (Universitas Catholica Lovaniensis, dissertationes 3/6) Louvain 1958.

Morton W. Bloomfield, The Seven Deadly Sins (Studies in Language and Literature) Michigan 1952.

Morton W. Bloomfield, Symbolism in Medieval Literature (Modern Philology 56, 1958), pp. 73-81.

Helmut de Boor, Die deutsche Literatur von Karl dem Grossen bis zum Beginn der höfischen Dichtung 770-1170 (Geschichte der deutschen Literatur 1), 2nd ed. Munich 1955.

J. Knight Bostock, Handbook on Old High German Literature, Oxford 1955.

Cecil Maurice Bowra, Heroic Poetry, London 1952.

Egon Brandenburger, Adam und Christus. Exegetisch-religionsgeschichtliche Untersuchung zu Röm. 5: 12-21 (1 Kor. 15) (Wissenschaftliche Monographien zum Alten und Neuen Testament 7) Neukirchen 1962.

Arnold Breymann, Adam und Eva in der Kunst des christlichen Alterthums, Wolfenbüttel 1893.

Robert B. Burlin, The Old English 'Advent.' A Typological Commentary (Yale Studies in English 168) New Haven/London 1968.

M. P. Buttel, Religious Ideology and Christian Humanism in German Cluniac Verse (Catholic University of America Studies in German 21) Washington 1948.

Cambridge Medieval History, ed. J. B. Bury, etc., 2nd ed. Cambridge 1924-36.

J. M. Campbell, Patristic Studies and the Literature of Medieval England (Speculum 8, 1933), pp. 465-78.

Harry Caplan, The Four Senses of Scriptural Interpretation and the Medieval Theory of Preaching (Speculum 4, 1929), pp. 282-90.

James Carney (editor and contributor), Early Irish Poetry (The Thomas Davis Lectures) Cork 1965.

E. K. Chambers, The Medieval Stage, Oxford 1903.

A. C. Charity, Events and their Afterlife. The Dialectics of Christian Typology in the Bible and Dante, Cambridge 1966.

Johan Chydenius, The Theory of Medieval Symbolism (Societas scientiarum Fennica, commentationes humanarum litterarum 27/2) Helsinki 1960.

Kenneth Clarke, Civilisation. A Personal View, New York/Evanston 1969.

Gustave Cohen, Le théâtre en France au moyen-age, Paris 1948.

J. Coppens, Le Protévangile. In: L. Cerfaux, J. Coppens and J. Gribomont, Problèmes et méthode d'exégèse théologique, Louvain 1950, pp. 45-77.

Mary Irma Corcoran, Milton's Paradise with Reference to the Hexaemeral Background (Diss. Catholic University of Washington 1945) Washington 1945.

Henrik Cornell, Biblia pauperum, Stockholm 1925.

G. G. Coulton, Five Centuries of Religion (Cambridge Studies in Medieval Life and Thought) Cambridge 1923-50.

Hardin Craig, English Religious Drama of the Middle Ages, Oxford 1955.

Thomas Wallace Craik, The Tudor Interlude, Leicester 1926.

Rudolf Cruel, Geschichte der deutschen Predigt im Mittelalter. Detmold 1879, repr. Darmstadt 1966.

L. W. Cushman, The Devil and the Vice in the English Dramatic Literature before Shakespeare, London 1900, repr. 1970.

Jean Daniélou, Sacramentum futuri. Etudes sur les origines de la typologie biblique, Paris 1950.

Neville Denny, Review of: Markham Harris, The Cornish 'Ordinalia' (Medium Aevum 40, 1971), pp. 305-9.

Frederick W. Dillistone, The Fall. Christian Truth and Literary Symbol. In: Comparative Literature. Matter and Method, ed. A. O. Aldridge, Urbana/Chicago/London 1969, pp. 144-57.

Ernst von Dobschütz, Vom vierfachen Schriftsinn. In: Harnack-Ehrung, Leipzig 1921, pp. 1-13.

F. Holmes Dudden, Gregory the Great. His Place in History and Thought, London 1905.

Burton Scott Easton, The Gospel According to St. Luke. A Critical and Exegetical Commentary, Edinburgh 1926.

Gustav Ehrismann, Geschichte der deutschen Literatur bis zum Ausgang des Mittelalters (Handbuch des deutschen Unterrichts an höheren Schulen 6) Munich 1922-35.

Oswald Erich, Adam-Christus. In: Reallexikon zur deutschen Kunstgeschichte, ed. Otto Schmitt etc., Stuttgart 1937ff., I, 157-67.

J. M. Evans, 'Paradise Lost' and the Genesis Tradition, Oxford 1968.

Joseph Feldmann, Paradies und Sündenfall (Alttestamentliche Abhandlungen 4) Münster/W. 1913.

Rodney W. Fisher, The Role of the Demonic in Selected Middle High German Epics, Diss. Cambridge 1968.

Angus Fletcher, Allegory. The Theory of a Symbolic Mode, Ithaca 1964.

Max Förster, Über die Quellen von AElfrics exegetischen 'Homiliae Catholicae' (Anglia 16, 1894), pp. 1-61.

Grace Frank, The Palatine 'Passion' and the Development of the Passion Play (PMLA 35, 1920), pp. 464-83.

Grace Frank, The Medieval French Drama, Oxford 1954.

Karl Fredrik Freudenthal, Gloria. Temptatio. Conversio. Studien zur älteren deutschen Kirchensprache (Acta Universitatis Gothoburgensis 65/2) Göteborg 1959.

Northrop Frye, The Typology of 'Paradise Regained.' In: Milton's Epic Poetry, ed. C. A. Patrides, Harmondsworth 1967, pp. 301-21.

Gordon Hall Gerould, The North-English Homily Collection (Diss. B.Litt., Oxford 1901) Lancaster/Pa. 1902.

J. de Ghellinck, L'essor de la littérature latine au XII. siècle (Museum Lessianum, sect. hist. 4/5) Brussels/Paris 1946.

Alan H. Gilbert, The Temptation in 'Paradise Regained' (Journal of English and Germanic Philology 15, 1916), pp. 599-611.

Louis Ginzberg, Die Haggada bei den Kirchenvätern und in der apokryphen Litteratur, Berlin 1900.

Louis Ginzberg, Book of Adam. In: The Jewish Encyclopaedia, ed. Isidore Singer etc., New York/London 1901-6, I, 179f.

Louis Ginzberg, The Legends of the Jews (various translators), Philadelphia 1913-38.

P. Glorieux, Pour revaloriser Migne. Tables rectificatives (Mélanges de science religieuse 9, cahier supplementaire) Lille 1952.

Martin Grabmann, Die Geschichte der scholastischen Methode, Freiburg/Br. 1909-11.

Robert M. Grant, A Short History of the Interpretation of the Bible, 2nd. ed. London 1965.

William M. Green, Initium omnis peccati superbia. Augustine on Pride as the First Sin (University of California Publications in Classical Philology 13/13, pp. 407-32) Berkeley/Los Angeles 1949.

Stanley B. Greenfield, A Critical History of Old English Literature, London 1966.

Julius Gross, Geschichte des Erbsündendogmas, Munich/Basle 1960-3.

Ernst Guldan, Eva und Maria. Eine Antithese als Bildmotiv, Graz/Cologne 1966.

S. Humphreys Gurteen, The Epic of the Fall of Man, New York 1896.

R. P. C. Hanson, Allegory and Event, London 1959.

R. P. C. Hanson, Tradition in the Early Church (The Library of History and Doctrine) London 1962.

Wolfgang Hempel, Übermuot diu alte. Der Superbia-Gedanke und seine Rolle in der deutschen Literatur des Mittelalters (Studien zur Germanistik, Anglistik und Komparistik 1) Bonn 1970.

Norman Hinton, Anagogue and Archetype. The Phenomenology of Medieval Literature (Annuale Medievale 7, 1966), pp. 57-73.

Donald R. Howard, The Three Temptations. Medieval Man in Search of the World, Princeton 1966.

Bernard F. Huppé, Doctrine and Poetry, Augustine's Influence on Old English Poetry, New York 1959.

Heinz G. Jantsch, Studien zum Symbolischen in frühmittelhochdeutscher Literatur, Tübingen 1959.

C. G. Jung, Psychologie und Alchemie, Zurich 1944.

C. G. Jung and M.-L. von Franz, Mysterium coniunctionis. Untersuchung über die Trennung und Zusammensetzung der seelischen Gegensätze in der Alchemie, Zurich 1955 -7.

Josef Andreas Jungmann, Missarum sollemnia. Eine genetische Erklärung der römischen Messe, 4th ed. Freiburg/Br. 1958.

R. E. Kaske, Patristic Exegesis in the Criticism of Medieval Literature: the Defense. In: Critical Approaches to Medieval Literature, ed. Dorothy Bethurum (Selected Papers from the English Institute, 1958 -9) New York 1960, pp. 27 -60.

James F. Kenney, The Sources for the Early History of Ireland. Ecclesiastical. An Introduction and Guide, revised ed. Ludwig Bieler, Dublin 1966.

W. P. Ker, Epic and Romance, London 1897.

W. P. Ker, The Dark Ages, London 1904.

Søren Kierkegaard, Begrebet angest, 1855, transl. Walter Lowrie, The Concept of Dread, Princeton 1944.

Watson Kirkconell, The Celestial Cycle: The Theme of 'Paradise Lost' in World Literature, Toronto 1952, repr. New York 1967.

Karl Klimke, Das volkstümliche Paradiesspiel und seine mittelalterlichen Grundlagen (Germanistische Abhandlungen 29) Breslau 1902.

Klaus-Peter Köppen, Die Auslegung der Versuchungsgeschichte unter besonderer Berücksichtigung der alten Kirche (Beiträge zur Geschichte der biblischen Exegese 4) Tübingen 1961.

Karl Künstle, Ikonographie der christlichen Kunst, Freiburg/Br. 1926 -8.

M. L. W. Laistner, Some Early Medieval Commentaries on the Old Testament (Harvard Theological Review 46, 1953), pp. 27 -46.

M. L. W. Laistner, Thought and Letters in Western Europe AD 500 to 900, 2nd ed. London 1957.

G. W. H. Lampe, Typological Exegesis (Theology 56, 1953), pp. 201 -8.

G. W. H. Lampe, The Reasonableness of Typology. In: Essays on Typology, ed. G. W. H. Lampe and K. J. Woolcombe (Studies in Biblical Theology 22) London 1957.

G. W. H. Lampe (editor), The Cambridge History of the Bible II. The West from the Fathers to the Reformation, Cambridge 1970.

Artur Michael Landgraf, Einführung in die Geschichte der theologischen Literatur der Frühscholastik, Ratisbon 1948.

Jean Leclerq, L'amour des lettres et le désir de Dieu, Paris 1947.

Hans Günther Leder, Die Auslegung der zentralen theologischen Aussagen der Paradieserzählung (Gn. 2: 4b -3:24), Diss. Greifswald 1961.

M. Dominica Legge, Anglo-Norman Literature and its Background, Oxford 1965.

A. Leitzmann, Zum 'Anegenge,' (Zeitschrift für deutsches Altertum 77, 1940), pp. 104 -7.

Israel Lévi, Eléments chrétiens dans le 'Pirké Rabbi Eliézer' (Revue des études juives 18, 1889), pp. 86 -9.

Barbara Kiefer Lewalski, Milton's Brief Epic. The Genre, Meaning and Art of 'Paradise Regained,' Providence/London 1966.

Ernst Lohmeyer, Die Versuchung Jesu. In: Urchristliche Mystik, 2nd ed. Darmstadt 1958, pp. 81 -122.

Robert Longsworth, The Cornish 'Ordinalia.' Religion and Dramaturgy, Cambridge/Mass. 1967.

Odon Lottin, Psychologie et morale aux XIIe et XIIIe siècles, Gembloux 1942 -60.

Henri de Lubac, Exégèse médiévale. Les quatre sens de l'Ecriture (Théologie 41 -2 and 59) Lyons 1959 -64.

Emile Mâle, L'art religieux de la fin du moyen age en France, 3rd ed. Paris 1925.

Emile Male, L'art religieux du XIIe siècle en France, Paris 1922.

J. M. Margeson, The Origins of English Tragedy, Oxford 1967.

Millard Meics, French Painting in the Time of Jean de Berry. The Late 14th Century and the Patronage of the Duke (National Gallery of Art: Kress Foundation Studies in the History of European Art) London 1969.

Volker Mertens, Das Predigtbuch des Priesters Konrad (Münchener Texte und Untersuchungen 33) Munich 1971.

Paul Meyer, Les manuscrits des sermones français de Maurice de Sully (Romania 5, 1876), pp. 466 -87.

J. H. Miller, Literature and Religion. In: Relations of Literary Study. Essays on Interdisciplinary Contributions, ed. James Thorpe, New York 1967, pp. 111 -26.

Wilhelm Molsdorf, Christliche Symbolik der mittelalterlichen Kunst (Hiersemanns Handbücher 10) Leipzig 1926.

Olin H. Moore, The Infernal Council (Modern Philology 16, 1918/9), pp. 169 -93.

Minnie Cate Morrell, A Manual of Old English Biblical Materials, Knoxville 1965.

195

Joseph Albert Mosher, The Exemplum in the Early Religious and Didactic Literature of England (Columbia University Studies in English) New York 1911.

Brian Murdoch, The Garments of Paradise. A Note on the 'Wiener Genesis' and the 'Anegenge' (Euphorion 61, 1967), pp. 375 -82.

Brian Murdoch, Review of: Das Anegenge, ed. Dietrich Neuschäfer (Modern Language Review 64, 1969), pp. 445 -7.

Brian Murdoch, The Fall of Man.A Middle High German Analogue of 'Genesis B' (Review of English Studies NS 19, 1968), pp. 288 -9.

Brian Murdoch, The Fall of Man in the Early Middle High German Biblical Epic (Göppinger Arbeiten zur Germanistik 58) Göppingen 1972.

Brian Murdoch, Theological Writings and Medieval German Literature (Neuphilologische Mitteilungen 71, 1970), pp. 66 -82.

Brian Murdoch, The Production of Concordances from Diplomatic Transcriptions of Medieval German Manuscripts. In: The Computer in Literary and Linguistic Research ed. Roy A. Wisbey, Cambridge 1972, pp. 35 -44.

Brian Murdoch, Zu einer quellenbestimmten Lexikologie des Altdeutschen (Doitsu Bungaku Ronko/Osaka 13, 1971), pp. 43 -63.

Brian Murdoch, An Early Irish Adam and Eve. 'Saltair na Rann' and the Genesis Tradition (Medieval Studies 1973, in press).

Brian Murdoch, The River that Stopped Flowing (Southern Folklore Quarterly 1973, in press).

Benjamin Murmelstein, Adam. Ein Beitrag zur Messiaslehre (Wiener Zeitschrift für die Kunde des Morgenlandes 35, 1928), pp. 242 -75 and ibid. 36, 1929, pp. 51 -86.

Donald A. McKenzie, Otfrid von Weissenburg, Narrator or Commentator? A Comparative Study (Stanford University Series, Language and Literature 6/iii, pp. 117 -96) Stanford 1946.

Alan McKillop, Illustrative Notes on 'Genesis B' (Journal of English and Germanic Philology 20, 1921), pp. 28 -38.

Robert E. McNally, The Bible in the Early Middle Ages (Woodstock Papers 4) Westminster/Md. 1959.

Bernd Naumann, Dichtung und Publikum in deutscher und lateinischer Bibelepik des frühen 12. Jahrhunderts (Erlanger Beiträge zur Sprache und Kunstwissenschaft 30) Nuremberg 1968.

Anthony Nemetz, Literalness and the *sensus litteralis* (Speculum 34, 1959), pp. 76 -89.

Friedrich Ohly, Vom geistigen Sinn des Wortes in Mittelalter (Zeitschrift für deutsches Altertum 89, 1958/9), pp. 1 -23.

W. J. O'Shea, Homily. In: The New Catholic Encyclopaedia, New York etc. 1967, VII, 113 -5.

G. R. Owst, Preaching in Medieval England (Cambridge Studies in Medieval Life and Thought) Cambridge 1926.

G. R. Owst, Literature and Pulpit in Medieval England, Oxford 1933.

Jack Horace Parker, Gil Vicente (Twayne World Author Series 29) New York 1967.

C. A. Patrides, Milton and the Christian Tradition, Oxford 1966.

Frederick P. Pickering, Literatur und darstellende Kunst im Mittelalter (Grundlagen der Germanistik) Berlin 1966.

A. L. Plumhoff, Beiträge zu den Quellen Otfrids (Zeitschrift für deutsche Philologie 31, 1899), pp. 464 -96 and ibid. 32, 1900, pp. 12 -35.

Elisabeth..Marie Pope, 'Paradise Regained.' The Tradition and the Poem, Baltimore 1947.

Bernhard Poschmann, Die abendländische Kirchenbuße im frühen Mittelalter (Breslauer Studien zur historischen Theologie 16) Breslau 1930.

E. Prosser, Drama and Religion in the English Mystery Plays. A Revaluation (Stanford Studies in Language and Literature 23) Stanford 1961.

Johannes Quasten, Patrology, Utrecht 1950 -60.

Esther Casier Quinn, The Quest of Seth for the Oil of Life, Chicago 1962.

Frederick J. E. Raby, A History of Christian-Latin Poetry from the Beginnings to the Close of the Middle Ages, 2nd ed. Oxford 1953.

Gerhard von Rad, Das erste Buch Mose (Das Alte Testament Deutsch 2) Göttingen 1953.

Ernst Ranke, Das kirchliche Perikopensystem, Berlin 1847.

Johannes Rathofer, Der 'Heliand.' Theologischer Sinn als tektonische Form (Niederdeutsche Studien 9) Cologne/Graz 1962.

Louis Réau, Iconographie de l'art chrétien, Paris 1955 -9.

Leonie Reygers, Adam und Eva. In: Reallexikon zur deutschen Kunstgeschichte, ed. Otto Schmitt etc., Stuttgart 1937ff., I, 126 -56.

D. W. Robertson Jr, A Preface to Chaucer. Studies in Medieval Perspectives, Princeton.1951.

D. W. Robertson Jr and Bernard F. Huppé, 'Piers Plowman' and Scriptural Tradition, Princeton 1951.

Lutz Röhrich, Adam und Eva. Das erste Menschenpaar in Volkskunst und Volksdichtung, Stuttgart 1968.

H. V. Routh, God, Man and Epic Poetry, Cambridge 1927, repr. New York 1968.

Heinz Rupp, Deutsche religiöse Dichtung des 11. und 12. Jahrhunderts, Freiburg/Br. 1958.

William Salloch (Bookseller), Catalogues of Medieval Works, Ossining 1970-1.

Felix Scheidweiler, Studien zum 'Anegenge' (Zeitschrift für deutsches Altertum 80, 1943), pp. 11 -45.

Gertrud Schiller, Ikonographie der christlichen Kunst, 2nd ed. Gütersloh 1969.

Gerhard Schmidt, Die Armenbibeln des XIV. Jahrhunderts, Graz/Cologne 1959.

Anton E. Schönbach, Übermuot diu alte (Zeitschrift für deutsches Altertum 38, 1894),pp. 136 -7.

Edward Schröder, Das 'Anegenge.' Eine literarhistorische Untersuchung (Quellen und Forschungen 44) Strasbourg/London 1881.

Klaus Schulz, Art und Herkunft des variierenden Stils in Otfrids Evangeliendichtung (Medium Aevum 15) Munich 1968.

Julius Schwietering, Typologisches in mittelalterlicher Dichtung. In: Festgabe Gustav Ehrismann, ed. Paul Merker and Wolfgang Stammler, Berlin/Leipzig 1925, pp. 40 -55.

Robin Scroggs, The Last Adam. A Study in Pauline Anthropology, Philadelphia/Oxford 1966.

Reinhold Seeberg, Lehrbuch der Dogmengeschichte, 2 -3rd ed. Leipzig 1913 -23.

Marius Sepet, Le drama chrétien au moyen age, Paris 1878.

St John D. Seymour, The Book of Adam and Eve in Ireland (Proceedings of the Royal Irish Academy 36/C, 1921 -4), pp. 121 -33.

St John D. Seymour, Notes on Apocrypha in Ireland (Proceedings of the Royal Irish Academy 37/C, 1924 -7), pp. 107 -17.

T. A. Shippey, Old English Verse (Hutchinson's University Library) London, 1972.

Albert Siegmund, Die Überlieferung der griechischen christlichen Literatur in. der lateinischen Kirche bis zum 12. Jahrhundert (Abhandlungen der Bayerischen Benediktinerakademie 5) Munich 1949.

E. Sievers, Zum 'Heliand' (Zeitschrift für deutsches Altertum 19, 1876), pp. 1 -76.

Theodore Silverstein, Allegory and Literary Form (PMLA 82, 1967), pp. 28 -32.

Samuel Singer, Zu Wolframs 'Parzival.' In: Festgabe für Richard Heinzel, Halle/S. 1898, pp. 353 -456.

Samuel Singer, Dogma und Dichtung des Mittelalters (PMLA 62, 1947), pp. 861 -72.

Arthur R. Skemp, The Transformation of Scriptural Story, Motive and Conception in Anglo-Saxon Poetry (Modern Philology 4, 1906/7), pp. 423 -70.

John Skinner, A Critical and Exegetical Commentary on Genesis (International Critical Commentary), 2nd ed. Edinburgh 1930.

Beryl Smalley, The Study of the Bible in the Middle Ages, 2nd ed. Oxford 1952.

C. Soetemann, Deutsche geistliche Dichtung des 11. und 12. Jahrhunderts (Sammlung Metzler 33) Stuttgart 1963.

Ceslas Spicq, Esquisse d'une histoire de l'exégèse latine au moyen age (Bibliothèque Thomiste 26) Paris 1944.

Eric Gerald Stanley (ed.), Continuations and Beginnings. Studies in Old English Literature, London 1966.

Friedrich Stegmüller, Repertorium biblicum medii aevi, Madrid 1941 -60.

Wolfram von den Steinen, Homo caelestis. Das Wort der Kunst im Mittelalter, Berne/Munich 1965.

Hermann Strack and Paul Billerbeck, Kommentar zum Neuen Testament aus Talmud und Midrasch, Munich 1922 -8.

Robert Stroppel, Liturgie und geistliche Dichtung zwischen 1050 und 1300 (Deutsche Forschungen 17) Frankfurt/M. 1927.

E. F. Sutcliffe, Some Footnotes to the Fathers (Biblica 6, 1925), pp. 205 -10.

Hilda Swinburne, The Selection of Narrative Passages in Otfrid's 'Evangelienbuch' (Modern Language Review 53, 1958), pp. 92 -7.

John Taylor, The Universal Chronicle of Ranulf Higden, Oxford 1966.

Valentin Teuber, Über die vom Dichter des 'Anegenge' benutzten Quellen (Beiträge zur Geschichte der deutschen Sprache und Literatur 24, 1899), pp. 249-360

Paul Teyssier, La langue de Gil Vicente, Paris 1959.

E. Crewdson Thomas, History of the Schoolmen, London 1941.

J. J. M. Timmers, Symboliek en iconographie der Christelijke kunst (Romens Compendia) Roermond/Maaseik 1947.

Charles Cutler Torrey, The Apocryphal Literature. A Brief Introduction, New Haven 1945.

Hope Traver, The Four Daughters of God. A Study of the Versions of this Allegory (Bryn Mawr College Monographs 6) Bryn Mawr 1907.

G. Turville-Petre, Origins of Icelandic Literature, Oxford 1953.

Rosamond Tuve, Allegorical Imagery. Some Medieval Books and their Posterity, Princeton 1966.

Dominic J. Unger, The First-Gospel. Genesis 3: 15 (Franciscan Institute Publications, Theology Series 3) St Bonaventura/Louvain/Paderborn 1954.

E. E. Wardale, Chapters on Old English Literature, London 1935, repr. New York 1965.

Leonhard Weber, Hauptfragen der Moraltheologie Gregors des Grossen (Paradosis 1) Fribourg/Sw. 1947.

Sarah Appleton Weber, Theology and Poetry in the Middle English Lyric, Ohio 1969.

Josef Weisweiler Buße, Bedeutungsgeschichtliche Beiträge zur Kultur- und Geistesgeschichte, Halle/S. 1930.

John Edwin Wells, A Manual of the Writings in Middle English 1050 -1400, New Haven/London 1916 -41.

J.-Th. Welter, L'exemplum dans la littérature religieuse et didactique du moyen age, Paris/Toulouse 1927.

Wilfried Werner, Studien zu den Passions- und Osterspielen des deutschen Mittelalters (Philologische Studien und Quellen 18) Berlin 1963.

Norman Powell Williams, The Idea of the Fall and of Original Sin (The Bampton Lectures 1924) London 1927.

H. B. Willson, Echoes of St Paul in the 'Nibelungenlied' (MLN 84, 1969), pp. 699 -715.

Roy A. Wisbey, Review of: H. Jantsch, Studien zum Typologischen (Year's Work in Modern Language Studies 22, 1960), p. 314.

Rosemary E. Woolf, The Devil in Old English Poetry (Review of English Studies NS 4, 1953), pp. 1 -12.

Rosemary E. Woolf, The Fall of Man in 'Genesis B' and the 'Mystère d'Adam.' In: Studies in Old English Literature in Honor of Arthur G. Brodeur, ed. Stanley B. Greenfield, Eugene/Oregon 1963, pp. 187 -99.

Rosemary E. Woolf, The English Religious Lyric in the Middle Ages, Oxford 1968.

Rosemary E. Woolf, The English Mystery Plays, London 1972.

Herbert B. Workman, John Wyclif. A Study in the English Medieval Church, Oxford 1926, repr. Hamden/Conn. 1966.

C. L. Wrenn, A Study of Old English Literature, London 1967.

Richard Paul Wülcker, Das 'Evangelium Nicodemi' in der abendländischen Literatur, Paderborn 1872.

Karl Young, The Drama of the Medieval Church, Oxford 1933.

INDEX

a. *Primary sources*

Abelard, Peter 42, 141
Adam an Eve, Ethiopian Book of 152
Adam of Dore 154
Aelfric 56-8, 61, 64
Alain of Lille 33, 54
Alexander III 42
Alsfelder Passionspiel 120, 128, 142
Ambrose 9, 36f, 43, 59
Anastasius of Sinai 44
Anegenge 42, 78, 84-92, 112, 114, 130, 136, 140f., 174
Angelom of Luxeuil 41
Anselm of Laon 33, 42
Apocalypsis Mosis 26
Aquinas 29, 36, 39, 44, 47, 127
Arnamagnaean MS 169 62
Augustine 13, 29, 36, 172
Autun carvings 152
Ava, Frau 93, 102
Avitus, Alcimus 144

Bale, John 124f, 142f.
Bede 13, 31, 41, 44; 75, 81, 96, 129, 161
Bernard of Clairvaux 76
Bible, Antwerp 42
Bible, Bishops' 24
Bible moralisée 131, 165-9
Biblia pauperum 153-65
Blathmac 67-70, 75, 116, 152, 174
Blickling Homilies 58-60
Bodley MS 343 (Oxford) 61f.

Bonaventure 33
PsBonaventue — *see* Meditationes vitae Christi
British Museum MS Royal 18Bxxiii 55
Bruno of Asti 33, 127

Caedmon 70
Calvin, John 9, 37, 40f., 46, 124
Canterbury Cathedral, glass 156, 164
Carinthian Sermons (St Paul) 63
Cassian, John 29, 37-9, 44, 47, 56, 88f., 92, 106, 127
Catherine of Cleves, Hours of, 151
Cave of Treasures, Book of 152
Certaine sermons . . . (1547-71) 56
Chaucer, Geoffrey 10, 56
Chester Plays (Butchers') 108f., 119, 128-32, 142, 174
Christ and Satan (OE) 70-3, 114, 146, 172, 174
Christian of Lilienfeld 162
Christian of Stavelot 41
Chrysostom, John 31, 34, 106
PseudoChrysostom 34, 106, 137
Claude of Turin 10, 33
Claudian 139
Concordantiae Veteri et Novi Testamenti 156
Cursor Mundi 102
Cyril of Alexandria 34

Daniel (OE) 70

Deus de cuius principio et fine tacetur 42

Devils Parliament, see Parlamentum of Feendis

Donaueschinger Passionspiel 123

Druthmar, see Christian of Stavelot

Dublin MS Trinity College B.4.19 65

Erlösung 93, 102

Eton MS 177 156

Eucherius of Lyons 10

Euthemius Zigabenus 44

Expositio quattuor Evangeliarum (Irish Pseudo-Jerome) 31

Eystein Asgrimsson 103-5, 129

Fletcher, Giles 73, 113f., 146f.

Folengo, Teofilo 2, 113, 127f.

Garnier of Rochefort 43

Gawain and the Green Knight, Sir 10, 174

Genesis A (OE) 70

Genesis B (OE) 76, 137f., 140, 161

Gilbert (Giselbertus) 152

Glossa Interlinearis 42

Glossa Ordinaria 36, 42, 81

Greban, Arnoul 125-8, 142

Gregory the Great 29f., 39-45, 47, 51, 53, 56-60, 62, 64, 75, 80-3, 88f., 92, 96f., 99f., 106f., 108-10, 119-21, 125, 128f., 131, 135, 140, 146, 154f., 159, 166, 168f., 171

Gritsch, Johannes 30

Guibert of Nogent 54

Guide for Painters 151

Gundacker von Judenberg 102, 105

Haymo of Auxerre 36, 64

Haymo of Halberstadt 36

Hegge Plays (Weavers' Play) 121-3, 132, 135, 142, 173

Heidelberger Passionsspiel 120

Heliand 73-7, 79f., 103, 161, 171, 173

Higden, Ralph 108, 110, 129

Hilary of Poitiers 36f.

Hildebert of Lavardin 33

Hoffmann's Sermons (Austrian) 64

Homeric Hymn to Demeter 139

Honoré of Autun 42, 86f.

Hugh of Prato 30

Hugh of St Victor 41f.

Hugo von Trimberg 107

Innocent III 43

Irenaeus of Lyons 16, 29, 33-7, 43, 47, 89, 110, 138, 164, 168

Isaac de Stella 43

Isidor of Seville 96, 144

James of Voragine 29, 37, 45f., 95, 111f.

Jerome 32, 41

PseudoJerome 41 and see Expositio quattuor Evangeliarum

John of Howden 101

John of Werden 30

Jordan of Quedlinburg 30

Josephus, Flavius 96

Justin Martyr 9, 31

Kells, Book of 70, 150

Konrad, see Rolandslied

Konrad von Helmsdorf 45

Konrad (Priester) 54

Künzelsauer Fronleichnamspiel 132

Langland, William 10

Lebor Gabála Érenn 152
Livre de la Passion 103
Ludus Covetriae, see Hegge Plays
Luther, Martin 9

Maastricht Passion Play 142
Macé de la Charité 166
Maimonides, Moses 27f.
Martin of Léon 43
Maximus of Turin 33
Mayron, François 30
Meditationes Vitae Christi (PsBon-
    aventure) 150, 162
Meditations on the Life and Passion
    of Christ (ME) 101
Mercadé, Eustache 126
Michael de Carcano 30
Michel, Jean 127f., 138, 142, 162
Mielot, Jean 45
Milton, John 1, 7, 8, 12f., 19f.,
    20f., 23, 34, 42, 49, 65, 67, 71,
    83f., 90, 95, 109f., 113-17, 129,
    138f., 142, 146f., 163, 168,
    171f., 174f.
Mirk, John 51, 64f., 155
Miroure of Mans Saluacionne 45
Mulhouse, glass 164
Mystère d'Adam 136-8, 140, 145

Nibelungenlied 11
Nicholas of Verdun 154, 157
Nicodemus, Gospel of 139, 142
Northern Homily Collection 95,
    99f.
Norwich Cathedral, roof 163

Oberaltaich Sermons 64
Ordinalia (Cornish) 14, 132-6, 146,
    174
Orendel 93
Ormulum 95, 101f., 105, 163, 173

Otfrid von Weissenburg 76-84, 88,
    92, 96, 103, 106, 174

Parlament of Feendis 140, 142
Paschasius Radbertus 38
Passio Bartholomaei 31f., 34
Passion d'Amboise 125
Passion du Palatinus 142
Passion St. Geneviève 125
Passion de Semur 125f., 137, 142
Paterius 41
Paul the Deacon 42
Peter of Celle 43
Peter Comestor 13, 41, 161
Peter Lombard 41
Peter of Paludo 30
Peterborough Cathedral, glass 156,
    164
Pepysian Gospel Harmony 49
Philo of Alexandria 9, 57
Pictor in Carmine 45, 154-6, 164f.
Pirkê de Rabbi Eliezer 26f.
Provençale Passion 125

Raban Maurus 13, 31, 41, 75, 81
Ralph of Poitiers 42
Regensburg Paradise Play 141
Riga, Peter 166
Robert de Baron 139
Roberto Caracciola 30
Rolandslied 93, 174
Rota in Medio Rotae 156
Rupert of Deutz 33, 41

Sachs, Hans 141
Saelden hort, der 105-7, 127
St Albans Psalter 153
Saltair na Rann 26, 69, 136, 144,
    152, 166
St Galler Passionsspiel 128
Sannazaro, Jacopo 139

Santiago, carvings 153
Saulieu,carvings 152
Scholia Vetera (Greek) 44
Sententiae Anselmi 42
Sententiae Berolinenses 42
Sententiae Divinae Paginae 42
Slovo o Lazarevom Voskresenii 139
Smaointe Beatha Chríóst 150
South-English Legendary 95, 100
Southern Passion 101
Speculum Humanae Salvationis 29,
  45, 131, 149, 163-5
Speculum Sacerdotale 56
Spoerer Hans 158, 162f.
Stanzaic Life of Christ (ME) 46,
  100, 108-12, 129-31, 140, 174
Stockholm Homily Book 62f.
Suger of St Denis 154
Summa Theologiae (MHG) 84
Tacitus 75
Taio of Saragozza 41
Talmud, Babylonian 27
Tasso, Torquato 139
Tatian 49
Tertullian 32
Theodore Prodromus 44
Theodoret of Cyrus 31

Theophylactus of Achrida 44
Thomas Aquinas, see Aquinas

Udall, John 115
Ulrich of Lichtenfeld 161

Vicente, Gil 20, 120, 142-7, 173-5
Vida, Marco Giramolo 139
Vita Adae et Evae 25f.
Volospá 141
Vorauer Genesis 76, 136

Werner of St Blaise 43
Wilde Mann, der 90-2, 112, 140,
  155, 174
Wiener Genesis 83
William of Auvergne 43
Wulfstan 56f.
Würzburg Matthew-Commentary 41
Wyclif, John 43

York Plays (Locksmiths') 121-3,
  132, 173

Ysagoge in Theologiam 42
Ystoire de la Passion 102

Zachary Chrysopolitanus 41

*b. Secondary writers. Editors and translators of primary texts
are included here only when particular mention has been
made of their comments.*

Adrian, H. 106f.
Altaner, B. 40.
Anderson, M. D. 122, 163
Aubry-Vitet, E. 50
Auerbach, E. 14

Benskin, M. 2, 7, 65, 100
Bethe, H. 151

Bloomfield, M. W. 10, 56, 86
de Boor, H. 84
Bostock, J. K. 76f.

Campbell, E. 2
Caplan, H. 52-4
Carney, J. 67-9
Chydenius, J. 14

Clark, K. 67
Cornell, H. 154, 156, 158-60, 162, 164f.
Cruel, R. 51, 64
Cubbin, G. P. 2
Cushman, L. W. 162

Daniélou, J. 14
Denny, N. 133
Detzel, H. 153
Dillistone, F. W. 174

Erdmann, O. 81
Erich, O. 152
Evans, J. M. 7, 16, 27, 34, 40, 76, 108, 139

Fisher, R. W. 2, 93
Förster, M. 56
Foster, F. 111, 129
Frank, G. 125f.
Friedlander, G. 27
Frye, N. 117

Gazeus, A. 39
Ginzberg, L. 26
Glorieux, P. 10
Goppelt, L. 14, 25
Green, R. B. 150
Greene, D. 26
Grein, T. 70
Gurteen, S. H. 138

Hanson, R. P. C. 14
Harris, M. 133
Harroff, S. 2
Herford, R. T. 27
Hopkins, G. M. 69
Howard, D. R. 9f., 28f., 31, 34f., 40-3, 57, 108
Huerta-Viñas, F. 2

Hull, E. 26, 69
Huppé, B. F. 71f.
Hurst, P. 2

James, M. R. 154, 165
Jantsch, H. G. 14-17
Jenner, H. 133
Jung, C. G. 112

Kaske, R. E. 50
Kierkegaard, S. 18
Kirkconnell, W. 84, 128, 166
Klimke, C. 140
Köppen, K-P. 9, 24, 28, 31f., 34, 36f., 40, 44, 69
Laborde, A. 165
Leder, H. G. 25
Lévi, I. 26
Lewalski, B. K. 13, 34, 37, 42, 46, 172
Lohmeyer, E. 27
Longsworth, R. 14, 18, 132
de Lubac, H. 12

McIntosh, A. 100
McKenzie, D. 77
McKillop, A. 139
Maclaren, D. 2
McNally, R. E. 31
Mâle, E. 131
Margeson, J. R. 136
Mertens, V. 54
Meyer, W. 25f.
Miller, J. H. 11
Minis, C. 2
Moore, O. 139f.
Morris, R. 60
Mosher, J. A. 53, 96
Murdoch, B. 7, 11, 27, 40, 50, 53, 56, 76, 79, 86, 88, 104, 136, 140f.

Naumann, B. 172
Nemetz, A. 12
Neuschäfer, D. 85
Norris, E. 133f.

Ohly, F. 12
O'Shea, J. 51
Owst, G. R. 11, 49, 53, 123

Pächt, O. 131
Parker, J. H. 143, 146
Patrides, C. A. 7, 114f.
Pickering, F. P. 11, 131
Piper, P. 81
Plumhoff, A. L. 81
Pope, E. M. 8f., 24, 28f., 31, 34-6,
    40-2, 46, 65, 108, 113, 123, 127,
    150f., 153f., 162, 168, 173
Powell, S. 2

Quasten, J. 33
Quinn, E. C. 152

Ragusa, I. 150
Rathofer, J. 80
Reau, L. 150
Robertson, D. W. 10
Roy, E. 126, 139
Rupp, H. 84f.

Salloch, W. 30
Schiller, G. 150, 152

G. Schmidt 154, 156-8, 161
Schreiber, W. L. 156
Schröder, E. 42
Schulz, K. 77f.
Soltész, E. 156
Scroggs, R. 52
Seymour, St J. D. 67
Sievers, E. 75
Singer, S. 106f.
Small, J. 95f., 99
Smalley, B. 12
Spicq, C. 12, 29
Standring, B. 90
Stegmüller, F. 25
von den Steinen, W. 152
Studer, P. 145

Teuber, V. 89
Teyssier, P. 143
Traver, H. 141

Walker, R. 2
Weber, S. A. 19
Wells, J. E. 129
Wells, L. S. A. 25f.
Willson, H. B. 11
Wisbey, R. A. 14
Woolf, R. 10, 24, 101, 137, 139,
    162
Wrenn, C. L. 70f.
Wülcker, R. P. 70, 139

c. Biblical Passages

Genesis
1   160
3   24, 158
3: 1   12
3: 5   168
3: 15   53, 158
25: 29f.   18

25: 29-34 155
37: 28f.   15

Exodus
34: 28   25

Deuteronomy

9: 9	25
9: 18	25

Judges

6: 36-8	158

1 Kings

9: 5	25
9: 8	25
17: 34	164
17: 49	18, 164

Job

19: 25	144

Daniel

14: 1-40	164

Matthew

4: 1-11	29,52,135,138,*passim*
4: 1-4	166
4: 8-10	167
4: 9	128
4: 11	135
27: 33	151

Mark

1: 12f.	23

Luke

4: 1-13	23
4: 5	167

John

1: 35f.	166

Romans

5: 12	24, 34
5: 14	16, 19

2 Corinthians

11: 4	162

Philippians

2: 3	111

1 John

2: 16	10, 29, 35, 120, 130